THE OPEN HEAVEN

W. H. CADMAN

THE OPEN HEAVEN

*The Revelation of God in the
Johannine Sayings of Jesus*

Edited by
G. B. CAIRD

BASIL BLACKWELL
OXFORD
1969

631 11330 4

Library of Congress Catalog
Card Number 74–81078

PRINTED IN GREAT BRITAIN
BY A. T. BROOME AND SON, 18 ST. CLEMENT'S, OXFORD
AND BOUND BY THE KEMP HALL BINDERY, OXFORD

To Lilian

PREFACE

For over forty years William Healey Cadman devoted the greater part of his time, energy, erudition, and devotion to the study of the Fourth Gospel. As an ordinand I attended his lectures. None of us found them easy to follow, and not all stayed the course; but those of us who persevered to the end found that they left an indelible stamp on the mind. He was known to be writing a book, but nobody seemed to know whether it was to be a commentary or a book about the Gospel. Rumour had it that he was almost on the point of publication when the first fascicle of Bultmann's commentary appeared, and that he then felt compelled to wait until the rest came to his hands. Since it was known that C. H. Dodd was also working on the Fourth Gospel, we began to fear that Cadman on John, like so many other works on the same book, would be posthumous. After his death, his widow handed me the typescript, giving me a free hand to do whatever I thought necessary to make it ready for publication. As I read it, two things at once struck me. The first was how much I had owed to Cadman throughout the twenty years of my teaching career, not only to his ideas about the Fourth Gospel, but to the example of his exact observation and estimation of evidence. The second was that our student doubts about Cadman's book had their roots in his own mind; for he had never really decided whether he was writing a commentary or a book with a thesis to sustain. It was plain too that he was still unsatisfied with the form of his book, for he left notes of a number of changes which he had envisaged.

With the advice and encouragement of Mr. H. L. Schollick of Blackwell's who generously agreed to publish the book if I could make the necessary alterations, I have done my best to convert Cadman's manuscript into a book about the Gospel. Wherever possible I have allowed Cadman's own words and inimitable style to stand. But the task could not be performed without the supplying of a good many connecting links and the recasting of whole paragraphs and, in one or two instances, of whole chapters. Regretfully I have also excised some commentary material which did not seem to fit into a consecutive exposition. I have not attempted to indicate where Cadman ends and Caird begins. Those who pride themselves on their ability to determine the authorship of biblical texts may be able, with or without the use of a computer, to detect the seams for themselves. Throughout all the changes I have made, I have tried not to alter Cadman's ideas, even where I was not wholly in agreement with them. If at any point I have unwittingly misinterpreted him, I need only ask his readers' pardon, since I know that I have his already in advance.

The editing of this manuscript has been a labour of love and gratitude to a man whom all his colleagues and pupils remember with warm affection, not least for his having shared with them his enthusiasm for the Fourth Gospel and his insight into its meaning. Against all the current trends of New Testament scholarship Cadman maintained that, whatever might be learnt about the words and symbols of the Gospel from their history in Jewish or pagan thought, their meaning in the Gospel was what St. John intended them to mean, and that what he intended them to mean could be discerned only by reading and rereading the Gospel. It was he who taught us to see in the great Christological word-themes of life and light, love, glory and truth, sending, abiding, and indwelling a set of almost synonymous terms, which the evangelist used deliberately in rapid interchange, so that the one might illumine the other and all might be filled with new meaning. From him we learnt that the Cross was as central to the theology of St. John as to that of St. Paul, and that he was a man to whom history mattered vitally because he believed that it mattered to God. If ever I have found myself disagreeing with Cadman's conclusions, it has always been because I wanted to carry the principles I learnt from him a little further than his native caution would allow him to go.

Mansfield College,   G. B. CAIRD
Oxford, 1968

CONTENTS

B

PART I

THE NATURE OF THE REVELATION GIVEN BY JESUS

Jesus in St. John's Gospel claims to reveal that which He has seen in His Father's presence or has heard from Him. 'I speak the things which I have seen with my Father' (viii. 38). 'The things which I heard from Him, these things speak I to the world' (viii. 26). 'He that cometh from heaven is above all. What he hath seen and heard, of that he beareth witness; and no man receiveth his witness' (iii. 31). If we are to grasp the essential character of the Christian Faith as presented in St. John, we must be at pains to read such utterances in the way he intended them. At one time it was the prevailing opinion that the things which Jesus speaks to the world, or to which He bears testimony, are things which He had seen and heard in heaven before the Incarnation. Such utterances as those which have just been quoted seemed to make this view so self-evidently right that it was hardly thought necessary to argue the case for it. Thus, in a treatment of the Fourth Gospel in his book *Kyrios Christos* (1921), Bousset wrote: 'The Son proclaims what He has heard (seen) in the Father's presence in eternity' (p. 170), and he thought that the following passages should be understood from that standpoint—i. 18, iii. 11, iii. 32, vii. 16, viii. 26, viii. 28, viii. 38, viii. 47, xii. 49, xiv. 10.

Zahn and Holtzmann held that a distinction should be made between passages in which the term used is 'see' and those in which it is 'hear', the former being intended to refer to the pre-incarnate life of Jesus and the latter to apply, at least in most cases, to the time of His life on earth.[1] Bultmann has argued for a different distinction,[2] between passages in which a present tense occurs, referring to the earthly life of Jesus, and passages in which there is a perfect or an aorist used, where the reference is to His pre-existence. Bultmann remarks that such passages raise expectation that great discourses and sayings of Jesus telling of what He had seen or heard in that heavenly world will appear in the Gospel, but

---

[1] See Zahn, *Kommentar zum N. Testament*, p. 345, note 49; H. J. Holtzmann, *Neutestament. Theol.*, II, p. 453.
[2] *Das Evangelium des Johannes*, pp. 190 ff., 103 f.

that this does not happen; and he thinks that the recourse to the notion of pre-existence in the passages in question should be treated only as a way of laying claim to the utmost authority for the person of Jesus and the revelation which He brings. This suggestion of Bultmann does less than justice to the Johannine concept of revelation, but it draws attention to a serious weakness in the view represented by the quotation from Bousset. If St. John thought of Jesus as bringing from heaven a revelation already complete, should we not expect to find it having to do with previously existing and always existing divine things? The great discourses and sayings in the Gospel, however, cannot be made to yield up their secret if they are approached in this way. Their main burden is the eschatological significance of the human divine person of Jesus, of His passion, and of His resurrection. If on the other hand we start with the actual content of the Gospel, we shall naturally assume that the person and activity of Jesus are not simply the media for the conveying of revelation, but are integral to the revelation itself.

But if the things which Jesus saw and heard with His Father relate exclusively to the significance of His earthly person and activity, ought we not to think of the seeing and hearing themselves as part of His earthly experience? This view would find support in a number of sayings in the Gospel. 'I am in the Father and the Father is in me' (xiv. 10, 11; x. 38). 'He that sent me is with me; he hath not left me alone; for I do always the things that are pleasing to him' (viii. 29). 'I am not alone, because the Father is with me' (xvi. 32). With this choice in mind, then, let us examine in turn the passages which speak of Jesus as hearing or seeing God.

In v. 30 the present tense shows that no question of a hearing before the Incarnation arises: 'I can of myself do nothing: as I hear, I judge: and my judgement is righteous; because I seek not mine own will, but the will of him that sent me.' But in other passages past tenses are used. 'I have many things to speak and to judge concerning you: howbeit he that sent me is true; and the things which I heard from him, these speak I unto the world . . . as the Father taught me, I speak these things' (viii. 26, 28). 'I speak not from myself; but the Father which sent me hath given me a commandment what I should say, and what I should speak . . . the things therefore which I speak, even as the Father hath said unto me, so I speak' (xii. 49 f.). 'I have called you friends: for

all things that I heard from my Father I have made known unto
you' (xv. 15). The use of aorists and perfects here could in itself
be taken as an indication that the sayings allude to a 'hearing' in the
pre-incarnate life of Jesus, but the improbability of this appears in
another passage in which the ideas of hearing and seeing occur
together. 'I speak the things which I have seen with my Father:
and ye also do the things which ye heard from your father. . . . But
now ye seek to kill me, a man that hath told you the truth, which I
heard from God' (viii. 38, 40). The hearing of the Jews from their
father the devil is clearly conceived to have taken place on earth,
and the natural inference is that this holds also for the seeing and
hearing of Jesus. Would the two 'hearings' have been compared if
that of Jesus belonged to his pre-incarnate existence? Would this
not have made them too dissimilar for comparison?

When we turn to sayings about the seeing of Jesus, the same
pattern is repeated. 'The Son can do nothing of himself, but what
he seeth the Father doing' (v. 19). It is clear from the tense that
the seeing belongs to the historical life of Jesus. The standpoint
is the same in the words which follow: 'for what things soever he
doeth, these the Son also doeth in like manner. For the Father
loveth the Son, and sheweth him all things that he himself doeth.'
And when it is added in v. 20, 'and greater works than these will
he show him that ye may marvel', the thought of a continuous
'showing' by the Father, and of a continuous 'seeing' by the Son
on earth, is unmistakable. Other passages in which past tenses are
used may seem to encourage expectation that the great discourses
of Jesus will convey the content of the seeing of God which He had
enjoyed before the Incarnation. 'Not that any man hath seen the
Father, save he which is from God' (vi. 46). 'He that cometh from
heaven is above all. What he hath seen and heard, of that he
beareth witness; and no man receiveth his witness' (iii. 31 f.).
But we must pause to consider what kind of seeing of God is here
in question, particularly in view of the evidence of viii. 38 to which
we have just alluded. When it is said of others before Jesus that
they have not seen God, what is denied of them is that they have
had that apprehension of the divine being and will towards men
from which the utterances of Jesus proceed; not only so, but, as we
should understand, they could not have had it. For the substance
of the utterances is that He Himself was the expression, the embodiment, of the eschatological saving action of God; that the

creation of His manhood within the Godhead, His dying, and His resurrection were this divine action in operation; that in these events the love of God for man was put forth to the full. To be sure, then, no one amongst men hitherto had seen God in such wise as Jesus made possible. In the absence of these events He could not have been seen, as now He had been seen by Jesus, as now He could be seen by others through Him. The revelation conveyed in the discourse in the sixth chapter of the Gospel in particular is, as we shall see, not of divine things which had always been true, but which had hitherto remained unperceived by men; it is of an action of God, a present action, the action taking place in the creation of the divine-human person of Jesus, in His dying, and in His resurrection. It is revelation both of the factual character of the action and of its meaning for the world.

Thus far the discussion has established three points: that Jesus sometimes speaks of seeing and hearing God not only as a present, but as a continuous experience; that there is nothing in the passages where a past tense is used which forbids us to ascribe this past seeing or hearing to the same earthly setting; and that the content of what Jesus has seen and heard is not some changeless eternal truth, but the meaning of His own historical existence for Himself and for men.

There is a further piece of evidence in the Gospel which strengthens the conviction to which we are moving. Although he ignores the baptismal rite, the Evangelist reports the testimony of the Baptist that the Spirit descended as a dove upon Jesus and 'abode upon him' (i. 32). In vi. 63 the idea is present that the Spirit was operative in the words spoken by Jesus in the preceding discourse, though the bestowal of the gift of the Spirit to believers required His death and resurrection (vii. 39; cf. xiv. 16 f., xiv. 26, xv. 26, xvi. 7 ff., xvi. 13 f.). And in iii. 34 the ability of Jesus to speak the words of God is expressly attributed to the presence of the Spirit: 'For he whom God hath sent speaketh the words of God: for he giveth not the Spirit by measure.' These three passages together strongly suggest that the Gospel does not derive the content of the words of Jesus, i.e. the revelation accomplished by Him, from His having seen the Father or heard things from Him before the Incarnation.

The question has been raised how it is that 'the bearer of the Logos within him, the cherished companion of the Father's

eternity, whom the Father loved so deeply that he gave all things
into his hands needed another revealer constantly "upon" him to
see that he spoke the right words,' and it has been thought that
there is evidence here of two 'different interpretations of the
person of Jesus, one from the traditional side in the language of
Hebrew idiom, the other from the Greek side, which cannot really
be combined.'[3] Such a dichotomy would obscure the true character of the revelation St. John wishes to describe, a revelation concerning the eschatological action of God, of which the first expression was the establishment of a relationship of reciprocal
'in-being' between Himself and manhood in Jesus, and the end
the incorporation into it of others, of all who believed, which was
what it meant for them to have eternal life. It is certainly not
meant in St. John that anyone could come into the possession of
eternal life through knowledge of 'the only true God, and him
whom thou didst send, even Jesus Christ' (xvii. 3), so long as the
knowledge in question is thought to be of truths about God
which the incarnate Logos had been able to impart from the content of His own knowledge of God in His pre-existence. The
familiar words in xvii. 3 have often been misunderstood. The
knowledge there spoken of is knowledge made possible by the
eschatological action of God displayed in the person, words, signs,
and victorious dying and rising of Jesus. But the discourses and
sayings in which Jesus expounds the eschatological significance of
His own life, death, and resurrection are said to have been uttered
under the direction of the Spirit. We are expected then to understand that He owed to the Spirit the knowledge of Himself—the
knowledge, that is to say, that in respect of His manhood he had
been created at the Incarnation in union with the Logos and in a
relation of shared life with the Father (cf. v. 26), and that through
His manhood life was to be offered to the world. As Jesus was
both brought to self-knowledge and sustained in it by the Spirit,
it is intelligible that, in the seeing and hearing passages which we
have had before us, not only the aorist and perfect but the present
tense of the verbs should be used.

Some students of St. John have been of opinion that the Evangelist intended his readers to think that the descent of the Spirit
upon Jesus was actually the moment of the Incarnation.[4] How could

---

[3] Carpenter, *The Johannine Writings*, p. 364.
[4] See for example F. C. Burkitt in *Church and Gnosis*, p. 98 f., and more

an already incarnate Logos have needed the Spirit to enable Him to
'speak the words of God' (iii. 34)? And further, it has been
doubted whether the Evangelist is likely to have distinguished at
all clearly the relations of the Logos and the Spirit, on the grounds
that Justin Martyr, who had lived at Ephesus, evidently did not
do so.[5] Referring to Luke i. 35 ('The Holy Ghost shall come upon
thee, and the power of the Most High shall overshadow thee'),
Justin declares that it is not lawful to understand by the Spirit
and the Power of God anything else than the Logos (1 *Apol.*
xxxiii). Again, in the Shepherd of Hermas (*Simil.* V. vi. 5) it is
said: 'The Holy pre-existent Spirit, which created all creation,
God made to dwell in the flesh which He chose.' Compare also
II Clement ix. 5: 'Christ, the Lord who saved us, became flesh and
called us, though He was first of all Spirit.' But this difficulty is
wholly obviated by the understanding of the Gospel we are here
advancing.

We are now in a position to consider one more of the passages
in St. John which have formed the basis of the view we are criticiz-
ing adversely. 'No man hath seen God at any time; the only
begotten Son, which is in the bosom of the Father, he hath
declared him' (i. 18). It is not said here directly, but it is clearly
implied, as in vi. 46, that the only begotten Son has seen God.
Because the only begotten Son had seen God, He was able, so we
are to understand, to declare Him. Is this to say that, because He
had seen God, He knew the thoughts and purposes of God
concerning man? Yes to be sure, but more than that. He knew
that these purposes were given effect in Himself. Hence it is that,
in order to 'declare' God, He had to so great an extent to declare
Himself. The discourses and sayings in which He did so were
'words of God' uttered in consequence of His having received the
Spirit (cf. iii. 34). So then, if we go on to connect His having seen
God with His reception of the Spirit, it is under the guidance of
the Gospel itself. In coming through the Spirit to know Himself,
to know that in Him manhood had been taken into union with the
Logos, in order that that union might subsequently be extended
to all humanity, He had seen God. To know Himself was, in His
case, to see God. And so, correspondingly, we find that in declar-

fully in the *Expository Times*, February 1927; and R. Seeberg's essay '*O λόγος
σὰρξ ἐγένετο* in *Festgabe für A. von Harnack*, 1921, pp. 272 ff.

---

[5] See Carpenter, op. cit., p. 364 f.

ing or revealing Himself he was providing for others the possibility of seeing God. 'He who hath seen me hath seen the Father' (xiv. 9).

We may then abide by this, that His seeing of God and His knowledge of Himself as man in mutual indwelling with God are two aspects of the one experience to which He was brought by the Spirit. In that case, the question whether or not we are to suppose that His seeing of God which is implied in i. 18 had taken place before the Incarnation answers itself.

Behind the statement that no man has seen God at any time lies the explanatory thought that no man could have seen Him until He had willed and accomplished the Incarnation; before that He had not so revealed Himself that He could have been 'seen' by anyone. The sharp antithesis in the immediately preceding verse of the Prologue—'the law was given by Moses; grace and truth came by Jesus Christ'—suggests that Moses especially is being contemplated. Of him it was told that God had let him see Him and had spoken to him face to face and mouth to mouth (Ex. xxiv. 9 f.; cf. xxxiii. 11; Num. xii. 8; Deut. xxxiv. 10). Carpenter (op. cit. p. 329 f.) remarked on i. 18 that 'the statement is a peremptory repudiation of the aims and claims of the mystery-religions'. Bultmann rightly insists that the Jews are included in the scope of the pronouncement, but adds that Gnosticism and, in fact, any way of trying to obtain knowledge of God outside the revelation given in the incarnate Logos is being repudiated (*Das Evangelium des Johannes*, p. 53 f.). This observation of Bultmann goes too far. He is not a God hitherto wholly unknown to whose self-revelation in Jesus appropriate response is yielded. But the point is well taken that the truth revealed in Jesus is inseparably bound up with His own historical existence.

The metaphor 'in the bosom of' denotes intimate fellowship. But there are three possible ways of taking the clause in which it stands. The Evangelist could be reverting to the first verse of the Prologue: He who in the beginning was in intimate communion with the Father disclosed when He was incarnate His previous knowledge of Him (for the present participle denoting past action cf. xii. 17). He could be looking back from his own time to the period of Jesus' earthly life: He who in His incarnate existence could be said never to have left the Father's side was therefore able to disclose Him. Or he could be writing from his own stand-

point of time: He who now, in consequence of His ascension, is
in closest communion with the Father, has now disclosed Him, as
He could not effectively disclose Him before His own passion and
the subsequent gift of the Spirit (see the discussion on xvi. 28–30
and viii. 12–14). The first possibility would lead us straight back
to the point from which we started, that what Jesus disclosed was
truths learnt from God in His pre-incarnate existence as Logos;
but in the next chapter we shall see that this is not what John
meant. Between the second and third possibilities we do not for the
present need to choose, since each yields a thoroughly Johannine
sense.

The designation of Jesus as Son of God is of course, in the
abbreviated form 'the Son', very common in the Fourth Gospel;
more precisely—and this should be borne in mind in connexion
with the familiar shorter form—He is 'the only Son' (i. 18; iii. 16,
18; cf. I John iv. 9); there were no other sons of God in the same
sense as Jesus was His Son. And God accordingly was His Father
in a peculiar way. 'My Father' is an expression which occurs
frequently on the lips of Jesus. Of believers, to be sure, as of
Jesus Himself, God is Father and God; yet, as the phrasing in
xx. 17 suggests, it is with a difference: 'I ascend unto my Father
and your Father, and my God and your God.'

The title 'Son of God' (for which the Fourth Evangelist had
Christian tradition to draw upon), as a designation of the King of
Israel and the Messiah, had a history in the Old Testament and
Judaism;[6] and in the old pagan world it was used of various
historical figures.[7] In its several applications it marked the bearer
or claimant as one who brought 'salvation' to man, however in
particular the salvation might be conceived. The properly
Johannine usage of the title is to be understood agreeably to the
content of the salvation which Jesus brings in this Gospel. It is
associated here more than once with the title 'Christ' (xi. 27;
xx. 31), the intention being to let each designation contribute
something to the understanding of the Johannine sense of the
other. Jesus, so the combination is meant to suggest, is the Christ
—that is to say, the One who brings the eschatological salvation—
because He is the Son of God; the relationship to God on account

---

[6] Strack-Billerbeck, III, p. 15 ff.
[7] G. P. Wetter, *Der Sohn Gottes*, 1916; Deissmann, *Light from the Ancient
East*, pp. 346 ff.; J. Bieneck, *Sohn Gottes*, 1951, pp. 27 ff.

of which He is called His Son makes Him the Christ, the One in whom eschatology comes to fulfilment. But further, the linking together of the two expressions is an intimation to the readers of the Gospel that they should take the recurring title 'Son of God' or 'the Son' to imply that the bearer of it is the fulfiller of eschatology.

There is some misapprehension of the thought of the Gospel when, as is often done, the expression is treated as interchangeable with 'the Logos'. It is not that there is failure to notice that in the body of the Gospel the incarnate figure is not called 'the Logos'; but it is supposed to be in accordance with the mind of the Fourth Evangelist to speak of 'the Son' in connexion not only with the incarnate but the pre-cosmic or pre-incarnate Logos as well. We find, for instance, the statement: 'the Son is eternal', with viii. 58 and xii. 41 quoted in support.[8] Or again: 'Christ . . . is the unique Son, not because He is the only Son of God that there ever can be; nor because He has something that other sons cannot have; but because Sonship with Him is eternal; He has been the Son so long as there has been a Father to have a Son.'[9]

Such statements might appear to gain some support from the prayer of chapter 17. The prayer is spoken by the Son to the Father and contains a reference to 'the glory which I had with thee before the world was' (v. 5), and to the love with which 'thou lovedst me before the foundation of the world' (v. 24). But this appearance is illusory. Jesus is aware that as Son He is the One in whom the Logos has become incarnate, that His life has thus become continuous with that of the Logos, and that He can speak of Himself as bearer of an eternal glory and recipient of an eternal love. But that is not to say that the title 'Son' can properly be used of His pre-incarnate state. On the contrary, if Son and Logos were interchangeable terms, it would make nonsense for the Son to pray for a glory which was already His eternal possession. Even the man Jesus can hardly at this stage pray for such glory for Himself, since according to this Gospel He has possessed it and manifested it throughout His ministry (i. 14; ii. 11). The prayer makes sense only because, as Son, Jesus is the bearer of the eschatological salvation through whose inclusive humanity, as we

[8] E. Gaugler, 'Das Christuszeugnis des Johannesevangeliums', in *Jesus Christus im Zeugnis der Heiligen Schrift*, 1936, p. 46.
[9] W. F. Lofthouse, *The Expository Times*, July 1932, p. 445.

shall see later, believers are to enter into the glory of eternal life.

It is not a small matter to know how the Fourth Evangelist used the title 'the Son', 'the Son of God'. For is it not said: 'He that believeth on the Son hath eternal life' (iii. 36)? 'This is the will of my Father, that everyone that beholdeth the Son, and believeth on him, should have eternal life' (vi. 40). 'God so loved the world, that he gave his only begotten Son, that whosoever believeth on him should not perish, but have eternal life' (iii. 16). On the relation to God of the subject of the designation 'the Son' everything turns in St. John. How then is the reference of the term to be understood? Two passages may be mentioned which call in question the opinion that the pre-incarnate Logos was 'the Son of God' in the Fourth Evangelist's sense of the title. The first is v. 26: 'As the Father hath life in himself, even so gave he to the Son also to have life in himself.' There is nothing in the Prologue to show that the Father gave or granted to the pre-cosmic or pre-incarnate Logos to have life in Him; on the contrary, 'in him was life' (i. 4), that is, life was in Him in the beginning. But the Son in v. 26 is One who had had life imparted to Him by the Father.

The other passage which helps us to secure the standpoint from which to understand St. John's usage is x. 34 ff.: 'Is it not written in your law, I said, Ye are gods? If he called them gods, unto whom the word of God came (and the scripture cannot be broken), say ye of him, whom the Father sanctified and sent into the world, Thou blasphemest; because I said, I am the Son of God?' The claim of Jesus to be Son of God rests on His being the One consecrated and sent into the world by the Father. Now the sending into the world, here and elsewhere, could in itself be taken as a reference to the Incarnation, the sending of the Logos, though it more probably refers to Jesus' public mission, as in xvii. 18 ('As thou didst send me into the world, even so sent I them into the world'.) But it is almost impossible to make intelligible the thought of a consecration of the pre-existent Logos. The word denotes transference into the divine sphere or, when persons are in question, into close association with God. How could the Logos be consecrated, who was with God and was God? It is moreover to be noted that these verses constitute an argument *a minori ad maius*: 'If he called the inspired men of the Old Testament gods, on the ground that the Logos of God came to

them, how much more may I say that I am God's Son, seeing
that the Father consecrated me and sent me into the world?' The
argument requires that not only the two claims but the two
justificatory clauses should be comparable. But this suggests that
in the consecration of Jesus the Logos had come to Him, not for
occasional inspiration of Him, but for lasting union. Thus it is
not the Logos who is consecrated; it is the coming of the Logos
into the flesh of manhood that consecrates the man Jesus and gives
Him the right to the title 'Son' (cf. i. 14).

We may now ask once more what is the reference of the
designation 'the Son' or 'the Son of God' in St. John? And—
this more especially—why is it held in this Gospel that the Christian revelation is rooted in the revelation of the Father and the
Son? The two passages which we have been considering (v. 26
and x. 34–36) put us in the way of answering the first question:
the 'Son' is Jesus considered in respect of His manhood, Jesus the
incarnate Logos. If without proper support from St. John we
ascribe Sonship to the pre-cosmic or pre-incarnate Logos, we
make it the harder to realize that on the relationship with Himself
in which God willed that the man Jesus should be, everything
turns in the Gospel. It revealed the divine end for man, and much
more than that, it revealed the divine will actually exerted to
achieve it. Did the Fourth Evangelist conceive of a perpetual
love-relationship within the being of God, an always-existing God-
Logos relationship of love? He did; but what of that, for creaturely
man, unless the love by which the eternal order was constituted
overflowed to include him within itself? It had overflowed.
There in the manhood of Jesus stood the perfect expression of it.

The discussion so far of the use of the title 'the Son', 'the Son
of God', in St. John suggests that it is applied to Jesus for two
reasons: first, on the ground that to Him, considered in respect of
His manhood, God had willed the extension of the love-relationship
in which He ever had His being with the Logos; secondly, on the
ground that His inclusion in this relationship ensured that many
more, all who should come to believe in Him, could now be there
with Him. It asserts both that He is in this relationship Himself
and what it means for mankind that He should be so, namely,
the possibility now of others being where He is. Hence the title
'Christ', its significance re-interpreted in this way, is also His in
St. John. On account of the fact that He shared in the love-

relationship of God and the Logos, Jesus could be and was the One by whom God at once disclosed and realised His end for men. It is, we may hold, on account of the fact that there are these two strains of meaning combined in the title 'Son of God' that the Fourth Evangelist is careful not to say that believers are sons of God. Because, as being the Son of God, Jesus is also Christ, naturally He alone can be given the former designation. Perhaps now the saying alluded to at an earlier point becomes easier to understand: 'I ascend unto my Father and your Father . . .' (xx. 17). No one could share with Jesus to the full His Sonship; to no one could God become Father in the whole sense in which He was to Him. Still, we should not suppose, because in His case there was something unique in Sonship and divine Fatherhood, that the uniqueness extended also to His participation in the love-relationship of God and the Logos; this believers would share with Him,—it is what is meant in this Gospel by the eternal life promised to them.

It is enough now simply to add that the utterances, 'I and my Father are one' (x. 30; xvii. 11, 22), 'I am in the Father and the Father is in me' (xiv. 10 f.; x. 38; xvii. 21), and 'I am God's Son' (x. 36), are variations in expression of the same theme. (We notice how the claim in x. 36 to be God's Son is re-stated two verses farther on as 'the Father is in me and I am in the Father'). What we have just been observing about the significance for the world of the fact that Jesus is the Son of God—namely, that it makes Him the Christ—stands also for these other utterances, and we should understand them accordingly.

But all this carries with it the clear corollary that the union of the man Jesus with the Logos and therefore with the Father, with all the possibilities which this opens up for believers, is the content, and not simply the medium, of the revelation accomplished by Him.

2

THE INTERPRETATION OF THE PROLOGUE

In our discussion of the title 'Son' in the previous chapter we have assumed that this word ought to stand in the text of i. 18. But deeply rooted in the textual tradition is a variant reading: 'Only-begotten God'. Whether this variant was written by the Evangelist or not, it clearly shows a return to the thought of *v.* 1, and thus reflects a belief that *monogenes* was a fitting epithet to use of the pre-cosmic Logos.

We notice first that at *vv.* 1 and 2 the Evangelist had written about the pre-temporal relation of the Logos to God with a chosen phrasing which does not in itself show that he had had in mind either of the primary senses—uniqueness and derived being—which come into question for the term *monogenes* at *v.* 18.[1] The Valentinian Nous or Arche, also called Monogenes,[2] was unique amongst the Aeons in the Pleroma of that school, being 'the first begotten by God',[3] the one 'in whom the Father emitted the totality[4] in germ',[5] and alone able to comprehend him.[6] But in the absence of a system of Aeons resembling the Valentinian in the outlook of the Fourth Gospel, the Evangelist could not have thought of the pre-temporal Logos as unique on a similar ground.

Is it more to the point that the Valentine Monogenes was derivative (he was the offspring of Bythos and Sige),[7] in company with 'the Son' in the Evangelium Veritatis,[8] the Logos of Philo,[9]

---

[1] See Büchsel, *T.W.N.T.*, IV, pp. 745–750; Hort, *Two Dissertations*, pp. 16 f.

[2] Irenaeus, *Adv. haer.* i. 1, 1; cf. Holl, in his edition of Epiphanius, *Panarion* 31, 10, 7.

[3] Irenaeus, ibid. i. 8, 5; Holl, ibid. 31, 27, 1 ff.

[4] 'Il s'agit toujours des Éons, au moins au premier plan' (Sagnard, *La Gnose Valentinienne et la Témoignage de Saint Irénée*, 1947, p. 312, note 1).

[5] Irenaeus, ibid. i. 8, 5.   [6] Irenaeus, ibid. i. 1, 1 and i. 11, 1.

[7] Irenaeus, ibid. i. 1, 1.

[8] Edited by Malinine, Puech, and Quispel (1956). Their numeration of lines is followed here, as in W. Till's translation of the writing in *Z.N.T.W.*, Heft 3–4, 1959, and in K. Grobel, *The Gospel of Truth*, 1960. In this Christian Gnostic work 'the Father of Truth', who was without beginning, uncreated, generated within His being a 'name' for Himself before producing the Aeons (38, 32 ff.). 'The name of the Father,' it is said, 'is the Son' (38, 6 ff.). By the term 'Son' is meant the otherwise incomprehensible God self-adapted to be knowable.

[9] Philo describes the Logos as begotten by the Father of the universe, and

C

and Wisdom?[10] Seemingly not. The thought of *vv.* 1 and 2 moves on the pre-temporal plane, describing how it had always been with the Godhead, not only how it was 'in the beginning'. In that case, effort to interpret these pronouncements about the Logos and God is at fault if it is based, in particular, on the Stoic distinction between a man's spoken word (*prophorikos logos*) and the thought (*endiathetos logos*) of which the spoken word was the expression,[11] the Logos then being taken to be God Himself become, by a self-effected differentiation within His own being, what He had not been eternally, that is to say, revealable (to man, once he had been brought into existence). The differentiation, the revealableness, had always belonged to the nature of God. The Evangelist calls it—calls that in God which would be revealable to man, knowable by him, when he came to be there to respond to God—the Logos. In two passages from the prayer in chapter 17 the pre-temporal Logos is conceived to have existed in a relation to God of love (*v.* 24) or glory (*v.* 5). The love or glory had always been constitutive in the being of God and on this account He would be self-revealable and self-communicable in the temporal order when He had made it.

It was not the intention of the Evangelist to make the Logos subordinate to God. In the body of the Gospel, to be sure, Jesus, loved by the Father (iii. 35; v. 20; x. 17) and loving Him (xiv. 31), one with the Father (x. 30; xvii. 11, 22), in the Father and having the Father in Him (x. 38; xiv. 10, 20; xvii. 21), is nevertheless subordinate to Him (v. 19; xiv. 28; xv. 9); but it is quite another matter when the incarnate Logos, Jesus considered in respect of His created manhood, is so presented.[12] Again, it can be seen that the Evangelist's conception of the Logos as underived in His being, eternal, subject and object of the interior love-relation

calls him His eldest son and His first-born (*De conf. ling.* xiv. 63; cf *De agric.* xii. 51). The Father begat the Logos and made him the unbreakable bond of the universe (*De plant.* ii. 9). The Logos is said to be God's 'name' (*De conf. ling.* xxviii. 146), and the name of God is 'the interpreting Logos' (*Leg. alleg.* III. lxxviii. 207). For Philo the Logos was God Himself thought of as having turned to the planning of the world perceived by our senses, before actually making it (*De opif. mundi* iv. 16, 19; vi. 24). Cf. also *De cherub.* ix. 28, where the Logos is regarded as 'conceived before all things'.

[10] Prov. viii. 22 ff.; Sirach i. 4, 9; xxiv. 8 f.

[11] Von Arnim, *Stoicorum Veterum Fragmenta*, II, p. 43, 13–20; p. 74, 3–6.

[12] On the created manhood of Jesus see Quick, *Doctrines of the Creed*, pp. 50, 110 ff., 179.

essential to the life of God, was not taken over from Philo, nor from Jewish thought about the pre-cosmic Wisdom and Torah;[13] it was his own, however much his mind may have been nourished on the way to it by knowledge of such speculations.

The statements in *vv.* 1 and 2 are to be pondered with recognition that the Evangelist had unexpressed reasons for making them. Soon he intended to introduce the historical figure of Jesus, in whom he held that the Logos so became incarnate that He, Jesus, shared in that love-relationship within the Godhead which had existed in the beginning and always; and then he proposed to let the theme be developed throughout the Gospel that everyone who believed in Jesus would share with Him forever in the same relationship. When he wrote these first two verses the Evangelist was laying the foundation of the Christian Faith as the Gospel in its entirety would set it forth.

So far as the Prologue is concerned, finding the notion of derived being in connexion with the pre-temporal Logos is simply an inference from the reading 'Only-begotten God' at *v.* 18, fostered by knowledge of those other sources already noticed; whilst the Gospel itself has material, in particular at v. 26 and xvii. 24 which tells against the rightness of doing so. *Monogenes* can be seen to be an appropriate term to use—at i. 14 and 18, and at iii. 16 and 18, its only other occurrences in the Gospel— once it is treated as an epithet not for the pre-temporal but for the incarnate Logos, with the ideas of derived being and uniqueness both contributing to its intended significance. For as manifested on earth in Jesus, the Logos had in His manhood derived being, and in view of what it means in St. John that the incarnate Logos should have been 'Christ', He was unique among men.

The variant reading we are considering must then have arisen when the Fourth Gospel had already gone into circulation. It is true that the earliest clear reference to i. 18 is found in the *Excerpta ex Theodoto* of Clement of Alexandria.[14] Monogenes, when first mentioned (6, 1 f.), is a proper name, the name of the Valentinian Aeon, another name for Arche, and 'is also called God, as likewise

---

[13] On the pre-cosmic Torah see Strack-Billerbeck, II, 353 ff.; III, 129–131: *T.W.N.T.*, II., pp. 1040 ff; Moore, *Judaism*, I, pp. 266 ff.

[14] Ed. Casey, 1934; Sagnard, *Les Extraits de Théodote*, 1948. Compare Ptolemaeus' exegesis of the Prologue (Irenaeus, *Adv. haer.* i. 8, 5; 1, 75–80 Harvey; 31, 27, 1 ff. Holl), where it is far from evident that the author found 'Only-begotten God' in his text of John i. 18. But see also Zahn, *G.K.* II, 957, note 4, and Hort, *Two Dissertations*, p. 31, note 1.

. . . he (i.e. John) shows', and there follows a citation of John i. 18 with the variant reading. The Valentinian exegetes were forcing on the Evangelist an interpretation he himself could never have intended. It might appear that, in spite of their misrepresentation, they provide good evidence for the presence of the variant in their text of the Gospel. But the appearance is deceptive, for we shall see that the Valentinians were in fact familiar with the other reading as well. At 7, 1 of the *Excerpta*, the Father, being unknown, is said to have 'emitted' Monogenes, to satisfy his desire to be known to the Aeons; and Monogenes is called 'the Son', because 'through the Son the Father was known'. Subsequently Monogenes is further defined as 'that of the Father which is comprehensible, that is to say, the Son'. And at 7, 3 it is observed that, after he had been emitted, Monogenes remained 'unique Son in the bosom of the Father'. It is noticeable that when (at 6, 1 f.) the deity of Monogenes is a matter of special interest and John i. 18 is used in confirmatory evidence of it, the reading 'God' appears in the quotation, but when (at 7, 1 ff.) it is a question of the role of Monogenes in revelation, and allusion is made to the same verse of the Prologue, the reading 'Son' is found.

An equally important textual question is raised by the punctuation of i. 3-4. Ought the words 'which came into being' (ὃ γέγονεν) to form the end of *v.* 3 or the beginning of *v.* 4? It was seemingly after the propounders of heretical opinions had found support for their views in the second possibility that the first became the favoured proceeding (see Hoskyns ad loc.), but this does not settle for us which of the two the Evangelist intended.

Let us first assume that he intended the words to go with *v.* 4. We must then choose between a variety of renderings.

(a) 'That which came into being—in it was life.' By life is then meant 'the vitalizing energy of all that exists'; but this is a meaning totally at variance with v. 26 and with the rest of the Gospel, where life is bestowed on men only through the coming, the death, and the resurrection of the incarnate Logos. It is also difficult to see how a general diffusion of life and light throughout mankind can be made to square with the subsequent references to darkness.

(b) 'That which came into being—in it He was life.' Here the Logos is being treated as immanent in the created universe, as in the Stoic philosophy. But this reading is open to the same objections as (a).

(c) 'That which came into being in Him was life.' The life which was eternally in the Logos went forth from Him by His will to issue in the created life of the world (so Bernard ad loc.). If it is right to hold that the eternal life of the Logos in St. John is a love-relationship within God, this understanding of the sentence would mean that the Logos, in Himself love, produced the life of the world out of His own blessed being; He did not cause it to be by sheer creation; He willed into existence another mode of His own life, but a mode of it which, for all its worth as an expression of the love which was the eternal being of the Logos, was subject to change, decay and death. But it is hard to believe that the Evangelist conceived of such created and transitory life as 'the light of men'.

(d) 'That which came into being in Him (i.e. the incarnate Logos) was life.' This is a proposal (Quick, *Doctrines of the Creed*, pp. 110 ff.) which lets 'life' have its normal Johannine sense: as the Father has life and has given it to the Son (v. 26), so believers, begotten again as children of God (i. 13; iii. 3 ff.), come to receive it. But it is harsh to see a reference to the Incarnation earlier than v. 5.

It would appear that v. 4 does not lend itself to satisfactory explanation if it is allowed to commence with 'that which came into being'. What then if we suppose that the Evangelist intended these words to belong to v. 3? In that case v. 4 begins with a statement not about creation but about the Logos: in the Logos was life. It is indeed still possible to construe this with what precedes, so that the words explain why it was that all things could be brought into being by Him; it was because 'in Him was life'. On this view, the life which was in the Logos is thought to be the power to produce the life which is in the natural world and in man, vitalizing energy, the creating and supporting source of all forms of temporal existence. But then life would here be ascribed to the Logos in a sense different from that of the Father, the Son, and believers in the body of the Gospel; it would not be 'eternal life'. There is also the improbability that the Evangelist would have gone on to say that this life was 'the light of men'. It is altogether more likely that at v. 4 the Evangelist has got past the thought of creation and is continuing his characterization of the Logos in anticipation and explanation of what he would represent Jesus to have been as the Gospel went on. Jesus, in whom he believed that the Logos had become incarnate, he intended to set forth as the giver of life to a world that had not got it. So now he explains why this was true of Him: 'in the Logos was life', and therefore also in Jesus, in whom the Logos became flesh, there was life, for imparting to men. If this was the Evangelist's motive in composing the first half of *v*. 4, he would not have intended life to be here understood differently from that life which Jesus gives to believers.

It is only this punctuation and this interptetation of it that make the second half of *v*. 4 intelligible, where it is said that the life which was in the Logos was the light of men; not the light they actually possessed, but the light for them. His life was to be their light. There is no lack of evidence in the Old Testament, later Judaism, the New Testament, and elsewhere, for the use of light as a symbol of beatitude or salvation in one sense or another, and this usage will put us on the right track here.[15] In using the term light as a symbol of the supreme blessedness the Fourth Evangelist knew that he would be understood. Here at *v*. 4 he is declaring that the true end of the creation of man was his participation in that light which was the life of the Logos. He has not yet begun to speak of the shining of the light, i.e. of the revelation to men of the nature of the felicity in which they were created to share.

The importance of this question of punctuation becomes apparent when we proceed to ask at what point in the succeeding verses the Evangelist begins to speak about the Incarnation. Is it at *v*. 5 or only at *v*. 14? Do *vv*. 5–13 refer to the activities of the pre-incarnate or of the incarnate Logos? *V*. 5 speaks of the light shining in the darkness; the shining is the revelation to men of the life which was always in the Logos, so that they might participate in it, if they would, and so come to the divinely willed end of their creation; and the darkness is the world of men which is called darkness because it has not the life which was in the Logos. There is no attempt to explain why a world which was brought into existence by the Logos should nevertheless be darkness.

Instead of the imperfect tenses hitherto employed in connexion with the Logos a present tense now appears: the light shines. Is perhaps the present used timelessly, to denote an activity of the

---

[15] E.g. Amos v. 18; Isa. ix. 1 f.; lx. 1; Enoch v. 7; Rom. xiii. 12; Eph. v. 8; Acts xxvi. 17 f.; I Clem. lix. 2; Acts of Thomas 28, 157; *Corp. Hermet.*, I. 32.

pre-incarnate Logos in revealing to men the life which was in Him? This might appear plausible, were it not that the next three verses introduce John the Baptist as a witness to the light. But the witness of John is to Jesus, the incarnate Logos, who is the light (i. 15; i. 19 ff.; viii. 12; ix. 5). Again, it is implied in v. 39–40 that until He to whom the Scriptures are there said to bear witness had come it was not possible for men to have life. Why not, if, before He became incarnate the Logos had already been revealing to men the life which was in Him? Why not, if, in the language of v. 5, the light had already been shining? There is a remarkable utterance in xv. 22–24, which is all in line with what would appear to be the thought of the Gospel on this matter: 'If I had not come and spoken unto them, they had not had sin: but now they have no excuse for their sin. . . . If I had not done among them the works which none other did, they had not had sin: but now they have both seen and hated both me and my Father.' That is, if the In-carnation of the Logos in Jesus had not taken place, and if Jesus had not in words and works revealed the fact and what it meant for men, namely, the possibility of their having life, the unrespon-sive Jews here referred to in particular, but regarded as typical of an unbelieving world, as always in St. John, would not have 'had sin'; they would have gone on walking in darkness, blind to God, but they would not have 'had sin', not in that definitive sense which settled their fate for ever. Before the coming of Jesus there was no revelation which could cause men to 'have sin' in this final, decisive sense; but this is just the situation which a revelation by the pre-incarnate Logos of the life which was in Him, a shining of the light, would have created for the unresponsive. 'I have come as light into the world, that no one who believes in me may remain in the darkness' (xii. 46). To be in the darkness was the only possibility for men before Jesus came. See also ix. 39–41, where again it is implied that up to the coming of Jesus men were in the darkness. The light was not shining yet; they could not see therefore, could not see God. So too in the last verse of the Prologue the meaning will be not simply that no one had in fact seen God at any time, but that until Jesus came no one could see Him for want of the needful revelation.

For these several reasons v. 5 is the point in the Prologue at which occurs the transition from statements about the pre-existent Logos to direct statements about Him as incarnate. The

Evangelist uses the present tense because he has in view not only the revealing activity of Jesus whilst He was on earth, which from his standpoint belonged to the past; in addition he is thinking of its prolongation in the Christian church after the death of Jesus, especially in the preaching of those for whom Jesus petitions the Father in xvii. 20. The preaching of the word, the Evangelist is implying, is the continued shining of the light in the darkness of the world. In it Jesus is present and active as the light of the world. In true Christian preaching that same light which John saw shining in Jesus shines on.

In the second half of *v.* 5, with the choice of the aorist, there is a reversion to the standpoint of the ministry of Jesus: the darkness did not grasp the light, so as to make it its own; and perhaps in addition we are to understand that the darkness did not prevail over the light, with primary reference to the conquest of the ruler of this world by the death and resurrection of Jesus (xii. 31 f.; xiv. 31).

The interpretation we have given to *v.* 5 is further strengthened when we read in *v.* 8 that the Baptist 'was not that light'. He is being contrasted not with the eternal Logos—nobody suggested he was that—but with Jesus (cf. i. 19 ff.). We are prepared therefore to find that the following verses describe that particular coming of the light into the world to which the Baptist was sent to bear witness. This at least will hold good, whatever we may decide about the syntax of *v.* 9. This verse may be taken to mean: 'The real light was in being that gives light to every man coming into the world.' There is no need to regard the final phrase as tautologous, since the Rabbis were fond of employing the expression 'every man coming into the world' as a circumlocution for 'all men'. But in view of the statement at iii. 19 that 'light has come to the world', it is more probable that the translation should be: 'The real light that gives light to all men was coming to the world,' the reference being, as at x. 36, to the public ministry of Jesus.

In the verses that follow there are two sets of parallel statements, each of which helps to explain the announcements in the other. 'He was in the world, and although He was creator of the world, the world did not know Him. He came to His own property, and those who were His own did not receive him.' His own property is the whole world of men He had created; they rightly belong to Him as being created by Him. Similarly those who received Him and so were given the right to become children of God are identical with the 'we' of *v.* 14 ('we beheld his glory'); for to behold the glory is to believe (cf. ii. 11). To those who did receive Him, who did recognise and acknowledge Him as the real light, who did appropriate His revelation of the life which was in Him, He gave the right to be children of God. It is important to notice that the giving of this right is described as an act different from and subsequent to the shining of the light and its reception. By His Incarnation Jesus had become Son of God and was therefore able to shine with the eternal light of the Logos; but this revelation could not of itself make it possible for others to enter the same relationship. He had still to *give* the right, and we shall see that this giving was the Passion. 'Children of God' is clearly meant to be a designation of those, but only of those, who receive the exchatological salvation, the life which Jesus brings.

Those who believed in His name became God's children or, as it is now further explained, were 'begotten of God'. There is reproof of obtuseness in what is said in this verse: the physical nature of human birth is no ground of objection to there being a process other than that of ordinary begetting by which God can have His children. Later in the Gospel the reader will be told that this process is an activity of the Holy Spirit, whose function is to lead believers into full realization and appropriation of the life and love of God revealed in Jesus (iii. 3 ff. and the Last Discourse). But this gift can only be bestowed through the Incarnation and Passion.

V. 14 gathers up all that has been said up to this point about the coming of the Logos into the world, but for the first time indicates the manner of His coming. Without ceasing to be the Logos, without ceasing to have in Him that life which was destined to give light to men, the Logos acquired manhood. The Evangelist and others like him know this because they have seen His glory, revealed in the discourses, signs, and above all in the dying and rising of Jesus. But what made their knowledge a saving knowledge was not just that they had been allowed to see the eternal glory which the Logos had always had in the presence of God (xvii. 5), but that they had seen this glory communicated to the man Jesus in such a way that in Him manhood was taken up into union with the Logos. In this union of the divine and human in Jesus the

Fourth Evangelist discerned the last things becoming present, eschatology in realization. It is to be noted that God is here, for the first time in the Prologue, called Father, because it is the incarnate Logos who is spoken of as His only Son.

The incarnate Logos is further said to be 'full of grace and truth'. 'Grace' expresses the idea of a favour which the Logos was able to render to man now that He Himself had acquired manhood. Attempts are still made to explain 'truth' here from the LXX sense of *aletheia*, the faithfulness of God to His covenant relation with His people (cf. Rom. iii. 3 ff.), and the clause as a whole on the basis on Exodus xxxiv. 6.[16] But we shall see later that *aletheia* has in this Gospel its normal Greek sense of 'reality', and denotes the reality of God's nature and purpose, and therefore also the reality of the destiny of man. It is another word for that love which is the life of God, and which he has designed to impart to men, to Jesus in the first instance by the Incarnation, and through Him to all believers. And the gift has in fact been imparted: 'from that of which He was full we have all received.'[17]

We have been told in *vv.* 6–8 of the testimony of John the Baptist to the presence in the world of that life which was the light of men; and we have taken this as proof that at *v.* 5 the Evangelist has already begun to speak of the Incarnation. He now reports in wording which emphasizes the authority and the continued applicability of the testimony (note the present tense) that this was the One—i.e. the Logos who had acquired manhood in Jesus, who 'dwelt among us,' whose glory believers had seen—of whom the Baptist had spoken. 'This is He of whom I said: "A follower of mine has taken precedence of me, because He existed before me." ' The Logos who had come to possess manhood was the Logos of *vv.* 1–4, and His attribute of pre-existence could therefore be transferred to the man Jesus.

Up to this point the incarnate Logos has not been identified by name, but now He is at last identified as Jesus Christ. It was not, as the Jews supposed, to the Law of Moses that men must go to discover the whole counsel of God, but to the gracious reality which had taken human form. Only from One who was the incarnate Logos, from His ministry in discourse, sign, voluntary

[16] Boismard, *Le Prologue de Saint Jean*, pp. 74–79; Barrett, *The Gospel according to St. John*, p. 139.
[17] See J. A. Robinson, *St. Paul's Epistle to the Ephesians*, pp. 255 ff.; C. F. D. Moule, *The Epistle of Paul to the Colossians*, pp. 164 ff.

dying, resurrection, and sending of the Spirit, came grace and truth. So would the Fourth Evangelist have wished his readers to understand the Prologue, once they had become familiar with the whole contents of the Gospel.

3

THE DESCENDING AND ASCENDING SON OF MAN

We have been arguing that the title 'Son of God' is applied in the Fourth Gospel to the human figure of Jesus, and that His Sonship is central to the revelation He is said to have given. In the fact that God, out of love for the world, had willed that now, for the first time, through the Incarnation, there should be a human being who shared in His own life (for this is in part what it meant for Jesus to be Son of God), lay the world's one hope of itself having eternal life. For St. John the Sonship of Jesus stood there objectively as the decisive expression of the will of God to bring to fulfilment His purpose for the world that it should have life. 'I came that they may have life and may have it abundantly' (x. 10). Further we have suggested that the divine Sonship of Jesus, except in so far as it made Him the Christ, is for believers an inclusive Sonship, becoming so through the Passion. This thesis might seem, however, to be called in question by the 'Son of Man' sayings, and to these we must now turn.

The first of the series is in i. 51: 'Verily, verily, I say unto you, Ye shall see the heaven opened, and the angels of God ascending and descending upon the Son of Man.' The promise is given with allusion to the story of the dream-vision of Jacob in Gen. xxviii. 'And he dreamed, and behold a ladder set up on earth, and the top of it reached to heaven: and behold the angels of God ascending and descending on it (*or* on him)' (Gen. xxviii. 12). We are not to suppose that Nathanael and the other disciples would see a literally opened heaven and angels in physical motion before their eyes. If the Fourth Evangelist had intended the promise to be understood in that way, he might have been expected to show some interest in its fulfilment. But no fulfilment of the promise, taken literally, occurs in the Gospel, and no wondering why not. We have to do with imagery. 'Heaven lying open' means 'God revealed'. But there are two ways of taking the imagery of 'the angels of God ascending and descending upon the Son of Man', for the Son of Man may here be compared either with Jacob or with the ladder in the story of Bethel. In the one case, we are being told that it is now possible to see God ('see the heaven opened'), because Jesus, as Son of Man, is in continuous communication with God. If on the other hand the Son of Man is being compared with the ladder, then Jesus, as Son of Man, is the means of connexion between earth and heaven, the medium for bringing about continuous communication between man and God.

J. Jeremias[1] has proposed that the saying should be interpreted in the light of certain late Jewish ideas about Gen. xxviii. 17 and 22, according to which the Bethel-stone was the place of the presence of God, the place above which was the door leading into heaven. Three things would then be asserted about Jesus in John i. 51: where He is, there is the presence of God; where He is, there is the door leading into heaven; where He is, there are the angels bringing down to earth the living word of God. Such were the things into which Nathanael and the others would gain insight. But is the Johannine saying really meant to suggest an analogy between Jesus and the stone of Bethel? It seems very doubtful.

A different interpretation of John i. 51 has been put forward by Odeberg (pp. 35 f.), making use of a rabbinic midrash on Genesis xxviii. 12, which assumes that Jacob had a heavenly counterpart or image, which was the ideal Israel. The passage runs: 'They were leaping and skipping over him, and rallying him, as it is said, "Israel in whom I glory" (Isaiah xlix. 3). "Thou art he whose image is engraved on high." They were ascending on high and looking at his image, and then descending below and finding him sleeping.'[2] According to Odeberg, the ascending and descending angels symbolize the opening up of communication between Jacob and his image in heaven, and he supposes that this piece of rabbinic interpretation underlies the Johannine utterance: the assurance given to the disciples that they would see the angels of God ascending and descending upon the Son of Man meant that they were to see the connexion being brought about between Himself as He was on earth and His mode of existence in heaven, His heavenly image. What should be said of this proposal? The thought of a connexion being brought about implies of course a broken connexion, or a connexion to be established. This, how-

---

[1] *Angelos*, 3 (1928), pp. 2–5.
[2] Bereshith Rabba lxviii. 18; cf. C. F. Burney, *The Aramaic Origin of the Fourth Gospel*, p. 116.

ever, is not a Johannine conception; on the contrary, Jesus in the Fourth Gospel is the incarnate Logos, one with the Father (x. 30; xvii. 11), having the Father in Him and Himself in the Father (x. 38; xiv. 20; xvii. 21); upon the factual character of this union everything turned for St. John. The theory of Odeberg starts off wrongly. The Johannine Christ had no heavenly counterpart, no image, from which on earth He was separated.

The saying in fact comprises two predictions. Nathanael and the others are to see (a) heaven opened and (b) angels ascending and descending. Are these parallel ways of expressing the one idea, that Jesus would be acting all the time in communion with God, that in Jesus Himself, in His divine-human person, in His whole work of revelation, God is manifest? Or does the second promise make a significant addition to the first, by asserting that Jesus is the medium by which the open heaven is to become a reality to men? It is more probably in accordance with the intention of the saying to start from the thought of the angels ascending and descending *on* rather than *to* the Son of Man, and to take the imagery to mean that a new intercourse between heaven and earth, between God and men, a new relation of shared life, would now set in, on account of the divine-human person and of the whole ministry of Jesus in uttered word, sign and Passion.

Nathanael had thought that a known eschatological figure would come and that in Jesus he had come. 'Rabbi, thou art the Son of God; thou art King of Israel' (i. 49; cf. i. 41). Here was faith in Jesus, faith of a kind; it is called faith in the story, but it was inadequate and needed to be put right. The saying in i. 51 is a promise that, from those first imperfect responses to Jesus, Nathanael and the other disciples would be taken on to true faith in Him as the One by whom God becomes manifest to men and shares His own life with them. But the implication is that this advance in faith cannot happen until a fuller revelation has been achieved than that which was at the time available to Nathanael.

Another difficult 'Son of Man' saying is that which occurs in iii. 13: 'And no man hath ascended into heaven, but he that descended out of heaven, even the Son of Man, which is in heaven.' In treating of *v.* 13 it is necessary to take into account the connected saying in *v.* 12: 'If I told you earthly things, and ye believe not, how shall ye believe, if I tell you heavenly things?' In the earlier part of the conversation with Nicodemus stress is laid on the necessity of a man's undergoing a new birth; as born of flesh, man is flesh, and therefore, if he is not to perish, he must be born anew. The earthly things which Jesus has told Nicodemus must then include this judgment on the natural state of man. By contrast the heavenly things are the divinely ordained destiny of man and the divinely ordained means by which that destiny is to be attained; and these are the things revealed in the great discourses and sayings of Jesus. The point is not that, having spoken of earthly things without being understood, Jesus will not speak of heavenly things, but that when He does speak of them, as speak of them He will, He will not find believing response. His witness to earthly things had to be received, if His witness to heavenly things was not to be unavailing. But the ability of Jesus to make this disclosure is now said to be grounded in the fact of the ascent of the Son of Man to heaven. The *kai* in *v.* 13, as often in St. John, is adversative,[3] 'and yet'; and the general sense of the utterance is: 'You will not accept my testimony to the heavenly things, and yet no one else can bear trustworthy testimony to them, because no one else has ascended into heaven.'

Although this verse makes reference to the descent of the Son of Man, we are not to suppose that the heavenly things were things known by Him in a pre-cosmic existence. His ability to speak of them depends not upon His descent but upon His ascent, which is treated as an already accomplished fact. How is this assertion to be made intelligible? One explanation, often adopted, is clearly to be ruled out, if we are intended to understand that it is the fact of His ascent to heaven which enables Jesus to reveal heavenly things. According to this proposal, the representation of our passage that Jesus had already ascended when the words were uttered should be regarded as merely reflecting the standpoint of believers after the earthly life of Jesus was over. For them, looking back, He had risen from the dead and ascended, and He was now in heaven;[4] and the saying has been given a form which made it agreeable to this element of their faith in Him. This cannot be right. We want an explanation of the ascent which will show how it could have brought to Jesus the knowledge of heavenly things which He conveys in His discourses. We have to try to make

---

[3] See Moulton and Howard, *Grammar of N. T. Greek*, II. iii, p. 469.

[4] It may be this misunderstanding of what is meant by 'ascended' that made the clause 'which is in heaven' textually uncertain, as being seemingly tautologous.

intelligible the ascent of Jesus into heaven as already a fact of His experience when He is said to have addressed Nicodemus. It need hardly be remarked that we are not expected to think of a literal ascent into a spatially conceived heaven. 'Heaven' is used to designate the immediate presence of God; and correspondingly, with regard to the ascent to heaven, it is not a question of an outward and visible proceeding. The Son of Man had ascended into heaven: He had come, that is to say, into the presence of God. There is no need for us to suppose that St. John is thinking of an ecstatic experience after the manner of Paul, who relates how he was once 'caught up even to the third heaven . . . and heard unspeakable words, which it is not lawful for a man to utter' (2 Cor. xii. 1–4). Of such experiences on the part of Jesus the Fourth Evangelist reports nothing. We are expected to understand that the authenticating ground of the witness of Jesus to the heavenly things was not ecstasy but His knowledge of His heavenly origin.

The descent of the Son of Man is one way of describing His origin in God, an idea which, as we shall see later, is conveyed in a variety of ways in the Gospel. His ascent to heaven is His coming, under the guidance of the Spirit, to a knowledge of that origin and of its implications for mankind. So interpreted the saying has close parallels in two other passages. 'I know him; because I am from him, and he sent me' (vii. 29). 'Not that any man hath seen the Father, save he which is from God, he hath seen the Father' (vi. 46). As having been brought by the Spirit to know His heavenly origin, and so to the self-knowledge disclosed in the Gospel, Jesus, the Son of Man, had already 'ascended into heaven', He had seen and constantly saw God, and therefore He could reveal Him and bear testimony to the heavenly things.

It is well-known that Bultmann[5] finds in the Johannine discourses and Prologue adaptations of a 'Gnostic' myth in which a heavenly Redeemer—Logos or Nous or Anthropos—was thought of as becoming incarnate. According also to W. Bauer[6] the 'Son of Man' passages in St. John reflect a current conception of a heavenly Man as redeemer, which is still to be observed in Gnostic, Hermetic, Mandaean, and Manichaean sources, with traces of it elsewhere. This is a suitable point at which to recall

[5] *Das Evangelium des Johannes* (1937–41), pp. 8–15, 38 ff., et passim; *Z.N.T.W.*, 1925 (Heft 1–2), pp. 100 ff.
[6] *Das Evangelium des Johannes* (3rd ed. 1933), pp. 42 f.

the opinions of these scholars, and to add a reason for doubting whether they are to be accepted.[7] Let it once be granted that the existence of Jesus as Son of Man before the Incarnation is not being implied in iii. 13, and then it becomes clear that the utterance is not evidence for the alleged relation of the Gospel to the myth. Naturally, the same is to be said of the whole group of Johannine sayings of Jesus in which the thought conveyed by the wording 'descended out of heaven' is expressed in different ways (cf. vii. 29; viii. 14, 23, 38, 42; xiii. 3; xvi. 27, 28, 30; xvii. 8).

We pass on to a consideration of the utterance in iii. 14–15; 'And as Moses lifted up the serpent in the wilderness, even so must the Son of Man be lifted up: that whosoever believeth may in him have eternal life' (cf. Num. xxi. 8–9). The connexion of thought with the two preceding verses seems to be that the bearing of His witness to the heavenly things by the Son of Man, which not even His disciples were as yet ready to believe, had to be followed by His Passion, if the purpose of the witnessing, indicated in v. 15, was to be achieved.

According to Hippolytus (*Refut.* v. 16), the Ophite Gnostic sect of Peratae found in the pre-incarnate Logos of St. John's Prologue the perfect Serpent of their doctrine, and—making reference to John iii. 14—in Jesus the appearance thereof. It is also interesting to notice that Philo, in the course of a treatment of the serpent made by Moses as typifying one of the cardinal virtues, temperance, used the expression '*logos* of temperance', from which it looks as if he had in mind a connexion between his Logos and the serpent of Moses (*Leg. Alleg.* II, 79–81). However, it does not appear that the brazen serpent itself is supposed in St. John to have been mysteriously significant in relation to the Son of Man; it is rather the action of Moses in setting it upon a pole that is regarded as a foreshadowing of the Crucifixion.[8] The expectation is that the words 'lifted up' will not be read without recollection of the procedure when a condemned man, about to die by crucifixion, was laid down, fastened to the crossbeam, and then

---

[7] For other reasons see Menoud, *L'évangile de Jean d'après les recherches récentes*, (1947), pp. 41 f.

[8] Cf. Mishnah, *R. H.*, iii. 8: 'But could the serpent slay or the serpent keep alive!—it is, rather, to teach thee that such time as the Israelites directed their thoughts on high and kept their hearts in subjection to their Father in heaven, they were healed; otherwise they pined away.' (Danby's translation). It seemed to Manson (*J.T.S.*, 1945, p. 130) that the passage was intended to rebut early Christian, including the Johannine, understanding of Numbers 21.

D

raised with it from the ground (cf. xii. 32 and the comments of
the Evangelist in xii. 33 and xviii. 32) into position on the upright
stake. The verb, however, is being applied to Jesus in a figurative
as well as in this literal sense. The lifting up of the Son of Man,
which was at one and the same time His execution and His exaltation, was necessary for the possession of eternal life by the believer.

There are two other sayings in which the Crucifixion is
described as the lifting up of the Son of Man. The first comes at
viii. 28: 'When ye have lifted up the Son of Man, then shall ye
know that I am *he*, and that I do nothing of myself, but as
the Father taught me, I speak these things.' The expression
'I am' (as in viii. 24 and xiii. 19, where also no predicate is added)
must be held to have concentrated in it the full content of Johannine belief in Jesus, for the implication is clear enough that upon
believing 'that I am' depends the possession of eternal life. 'Ye
are from beneath; I am from above; ye are of this world; I am not
of this world. I said therefore unto you, that ye shall die in your
sins: for except ye believe that I am (*he*), ye shall die in your sins.'
(viii. 23-24). The formula 'I am' seems to have been taken from
the Old Testament[9] (Deut. xxxii. 39; Isa. xli. 4; xliii. 10; xlvi. 4;
xlviii. 12), and laden with the distinctive meaning of the Son of
Man sayings in the Gospel. In asking Jesus 'Who are you?' the
Jews do indeed show that 'I am' was not intelligible to them.
They receive an answer which implies, whether we follow RV or
RVm at *v.* 25b, that the meaning of the title has already been
disclosed in previous utterances of Jesus, which he has addressed
to unreceptive minds up to this point in the Gospel, but with the
added warning that, after they have crucified Jesus, the knowledge
of Him they think they want but do not, they will have. It is
possible to hold that Jesus is giving the Jews, unreceptive though
they are, crucify Him though they will, an assurance that after
His death they will come to believe in Him. But the announcement
is made in a quite unqualified manner, so much suggesting the
inevitability of their knowledge, that their situation would then
lose much of its seemingly unquestionable gravity. They may
carry their refusal of Jesus to the last extreme, and it will not
matter in the end; for know Him they will, and knowing find
salvation. The more natural interpretation of the words is that the

---

[9] On the attempt of G. P. Wetter to establish a pagan-hellenistic origin for it
in St. John see F. Büchsel, *Johannes und der hellenistische Synkretismus*, pp. 37 f.

knowledge spoken of is the catastrophic knowledge—borne in upon the Jews at the 'last day'—that their rejection of Jesus had established their origin from the Devil (viii. 44, 47) and brought them to ruin in common with him. If this is so, then the title 'Son of Man', here as in v. 27 ff., includes the idea of Jesus as judge. The life-giver is transformed into the judge by all to whom He comes ineffectively. Let them not suppose that they had nothing to fear from their now established ignorance of Him. The alternative to the salvation He offered was divine judgment and there was much that He could say about them and their calamitous lot (viii. 26a: 'I have many things to speak and to judge concerning you'). It was however not the fact that Jesus could say it, as if on His own authority, but the reliability of Him who had sent Him (viii. 26b: 'he that sent me is true'), from whom He had heard the things that He spoke to the (unbelieving Jewish) world, that made fateful their refusal of Him. When the Jews came to understand that Jesus was the Son of Man, they would know then that His mission now was not a self-appointed one and therefore without divine authority, but that He acted in it as the Father taught Him.

The only other saying of Jesus in which the Crucifixion is described as a lifting up is also to be regarded as spoken of the Son of Man. 'Now is the judgement of this world: now shall the prince of this world be cast out. And I, if I be lifted up from the earth, will draw all men unto myself. But this he said, signifying by what manner of death he should die.' (xii. 31–33). The dying of the Son of Man would bring to pass 'the judgement of this world': it would dethrone 'the ruler of this world' and determine the fate of those in it who showed that they belonged to him by their rejection of Jesus; and as for all others—all Gentiles and Jews who are described in the Gospel as 'given' by the Father to Jesus —it would enable Him to 'draw' them to Himself. From the time of the Crucifixion the Devil would produce no more children, no more men owing their origin to him and therefore unable to believe in Jesus (viii. 43–47). The casting out of the Devil from the world would bring freedom to man—to use it if he would—to be 'drawn' by Jesus to Himself. The phrasing 'I will draw' and 'unto myself' is deceptively simple. The first person singular must be understood to include the activity of Jesus in the coming apostolic mission (cf. x. 16; xvii. 18 ff.); and the sense of 'unto myself' is

no less than 'into my own union with the Father' (cf. xiv. 3). Of
this so wonderful appointment for man the death of Jesus and the
apostolic preaching were the prerequisites; only by dying, and only
with believers, could He share His union with the Father.

What is said in xii. 31–33 should be kept in mind at the reading
of the words 'I have overcome the world' (xvi. 33): Jesus by His
dying casts out 'the ruler of this world' and acquires it for Himself;
its future rests with Him. The perfect indicative is used because
the victory over Satan which the Passion secures is seen as already
achieved and permanent.

We have already made use of the saying at v. 26 to prove that
by 'the Son' St. John means not the pre-existent Logos, who
eternally possessed life in Himself, but the man Jesus, to whom
the Father gave 'to have life in himself'. We must now take note
of the succeeding verse: 'and he gave him authority to execute
judgement because he is the Son of Man.' Here there is no
question of a pre-existent Son of Man: He is the human figure, to
whom God has imparted the authority to be revealer and therefore
also judge of those who repudiate the revelation. This inference
finds support in vi. 27: 'Work not for the meat which perisheth,
but for the meat which abideth unto eternal life, which the Son of
Man shall give you: for him the Father, even God, hath sealed.'
The Son of Man not only has food which abides unto eternal life,
but is that food: He is 'the bread of life'. And of both Son of
Man and bread of life it is said that they 'come down from heaven
(vi. 33, 38, 41, 50, 51; cf. iii. 13). But it cannot be held that He
pre-existed either as Son of Man or as bread of life, for the bread
is subsequently said to be his flesh (vi. 52), his human life created
by God in union with the Logos and surrendered to death for the
life of the world. Further discussion of this saying and the 'Son
of Man' sayings at vi. 53 and vi. 62 must be deferred until we deal
with the chapter as a whole.

In the story of the man born blind Jesus puts to the healed
man the question: 'Do you believe in the Son of Man?' (ix. 35).
The man had owned to a belief that Jesus was a prophet (v. 17),
and that He had a divine mission (v. 33). For all that he had not yet
grasped the true meaning of the action of Jesus in healing him.
The act of healing had been a 'sign' (v. 16), and signs in St. John
are revelation of the 'glory' of Jesus (ii. 11), that is to say, of the
relationship of 'in-being' existing between Himself and the

Father (x. 38; xiv. 20; xvii. 21). This mutual relationship between God and the Logos, into which the manhood of Jesus was taken up through the Incarnation, underlies all the recurrent word-themes of St. John's Christology. In the present instance it is intimated first of all that in performing the sign Jesus was revealing Himself to be the light of the world; that is, He was revealing that the life of the Logos which was to be the light of men (i. 4) had in Him taken human form. Thus at the climax of the story when Jesus seeks from the healed man a statement of belief beyond anything he has so far offered, it is discernment of what the sign has disclosed that He wants from him, but He asks for it in terms of a confession of Himself as Son of Man. We are bound therefore to conclude that the Evangelist intended the title 'Son of Man' to be yet another expression of the union of Jesus' manhood with the Father.

The healed man's confession is followed by further words about judgement: 'For judgement came I into this world, that they which see not may see; and that they which see may become blind. Those of the Pharisees which were with him heard these things, and said unto him, Are we also blind? Jesus said unto them, If ye were blind, ye would have no sin: but now ye say, We see: your sin remaineth.' (ix. 39–41). Those who lack sight are those who know that they walk in darkness and need the light of life; and they are promised that they will find it in the Son of Man. Those who are said to see are those who are unaware of the darkness they walk in; by their misuse of the opportunity to discover the light of life in the Son of Man they are made 'blind', i.e. they come to know—when it is too late—that they do 'walk in darkness'. From the encounter with the Son of Man comes either enjoyment of the light of life or blindness (cf. xii. 35: 'Walk while ye have the light, that darkness overtake you not; and he that walketh in the darkness knoweth not whither he goeth.') The Pharisees are being told that, if they have only darkness to walk in, which is all they do have, if Jesus is not what He claims to be, there is no sin in not believing in Him (cf. xv. 22). But the truth is that they have the light of the world in their midst, as the words of Jesus and the sign disclose; yet they will not acknowledge that apart from Him they 'walk in darkness' (but now ye say, 'We see'). Not to believe in Him, when the facts about Himself and their own situation are what they are, is sin for which there is no remedy ('your sin remaineth').

There remain to be considered the utterances in which the title 'Son of Man' is used in connexion with the term 'glorify'. In contrast to the earlier pronouncements by Himself (ii. 4; vii. 6, 8) or by the Evangelist (vii. 30; viii. 20) that His hour or time had not yet come, Jesus declares in xii. 23: 'The hour is come, that the Son of Man should be glorified.' Later we read: 'When therefore he (Judas) was gone out, Jesus saith, Now is the Son of Man glorified, and God is glorified in him; and God shall glorify him in himself, and straightway shall he glorify him' (xiii. 31–32). The former saying belongs to the incident of the Greek-speaking non-Jews attracted to Judaism and now wanting to see Jesus—a development which has other significance for Him than it has for them: for Him it means that the time has now come when prophetic anticipation is to be fulfilled through Himself and the Gentiles are to be embraced within the salvation He brings (cf. Mic. iv. 1–5; Isa. xi. 10; xlii. 1–8; xlix. 6; Zech. viii. 20–23). There follows at once the utterance: 'Except a grain of wheat fall into the earth and die, it abideth by itself alone; but if it die, it beareth much fruit.' Unless He died, the life that was in the Son of Man would remain in Him alone, but if He died He would become 'the bread of life' to Gentiles no less than to Jews. From all this it is clear that the glorification of the Son of Man is His death.

But what is meant by the word 'glorify' in the quoted passages? Before we attempt to answer this question, it will be well to observe the extent to which the uses of the noun 'glory' as well as the verb 'glorify' can vary in this Gospel.

(a) There is a glory which the Logos is said to have possessed in the presence of God before the creation of the world (xvii. 5).

(b) There is a glory of the incarnate Logos, revealed by Jesus, and observed by his disciples (i. 14; ii. 11).

(c) There is a glory of God revealed in the raising of Lazarus, but presumably also in the other signs of Jesus (xi. 40).

(d) There is a glory to be given by Jesus to those who believe in Him (xvii. 22).

(e) There is the glory of Jesus' exalted state, which believers are ultimately to behold (xvii. 24).

In all the passages mentioned above it is the noun that is used, but there are further variations on the theme of glory which are expressed by the use of the verb.

(f) There is a glory which Jesus lacked during His ministry but would receive or win through His death (xii. 23; xiii. 31; xvii. 1), or through the active faith of the disciples (xvii. 10).

(g) There is a glory which the Father lacked, to be supplied by the Son (xiii. 31; xvii. 1).

(h) There is a glory which the Father wins for Himself (or for His name) in the ministry and death of Jesus (xii. 28), in the subsequent activity of Jesus in the disciples (xiv. 13), and in the mission of the disciples themselves (xv. 8).

The glory which the Logos eternally shared with God was by the Incarnation imparted to the man Jesus in such a way that everything He said and did, but particularly His signs (ii. 11) manifested both His glory (i.e. the fact of His union with the Logos) and the glory of God (xi. 40). There are two passages in the Gospel which the commentators and the authors of monographs or of articles on *doxa* appear not to have thought of turning to account. 'If I do not the works of my Father, believe me not. But if I do them, though ye believe not me, believe the works: that ye may know and understand that the Father is in me, and I in the Father' (x. 37–38). 'Believe me that I am in the Father and the Father in me: or else believe me for the very works' sake' (xiv. 11). 'Works' and 'signs' are nearly, though not quite synonymous in this Gospel. Thus in the story of the man born blind Jesus says: 'Neither did this man sin nor his parents: but that the works of God should be manifest in him' (ix. 3); and later in the story the healing is called a sign (ix. 16). Now the signs are said in ii. 11 to be a revelation of Jesus' glory, and the works are said in x. 37 f. to reveal the mutual indwelling of Jesus and the Father: Jesus is 'in' the Father and the Father 'in' Him. It would seem to follow then that the glory which Jesus possessed and revealed in His ministry, and which others could see and ultimately share, was His union with the Father, the union of His manhood with Godhead. Naturally, glory, so conceived, does not belong to others until Jesus imparts it to them through their response of believing in Him; that is to say, in their case possession of it is a consequence of His Incarnation, of the Passion and the Resurrection, and of the words and works by which Jesus reveals the significance of these events.

When we turn to the passages in which the Evangelist uses not the noun 'glory' but the verb 'glorify', we are confronted with a problem. For Jesus prays to the Father to endow Him with glory and declares that the time has come for this glory to be bestowed upon Him. 'The hour is come, that the Son of Man should be glorified' (xii. 23). 'Now is the Son of Man glorified, and God is glorified in him; and God shall glorify him in himself, and straightway shall he glorify him' (xiii. 31–32). 'Glorify thy Son, that the Son may glorify thee' (xvii. 1). 'Glorify thou me with thine own self with the glory which I had with thee before the world was' (xvii. 5). Now—at this time of His Passion and because of it—the Son of Man will win for Himself glory. How may that be? The last of the four passages quoted makes it plain that the concept of glory expressed by the verb is the same as that expressed by the noun. But the glory which the Logos has with God before the world was is a glory which Jesus Himself already possesses and has manifested: He is already in the Father and the Father in Him. However, if glory can be used of that relationship, why not also of a corresponding one between Himself and those who believe in Him? There is a supporting passage to quote: 'And the glory which thou hast given me I have given unto them; that they may be one, even as we are one; I in them and thou in me. . . .' (xvii. 22–23). 'I in them': in giving them His glory He comes to be 'in' them. Now that He dies, His union with the Father expands to include within it His disciples, and this adds a glory, a new union of love, to the glory He had already.

In the first half of xiii. 31 Jesus declares that this union with the disciples is already achieved, because He is speaking as though the Passion were already accomplished. In the second half of the verse He adds that God will win for Himself glory by means of the Son of Man. Jesus is in union both with Him and—now at last —with the disciples. God has therefore also come into union with them. The relationship of reciprocal 'in-being' is no longer confined to Him and Jesus; the Passion brings believers into it, and the Son of Man and God are thus glorified together.

In the following verse the tense changes from an aorist to a future: 'and God shall glorify him in himself, and straightway shall he glorify him.' The aorist indicated that the glorification of the Son of Man, which consisted in His drawing of believers through the Cross into union with Himself and therefore with the Father, was deemed to be complete at the moment of Judas's departure. But now we read of a future glory also. It is possible that the Evangelist is simply repeating as a promise what he has stated as a fact, but more likely that the new statement carries the argument further. God will bestow glory on Jesus in some Johannine sense not wholly covered by the previous verse. Jesus is in the Father, and that is His glory; His dying enables Him to be in believers also, and that adds to His already existing glory; and a still more complete 'glorifying' awaits Him in God. How may we proceed now? More than one possibility of interpretation would appear to be open for consideration. It may be implied that the union of Jesus with believers, as conceived in v. 31, is not yet all that it can be and will be; or that Jesus Himself had yet to enter a perfection of union with the Father exceeding that which He now enjoys. In the Father though He is, He declares repeatedly that He 'goes' or 'comes' to Him, as if He would say that His crowning act of obedience to Him at the Cross would bring Him even nearer to the Father (cf. x. 17 f.), still more completely into union with Him; and it may be that this is the sense in which the Father has yet to glorify Him. These two possibilities are not, however, mutually exclusive, and indeed may well be regarded as complementary; for if the glorification already achieved is the union of Jesus with believers, then any future access of glory for Himself will be a deeper union with the Father which He can share with them.

Further light on this theme is provided by the prayer of xvii. 1, 5: 'Father, the hour is come; glorify thy Son, that the Son may glorify thee. . . . And now, O Father, glorify thou me with thine own self with the glory which I had with thee before the world was.' In trying to grasp the meaning of this petition we reflect that Jesus is already glorified in the sense that He is in the Father, and already glorified in the sense that He is in believers (xiii. 31). Would it not appear then that the words of the prayer are to be regarded as a request for the fulfilment of the promise in xiii. 32? It will be noticed that, since the glory prayed for in xvii. 5 is the glory of the Logos before the creation of the world, the recipient is to be Jesus considered in respect of His manhood. But we cannot stop here without implying that the Incarnation of the Logos involved the relinquishment of His glory; whereas the Gospel tells us that the ministry of the incarnate Logos was the revelation of His glory. Within the Godhead before the creation of the world there was, and ever continues to be, a glory-relation-

ship, which is also contemplated in xvii. 24, with only a variation
of the phrasing, as one of love: '. . . thou lovedst me before the
foundation of the world.' Into this relationship—fully now at
last, because He accepts the Cross (x. 17)—the Father is to draw
Jesus. But not Jesus alone, since in the Cross His manhood is to
become inclusive of all who are to believe in Him.

Both these passages speak also of the glorifying of the Father
by the Son. The act by which Jesus imparts to others the glory He
has manifested, and so brings them into union with Himself and
with the father (cf. xvii. 22), is an enrichment of his own glory
but therefore also an enrichment of the glory of God. The glory
which was characteristic of the relationship between God and the
Logos was first extended to include the manhood of Jesus, and
then further extended to include all who belonged to Jesus.

The prayer in chapter 17 looks on ahead beyond the believers
who are more immediately contemplated in it. This is true in
particular of the petitions in v. 1 and v. 5. 'Neither for these only
do I pray, but for them also that believe on me through their
word. . . .' (xvii. 20). The dying of Jesus glorifies them all, the
few of the present, and the many to come. The petitions in v. 1
and v. 5 have a fulfilment at once—'straightway' (xiii. 32), 'the
hour is come' (xvii. 1)—but that is not all that may be said of
them. It would be a function of the Paraclete to promote in the
'glorified' the knowledge of their state: 'In that day ye shall know
that I am in the Father, and ye in me, and I in you' (xiv. 20). At
the last day itself, of which the expectation is alive in the Fourth
Gospel, whatever still stood between all the already 'glorified'and
their complete realisation of what Jesus had done for them when
He died would disappear, and theirs would be the final beatitude,
to which the utterance near the end of the prayer relates: 'Father,
that which thou hast given me, I will that, where I am, they also
may be with me; that they may behold my glory, which thou hast
given me: for thou lovedst me before the foundation of the world'
(xvii. 24). The glory which they are to discern, to discern per-
petually, is indeed His own glory in the sense of His union with the
Father, yet it is also His glory in the sense of His union with them
as won for them by His dying. They are to be with Him where He
is, with Him in that always-existing relationship of love within
the divine life, of which the word 'glory', here as in xvii. 5 is a
designation.

Throughout the Gospel the title 'Son of Man' regularly alternates with the titles 'Son' or 'Son of God'. There is the transition from 'Son of Man' to 'only Son' at iii. 13–16, and the reverse transition from 'Son' to 'Son of Man' at v. 22–27. In chapter 6 the two titles are to all appearance interchangeable. And we have just seen that what is declared as a fact about the Son of man in xiii. 31–32 becomes in xvii. 1–5 the theme of a prayer about the Son. But this is not to say that St. John ever uses either title in a purely formal way, without regard to its meaning and history. This is a point of some importance when we come to summarize the ideas which the Evangelist has brought to expression by means of the traditional title 'Son of Man'.

As Son of Man Jesus is the revealer of heavenly things, that is, of the divinely ordained destiny of man, of which His own life is the supreme example. He is the bringer of the eschatological salvation, the light of a world in darkness. Because men are judged by the response they make to the coming of the light, He is also the One authorized to execute judgement. His existence has its corporate aspect, since His glorification is the means of drawing believers into unity with Himself and therefore into unity with God. But He is able to be all this because He is in the first instance the Proper Man, man living as God intended him to live, in continuous communion with Himself, totally dependent on God's authority and totally obedient to His will. Elsewhere in the New Testament the ascription of the title 'Son of Man' to Jesus shows clear associations either with Daniel 7 (Mark xiv. 62; Rev. i.13) or with Psalm 8 (Heb. ii. 6 ff.; cf. I Cor. xv. 24 ff.), and it is proper to ask whether there is any trace of such a background to the usage of the Fourth Gospel. To be sure, St. John never actually cites either Old Testament passage. But it can hardly be coincidence that three of the ideas which are associated with the Johannine Son of Man are also found in Daniel 7, where the 'one like to a son of man' is the bearer of eschatological salvation, a corporate or representative figure, and the wielder of judgement. It seems plausible too that St. John, like the author of Hebrews, went behind Daniel and early Christian tradition to the basic Hebrew meaning of the phrase, and understood 'Son of Man' as a description of the perfect manhood of Jesus. But if we are right in so thinking, it is important to note that St. John envisages three distinct stages or phases in the development of that perfect manhood. By the Incarnation of the Logos God objectively took the individual manhood of Jesus into union with Himself. By the guidance of the Spirit Jesus subjectively entered into knowledge of His own heavenly origin and of God's purpose in sending Him, and entered so fully that He could be said to have ascended into heaven and indeed to be in heaven, in the bosom of the Father. By His glorification at the Passion, like the seed which by dying bears much fruit, His individual manhood ceased to be alone in the presence of God, but became a corporate, inclusive manhood into which others could be brought. And in this threefold action of God we are to see the heavenly things which it was the function of the Son of Man to reveal.

4

ESCHATOLOGY IN ST. JOHN'S GOSPEL

We have been arguing that what Jesus revealed, according to the Fourth Gospel, was that in Him the eschatological action of God was taking place, for the salvation or judgment of men. It is now time to take a closer look at the eschatology of the Gospel. So far we have concentrated on the titles 'Son' and 'Son of Man', which have often been interpreted in the past as though they had a timeless quality. That they are in fact eschatological titles is shown by their close association with the other title 'Christ', with which the Gospel begins and ends (i. 41, 49, 51; xx. 30–31; cf. iv. 26; vii. 41; x. 24–25). The same Jesus who was the incarnate Logos merges in the figure of the Messiah, making the final stages of resurrection, judgment, and eternal life in the drama of eschatology present realities. But this is not the whole truth about Johannine eschatology; for there is also the prospect of further fulfilment 'at the last day'. We may find first the one attitude adopted towards eschatology and then the other in a single passage. 'He that heareth my word, and believeth him that sent me, hath eternal life, and cometh not into judgment, but hath passed out of death into life. . . . The hour cometh, in which all that are in the tombs shall hear his voice, and come forth; they that have done good, unto the resurrection of life; and they that have done ill, unto the resurrection of judgment' (v. 24–29). 'He that eateth my flesh and drinketh my blood hath eternal life; and I will raise him up at the last day' (vi. 54). In xiv. 2–3 Jesus, it is said, goes to His Father's house to prepare abodes for believers; and He will come again and take them to be with Him where He is. The weight of meaning in the deceptively simple language of the verses is considered later, together with reasons for concluding that the promised coming again of Jesus was to be that expected at the last day. On the other hand, Martha is guided from the thought of resurrection at the last day to that of resurrection and life as made present facts for believers by Jesus. Judgment is conceived to be predominantly a proceeding of the present. 'He that believeth not hath been judged already, because he hath not believed on the

name of the only begotten Son of God' (iii. 18). 'For judgment
came I into this world, that they which do not see may see; and
that they which see may become blind' (ix. 39). 'Now is the judgment of this world; now shall the prince of this world be cast
out' (xii. 31). 'For the prince of this world has been judged'
(xvi. 11). Yet there is also a definitive judgment still to come.
'He that rejecteth me, and receiveth not my sayings, hath one that
judgeth him: the word that I spake, the same shall judge him in
the last day' (xii. 48; cf. v. 28 f.).

In senses which are more fully discussed in a later chapter,
Jesus gives promises to believers that, after His death but before
He raises the dead from their graves for life or judgment, before
He comes again to make good the assurances uttered in xiv. 3, He
will come to them, they will see Him, He will see them again. 'I
will not leave you desolate: I come unto you. Yet a little while,
and the world beholdeth me no more; but ye behold me: because
I live, ye shall live also. In that day ye shall know that I am in the
Father, and ye in me, and I in you' (xiv. 18 ff.). 'Ye heard how I
said to you, I go away and I come unto you' (xiv. 28). 'A little
while, and ye behold me not, and again a little while, and ye shall
see me' (xvi. 16 f.). 'Do you inquire among yourselves concerning
this, that I said, A little while, and ye behold me not, and again a
little while, and ye shall see me? . . . ye shall weep and lament, but
the world shall rejoice: ye shall be sorrowful, but your sorrow
shall be turned into joy. . . . I will see you again, and your heart
shall rejoice, and your joy no one taketh away from you' (xvi.
19 ff.). It would not be enough to refer the expressions in these
passages simply to the brief resurrection appearances of Jesus.
More meaning than that is required to account for the promises
that He would not leave believers bereft, and that 'in that day ye
shall know that I am in the Father, and ye in me, and I in you.'
We are to understand in addition that Jesus would become
continuously present within them as a fruit of His dying and of the
work of the Paraclete whom He would send to dwell in them.

The content of the 'word' of Jesus in St. John, summarily
described, ranges over the action of the Logos in acquiring manhood in Jesus, the dying and resurrection of Jesus, and the
revelation of the meaning of these three events in His discourses
and signs in the Gospel and in the sending and work of the Paraclete. That the function of the Paraclete in relation to the word

of Jesus is to expound it, and not to add to or complete it, is
explicitly stated at xvi. 13 ff. and implied at xii. 48, where the
basis of the judgment at the last day is made the word spoken by
Jesus. The events of the Gospel story and their explanatory
unfoldings together determine in some sense a present fulfilment
of eschatology in respect of resurrection and life in those who are
believingly responsive to the word of Jesus, whether presented to
them by Himself or by others subsequently (xiii. 20; xvii. 18 ff.),
and in respect of judgment in those who are not; and they also
determine a future, last day fulfilment of it in respect again of
resurrection and life or of judgment.

How may we understand the varying character of the 'realized
eschatology' in St. John, the movement of thought about it
between the present and the future? Are the sayings of 'the last
day' group out of harmony with the others? and are they therefore
perhaps the work of an interpolator? Yet why should a conjectured
reviser of the Gospel have allowed the two types of eschatological
sayings to stand there, even side by side in chapters 5 and 6, if he
had believed that they were discordant? Or are the futurist
sayings of the group not indeed additions to an earlier form of the
Gospel, but nonetheless only concessions to a Christian expectation which the Evangelist himself did not cherish?

It is to the point to observe that the act of Jesus in bringing
Lazarus from the dead is regarded in xi. 25 f., 43 f. as a revelation
of His will and power to raise believers who die, and this shows
that the promises He gives in vi. 39 ff. to do so 'at the last day'
would express authentic Johannine thought, even if they were
insertions made by a reviser. The world of change, decay, and
death would come to an end, and when it did Jesus would not let
believers who had died pass away with it; He would make them
participants in the eternal order of 'life' alone. The fourfold
assurance in chapter 6 and the story of the miracle in chapter 11
do cohere; so do both with the announcement in xii. 48, and all
three with that in v. 28 f. If a reviser had been at work in the last
of these verses, which began significantly with 'Marvel not at
this', he has produced safeguarding utterances, neither calling in
question the teaching of the preceding verses nor allowing it to
stand alone, in case it should be taken to express the whole truth of
its themes.

The problem raised by the existence of differing eschatological standpoints in St. John is not one which a hypothetical reviser of the Gospel has created; even if we were to admit his existence, we should have to say that he has interpreted Johannine eschatological thinking from itself, with true apprehension and not distortion of it. What may we then say in explanation of the varying outlooks? Shall we say that the hope of a future, definitive fulfilment of eschatology was too deeply rooted in primitive Christian theology not to find a place in the Gospel? This is likely to be so, provided that it be maintained that the hope is really alive in St. John along with the faith in the present realisation. But it amounts to little as an explanation of the two standpoints, which are due to a conception of the Last Things which made the two harmonious. How then are they held in unity in the Gospel?

A two-sided eschatology is not peculiar to St. John in the New Testament. Differences of emphasis and other variations apart, St. Paul had a similar eschatology, and it is less difficult in his case to understand the combination of the two elements; the clues are more obvious. Perhaps then St. Paul may ease the problem for us in the Fourth Gospel. 'There is, therefore, now no condemnation to them that are in Christ Jesus;' so St. Paul writes in Rom. viii. 1, meaning that for them the eschatological judgment is over. And yet we read in Rom. xiv. 10: 'We shall all stand before the judgment seat of God'; and in Gal. v. 5: 'We through the Spirit by faith wait for the hope of righteousness.' Again, the Christian, Paul can say, has already risen with Christ from the dead. 'For the death which he died, he died unto sin once: but the life that he liveth, he liveth unto God. Even so reckon ye also yourselves to be dead unto sin, but alive unto God in Christ Jesus' (Rom. vi. 10 f.). 'Wherefore if any man is in Christ he is a new creature; the old things are passed away; behold they are become new' (2 Cor. v. 17; cf. Col. iii. 1; Eph. ii. 5 ff.). Yet in Phil. iii. 8–14 Paul's longing is that 'I may know him and the power of his resurrection, and the fellowship of his sufferings, becoming conformed unto his death, if by any means I may attain unto the resurrection from the dead. Not that I have already obtained, or am already made perfect: but I press on . . . toward the goal unto the prize of the high calling of God in Christ Jesus.'

Paul allows us to follow him fairly easily in the movement of his thought to and fro, from already fulfilled to still unfulfilled eschatology, in the manner indicated by such passages as these. The divine saving act of Christ's death and resurrection took place, he believed, inclusively of believers. Thus in 2 Cor. v. 14, from the promise that 'one died for all', Paul infers the death of all: 'therefore all died'; they died as regards 'the flesh', and they so died, it is meant, when Christ died. 'I have been crucified with Christ' (Gal. ii. 20). The 'I' which had been crucified was 'the flesh', the old self in bondage to sin. 'They that are of Christ Jesus have crucified the flesh with the passions and the lusts thereof' (Gal. v. 6). When? At baptism (cf. Rom. vi. 6)? There is no mention of baptism in connexion with either of these passages from Galatians; but even if Paul had had baptism in mind, it would not have been to the exclusion of the historical event of the Crucifixion, held by him to have been a dying of all Christians as such with Christ, in virtue of His solidarity with them, of His inclusion of them in Himself. Inasmuch as they had died in respect of the flesh, having so died when Christ died, Paul could assure Christians that for them the judgment had already gone by. And it was for the same reason—the relationship of solidarity existing between Christ and themselves—that Paul could hold that Christians had risen when Christ rose from the dead. They formed with Him a kind of joint personality and therefore they had been with Him at the Cross for their deliverance from evil, and had passed with Him into His resurrection life. Now, true though Paul believed it to be that he himself, his converts, and other Christians had all died when Christ died and all risen when He rose, he did not mean that it was true of himself and of them in the same sense in which it was true of Christ at the moment of His death and resurrection. For the actual experience of 'dying to sin' and 'living to God' had been His alone (Rom. vi. 10). Yet, although it had to be His alone, it had been His in order that it might become the experience of all who with Him would make up His mystical body—that body of Christ which was Christ and His community together. It had once been delivered from all evil and raised up in perfection before God, but in advance of the knowledge of any except the chief member. 'For ye died, and your life is hid with Christ in God' (Col. iii. 3). Now, in the present, the other members were being conformed to Christ dying and risen. 'For we which live are alway delivered unto death for Jesus' sake, that the life also of Jesus may be manifested in our mortal flesh'

E

(2 Cor. iv. 11). At the last all would be wholly and veritably raised
up into His resurrection life. 'When Christ, who is our life, shall
be manifested, then shall ye also with him be manifested in glory'
(Col. iii. 4).

We can see how for Paul, without discord in his thought,
eschatology could be already realised, and yet unrealised; or
rather, strictly speaking, already realised, and yet now in the process
of realisation, and yet again still to be realised. The clues to the
unity of his thought are his belief that the crucial divine acts of
Christ's death and resurrection were inclusive of believers; that, in
the nature of the case, these saving events had taken place in
advance of their conscious participation in them; that by manifold
operations of the Spirit the participation of Christians in the
events was now in process of being actualized in their experience
(Rom. viii. 2-6, 12-17, 26 ff.; 1 Cor. ii. 12 ff.; xii. 3, 9 f.; Gal.
v. 16-25; vi. 8); and that finally, liberated entirely in manifest fact
from the flesh and sin, they would be drawn into Christ's own
resurrection life alone.

When we find the minds of Paul and John moving from realised
to still unrealised eschatology in a comparable fashion, there is a
presumption that it is not for wholly different reasons. In the
case of Paul the changes of standpoint become intelligible from his
manner of conceiving Christ's person corporately, inclusively: by
Him for others salvation had been gained and, as it were, concentrated in Himself for imparting to them as they believed; hence
for them the Last Things had already come hiddenly, were now
coming manifestly, and in this latter sense had still to come to the
full. Is it in a similar way that John's varying eschatology should
be understood? In each case salvation is only possible through
union with Christ: there is no doubt about that. It is also true
that in each case the union with Christ is made possible by divine
eschatological action. And it is true of John as well as of Paul that
in the first instance the person of Christ is the field of the action:
'I am the resurrection and the life' (xi. 25). With so much not in
doubt, it is to be expected that in John too in some manner Christ
is conceived inclusively of believers. It is indeed alleged by some
students of the Gospel[1] that the thought of the solidarity of
Christ and believers in what for Paul were the decisive saving
events, has no place in John, and that here is a cardinal point of

[1] E.g. A. Schweitzer, *The Mysticism of the Apostle Paul*, p. 354.

difference between the two. But to make a clean cut like this is a mistake. Thus a Johannine utterance which by implication is comparable in sense with Col. iii. 1 may be quoted from xiv. 20: 'In that day ye shall know that I am in my Father and ye in me and I in you.' To be in Christ is to be in Him who has passed victoriously through death, in Him as sharers of His risen life; and this, as we shall see, following upon a manner of joint dying with Him.

Can we then produce a Johannine utterance about the death of Christ to put beside, for example, 2 Cor. v. 14 ('one died for all, therefore all died'), where Paul means, as we have observed, that when Christ died all believers also died in respect of 'the flesh'? To some extent, it is true, the thought of the passage is un-Johannine. But then in Paul's eyes 'the old self', 'the flesh', was so bad that such life as was Christ's risen life was an impossibility for any man unless he first died in respect of 'the flesh', whereas in John the verdict on the natural state of some men—those who 'come to the light' when it is shining (iii. 21)—is different. Not that he held that there could have been hope of eternal life even for these, if there had been no coming of Christ, no Incarnation, no passion and resurrection, and no revelation by Christ in words and signs of the meaning of these events. They would then have remained in darkness and in death. 'As the Father raiseth the dead and quickeneth them, even so the Son also quickeneth whom he will. . . . The hour cometh, and now is, when the dead shall hear the voice of the Son of God; and they that hear shall live' (v. 21, 25). Still, for John, in some cases, many or few—how many or how few only the encounter with Christ discloses—the self is not so incapable of possessing eternal life, once the possibility is there, that it can become fit only by dying, as it seemed to Paul. So we can understand why John does not go all the way with Paul in asserting a joint dying of believers and Christ.

Nevertheless, if not wholly in Paul's manner, he does conceive that Jesus was not alone at the Cross; believers too were there with Him, having its meaning made over to them. He is the real Vine; but not apart from them, and not to the exclusion of the significance of His death. However, the passage in which the thought of Christ's inclusion of believers in His act of dying is most clearly discernible is one from the prayer in chapter 17: 'And for their sakes I sanctify myself, that they themselves also may be sanctified in truth' (xvii. 19). We ought to allow the following considerations to guide us in interpreting the utterance. First, said at such a moment, when Jesus is about to lay down His life, 'I sanctify myself' should be taken to mean 'I in dying consecrate myself'. Secondly, according to John Jesus was at once a human figure and the Logos who was with God and was God (i. 1). In what sense could it be said of Him that He sanctified or consecrated Himself? As we have already seen, to sanctify means to separate from the profane and to transfer to the divine sphere, and this is a concept which can properly be applied to the manhood of Jesus, but not to the eternal Logos. The man Jesus in dying separates Himself from 'the world', from the darkness, and transfers Himself wholly into the divine sphere, by perfecting the union in Him of that which was human with that which was divine, the union of His human will with the will and purpose of the Father.

What then is the case for regarding the passage as implying that Jesus died in solidarity with believers? The purpose of the self-consecration of Jesus is explained to be in general 'for their sake' and specifically that they also may be 'consecrated in truth'. Earlier in the Gospel it is said that Jesus had been consecrated already: 'If he called them gods, unto whom the word of God came, . . . say ye of him, whom the Father sanctified and sent into the world, Thou blasphemest; because I said, I am the Son of God?' (x. 34 ff.). Here the allusion is to the moment of the Incarnation when the manhood of Jesus was brought into being in possession of life shared with the Father (v. 26), and was therefore separated from the world which had not life in it. Thus did the Father equip Him for His mission to give life to the world. As One already consecrated in this sense Jesus in xvii. 19 says, 'I consecrate myself'. United though He is already with the Father, sharing His life, here is another act of union. What significance attaches to this one? Certainly there is something distinctive in this 'consecration'; it is His own act, His act of complete self-offering in death to the Father, and it makes Him all the more the object of the Father's love: 'Therefore doth the Father love me, because I lay down my life' (x. 17). But this time a further element is added; for it is said that the consecration is 'for their sake', that they may be 'consecrated in truth'. Yet it is by the consecration of Himself, of His manhood, that they are so consecrated; His consecration is at the same time their own. He and they are so related, so bound together, that He can and does now act inclusively of them, can and does now make the perfected union of His manhood with the Father their union also. How this finding as to the relationship between Jesus and believers at the Cross, according to John, enables us to perceive the essential harmony of his eschatology within itself in much the same way as in the case of Paul's we shall observe as we proceed. For the moment we must turn to the remaining and related 'consecration' passage in John, which occurs two verses earlier in the prayer.

'Consecrate them by the truth: thy word is truth' (xvii. 17). It eases matters to observe that 'thy word' is said to be the truth in which believers are to be consecrated, and that in the course of the prayer it is also said, 'I have given them thy word' (v. 14), and 'they have kept thy word' (v. 6). We have to remind ourselves, then, in trying to understand the petition, that those for whom Jesus makes it are deemed to have knowledge of the truth, i.e. of the word of God as revealed by Jesus. For them there was consecrating power in this truth. We recall also that Jesus has himself claimed to be 'the truth' (xiv. 6; cf. viii. 32, 35, where 'the truth shall make you free' and 'the Son shall make you free' are interchangeable statements), and that in Him the Word has become flesh (i. 14); so that to be consecrated in truth can only mean being brought into union with Him. It is the clear implication of v. 19 that it would be the inclusive self-offering of Jesus which would cause them to be 'consecrated in truth'. The petition in v. 17 is made with the act of v. 19 in view, and upon it the fulfilment of the petition depends. But the act, the passion, is expected to achieve its declared purpose because those for whose sake Jesus dies are in possession of the 'word'. Just because they are in possession of it, Jesus in dying could cause them to be consecrated, that is, to be taken up into His own union with the Father as consummated at the Cross.

To be one who has been consecrated by Jesus means the same thing as to be one who has been given life by Him. For to have life is to participate in the relationship of reciprocal in-being between Jesus and the Father (x. 38; xiv. 20; xvii. 21). So we should not allow the terminology employed in xvii. 19 to conceal from us the fact that Jesus is speaking of His purpose to give, by His dying, life to men who had received the revelation which He has made. By His act in dying He would give them life, as a sure consequence of their being now in possession of the revelation. And what was true of them would also be true of all believers of a subsequent time. When through the preaching of others, after the ministry of Jesus, men were confronted with and appropriated the 'word', the consecrating power of His death would come into operation for them too. It is to the point to notice the reference to preachers of the Johannine 'word' in v. 18, and how in v. 20 those who would become believers 'through their word' fall within the scope of the petition 'consecrate them in the truth', and therefore within the range of efficacy of the death of Jesus which conditions its fulfilment. Both clauses of v. 18 may be read as if the term 'consecrated' stood there: 'As thou didst send me (consecrated) into the world, even so sent I them (consecrated) into the world' (cf. x. 36). That is, as the Logos took to Himself manhood in Jesus, and in so doing gave 'life' to Him that He might be able to impart it to men, so by dying Jesus gave 'life' to preachers of the 'word' as equipment for their mission in the world. (Cf. xx. 21–29, where the ideas of the prayer are adapted to form a mission charge to the disciples after they have been effectively united with Him and endowed with the gift of the Spirit.)

It appears then that not only the immediate disciples of Jesus but also those who would later become believers are to be included in the consecrating efficacy of His death. Appropriating response to the 'word' at any time causes those who yield it to become united with that manhood of Jesus which His passion established in complete union and harmony with the Father. We are now in a position to understand why it should be represented in the Fourth Gospel that the believer has eternal life, why it should be that in this regard eschatology is treated as already realised, whilst yet a definitive realisation is left outstanding. The utterance in xvii. 19 shows that the reason is in principle the same as it is in the case of the varying eschatological outlook of Paul— Christ's gift of life to believers, present and to come, in advance of their knowledge of what He has done for them, by His inclusion of them in His act of dying.

It is in respect of present and future judgment that we see most clearly the difference between Pauline and Johannine eschatology. When Paul said, 'There is therefore now no condemnation to them that are in Christ Jesus' (Rom. viii.1), his meaning was that everyone in solidarity with Christ at the

Cross had already undergone the eschatological judgment of God. There is no suggestion in John that Jesus Himself must undergo judgment, or that those who are united with Him in His death have in His representative person passed through that judgment. 'He that believeth on him is not judged: he that believeth not hath been judged already, because he hath not believed on the name of the only begotten Son of God. And this is the judgment, that the light is come into the world, and men loved the darkness rather than the light' (iii. 18 f.). The light is here a symbol of the eschatological salvation become a present possibility for men on account of the fact that Jesus was in the relationship of 'in-being' with the Father. This is what is meant when it is said that 'the light is come into the world'. This fact it is which brings to pass forthwith the judgment of those who do not discern and receive it when it is revealed, whether by Jesus in utterance and sign or by the preaching of others after Him.

The discussion of the utterance in xvii. 19 has shown that according to John those who make appropriating response to the revelation conveyed by Jesus thereby become so related to Him that He can and does by His dying incorporate them into His own union with the Father, thus causing them to have eternal life. Correspondingly, those whose attitude towards the revelation, when it is presented to them, does not cause them to be so related to Jesus lose the opportunity to have life. He cannot include them in Himself, and therefore He cannot give them life; He does not say of them, 'for their sake I consecrate myself'. To miss the gift of eternal life is to be judged. It is precisely because others come to the light and are not judged that Jesus is able to incorporate them into His own inclusive manhood. So then we can understand how it can be represented in John that the unbeliever is already judged, whilst the believer is already in possession of eternal life. Yet if we maintain that the expectation of a future and definitive fulfilment of eschatology is really alive in the Fourth Gospel, we shall not imagine that the believer's actual experience of eternal life was the fullest conscious experience of it that he would ever know, or that anyone who refused the revelation underwent at once the eschatological judgment with the only degree of awareness that he would ever know. Indeed, are we to suppose that those with whom the revelation proved to be unavailing were conscious at all of what had really happened to them?

The expectation in John of a future judgment should be taken to imply that it must come home to them 'on the last day'. This conclusive 'coming' of Jesus would have a meaning beyond what could be grasped beforehand; for it would produce an immense intensification of the effect of previous decision for or against Him.

John's eschatology is different from that of Paul, but no less self-consistent. The event in which the Logos took manhood in Jesus, disclosed Himself in sign and discourse, and consummated the union in the death and resurrection of Jesus, made resurrection and life present actualities in those who believed in Him (and judgment a reality in those who did not), but actualities which had to be made more evident in human experience by the work of the Paraclete, and fully so by Jesus at the last day.

Further light is thrown on the eschatology of the Gospel by a study of the verb 'believe' in Johannine usage. It occurs more than ninety times, and in the vast majority of them it is used either absolutely or of belief in Jesus (or God), without any indication of the intellectual content of the belief. Elsewhere men are called to believe in the Son (iii. 16, 36), or in the Son of Man (ix. 35); to believe that He is the Holy One of God (vi. 69), that He is in the Father and the Father in Him (x. 38; xiv. 10 f.), that 'I am' (viii.24; xiii. 19). But in none of these cases does the eschatological emphasis of the Gospel lie on the surface. For that we must turn to the three remaining instances. We have already drawn attention to the eschatological significance of the verse with which the Gospel ends. 'Many other signs therefore did Jesus which are not written in this book: but these are written that ye may believe that Jesus is the Christ, the Son of God: and that believing ye may have life in his name' (xx. 30 f.; cf. xi. 27). If signs reveal that Jesus is the Son of God, as the verse clearly implies, or that He is in the Father and the Father in Him (x. 38; xiv. 10 f.), then to believe is to discern and receive this significance in them, to see in Jesus the One in whom the Logos has become flesh. But the presence of the title 'Christ' shows that something more is involved. To believe is to discern in the person and work of Jesus the eschatological act of God. Similarly, when it is said of the sign at Cana that Jesus 'manifested his glory, and his disciples believed on him', they are being credited with having discerned, however inchoately, His relationship of mutual indwelling with the Father. But it is significant that John should have chosen to use the word 'glory' as one of his chief incarnational terms. For this was a word with a long eschatological history: it was part of Jewish expectation of the Last Things that in the end God would impart His own glory to His people Israel.

More important than either of these, however, is the group of passages which speak of believing that God has sent Jesus (v. 24, 38; vi. 29; xi. 42; xvii. 8, 21), or that He is 'from God' (xvi. 27, 30). We read these passages, perhaps, with some surprise, since they seem to require an inadequate response for the gaining of eternal life. In some of the utterances in question Jesus might appear to be only one of the many messengers of God; for John the Baptist is also described as 'a man sent from God' (i. 6), and the estimate of Nicodemus is clearly regarded as a less than adequate response: 'Rabbi, we know that thou art a teacher come from God: for no man can do these signs that thou doest, except God be with him' (iii. 2). Yet it is clear that for John salvation turns on believing that Jesus is sent from God. 'This is the work of God, that ye believe on him whom he hath sent' (vi. 29). To appreciate the thought which this demand is intended to convey, we should have in mind the fuller expression in x. 36: 'whom the Father sanctified and sent into the world.' We have already seen that by the consecration of Jesus is meant the uniting of manhood in Him with the Logos, so that He could say, 'The Father is in me and I am in the Father'. The clause 'him whom He sent' has this meaning clinging to it, and we are expected to understand the required belief accordingly, as perception and acceptance of it. But once again, it is significant that John should so often have used the word 'send' to express this Christological meaning. For it indicates that what believers are required to accept is not simply the status of Jesus, but the eschatological act of God, in which He has taken humanity into union with Himself, first by having the Logos assume manhood in Jesus, then by making His manhood inclusive of others. It is important to notice, too, that the same word[2] is used to give eschatological meaning to the subsequent mission, both of the Paraclete (xiv. 26; xv. 26, xvi. 7) and of the disciples (xvii. 8; xx. 21).

It is the interaction between the objective act of God in Jesus and the subjective response of believers that explains the varieties

---

[2] John actually uses two Greek verbs, but the difference between them in this Gospel, as with other lexical pairs, is purely stylistic.

of eschatology in the Fourth Gospel. From one point of view the
eschatological act of God was complete when Jesus died on the
Cross (xvii. 4; xix. 30); in Him all men were objectively drawn
into union with the Father. But on the other hand the work of
God cannot be said to be complete until, through the renewed
presence of Jesus with His disciples, through their preaching of
His word, and through the interpreting and convincing power of
the Paraclete, the finished work of Christ has been fully appropriated.

PART II

PART II

5

THE GLORY OF JESUS

In Part I we have stated, with a certain amount of supporting argument, the thesis of this book: that what Jesus in the Fourth Gospel reveals is not the eternal nature or truth of God, not even the eternal purpose of God, but rather the fact that this eternal purpose is being enacted in His own life and ministry and will reach its full accomplishment in His impending passion and its aftermath, the sending of the Spirit; that, when John speaks of Jesus as the only Son in the bosom of the Father, and when Jesus speaks of Himself as the Son of Man who is in heaven, these are to be understood as metaphorical descriptions of the close union with God enjoyed by Jesus during His earthly life; and that, when Jesus speaks of His having ascended to heaven, or having heard and seen heavenly things in the presence of His Father, He is referring to the process by which He came to know and to identify Himself with the will of God for Himself and incidentally for mankind.

But, as we have seen, this is not the way in which the Fourth Gospel has commonly been interpreted. In expounding so complex a work, it is easy enough to support a great variety of interpretations by a judicious selection of the evidence. In the present instance it will be clear that we have been relying very heavily on two passages (v. 26; x. 37–38), which have been treated as keys to unlock the secrets of the whole book. But we have also assumed that St. John's theological thought is self-consistent throughout, so that every statement he makes is to be understood in the light of parallel, but slightly different, statements elsewhere. Thus, for example, to believe that Jesus is the Son of God, the Son of Man, the Holy One of God, the Christ; to believe in His glory; to believe that He is in the Father and the Father in Him; to believe that the Father has sent Him—all these are variations on the one Christological theme, each of which must be used to throw light on the others. The difficulty with this kind of cross-reference is that it is all too easy to misinterpret any of the Johannine sayings by seeing it in isolation from its context. Accordingly, the rest of this book will be devoted to a systematic examination of the discourses of Jesus, to see whether they do in fact support the thesis we have advanced.

The first important pronouncement of Jesus comes at the end of the conversation with Nathanael. 'Ye shall see the heaven opened, and the angels of God ascending and descending upon the Son of Man' (i. 51). We have already dealt with this saying in some detail in the third chapter, but we must allude to it here again, because it is in some sense programmatic for the Gospel as a whole. Jesus has been talking to Nathanael in the second person singular, but changes to the plural because the promises here given are intended for all disciples; and they are to be both expounded and fulfilled in the subsequent episodes of the Gospel. We shall expect, then, as the Gospel proceeds, to be told in other terms or imagery what it means to see heaven opened and angels of God ascending and descending on the Son of Man.

The promise is immediately followed by the story of the wedding at Cana, about which the Evangelist comments: 'This beginning of his signs did Jesus in Cana of Galilee, and manifested his glory; and his disciples believed on him' (ii. 11). The word 'beginning' indicates that there are to be other signs recorded, and that what is said about the first will hold good also for other members of the series; and, by the same token, that what is said about the others will help to elucidate the first. In the properly Johannine sense of the term, a sign is a miracle having the special significance of being a revelation of the glory of Jesus. To regard the glory as the miraculous power by which He made the water wine is unsatisfying.[1] In so far as it was a miracle, there was no mistaking the occurrence of a sign by any who witnessed one; it was otherwise with its character as a manifestation of the glory of Jesus, for the servants saw the miracle, but only the disciples are said to have believed. Again, since the feeding of the people by Jesus is called a sign, it is presumably to be taken as a revelation of His glory. Is the glory here revealed the power by which the five barley loaves and the two fish are made to suffice for five thousand persons? It is shown that Jesus has such power; but although they know it they do not on that account see His glory. As appears from the discourse connected with the narrative of the

---

[1] As is done by H. Kittel in his monograph *Die Herrlichkeit Gottes* (1934), pp. 241f.

feeding, the glory of Jesus displayed in this miracle is that in Him which makes Him 'the bread of life' to believers. Yet to this the crowd is blind. 'Ye seek me, not because ye saw signs, but because ye ate of the loaves, and were filled' (vi. 26). They had seen the signs, but they had done so undiscerningly; they had not perceived the revelation concerning Jesus which the signs had conveyed. The signs in St. John have in common with the utterances of Jesus the purpose of awakening, or it may be of deepening, belief in Him, of eliciting, or of intensifying, the perception of His glory. 'Many other signs therefore did Jesus in the presence of His disciples, which are not written in this book: but these are written that ye may believe that Jesus is the Christ, the Son of God, and that believing ye may have life in his name' (xx. 30 f.)

The miracle in its deeper significance was a revelation of the glory of Jesus. What then is meant here by His glory? The best comment is to be found in xvii. 22 f.: 'And the glory which thou hast given me I have given unto them; that they may be one, even as we are one; I in them, and Thou in me. . . .' Jesus comes to be 'in' believers by the bestowal of His glory upon them, and they are brought by it into a union with one another like that which exists between Himself and the Father. Another instructive indication in the Gospel as to how a reader is to think of the glory of Jesus is given by the utterance in x. 37 f.: 'If I do not the works of my Father, believe me not. But if I do them, though ye believe not me, believe the works: that ye may know and understand that the Father is in me, and I in the Father'. From this it would appear that to see and believe in the glory of Jesus is to see and believe that the Father is in Him and He in the Father. The reader is not, however, expected to wait for these later sayings before he can understand what is meant by the glory of Jesus. He has already been told in the Prologue that, when the Logos became flesh, there were those who 'beheld his glory, such glory as befits an only Son'. When the disciples responded to the manifestation of His glory they were experiencing a beginning of the fulfilment of the promise given in i. 51. From their thoughts about Him as 'the Messiah' (i. 41), 'the Son of God, the King of Israel' (i. 49), they are drawn onwards by Jesus—so the Fourth Evangelist seems to be suggesting—to a vision of His glory, His union with the Father.

When we turn back from the Evangelist's comment to the story itself, we find that it contains a hint of a further disclosure by

Jesus, beyond what He is at present able to achieve. A marriage takes place in Cana of Galilee. The mother of Jesus is there; and He and His disciples are among the guests. She brings an embarrassing turn to the festive proceedings to the notice of her Son: 'They have no wine.' In answer to His mother Jesus says: 'Woman, what have I to do with thee? Mine hour is not yet come' (*v.* 4). The phrase with which Jesus resists His mother's suggestion is used in classical Greek and in the LXX (rendering a similar Hebrew one) to express protest or the refusal of a wish. The point however will not be—'What affair is it of ours that they have no wine?' He resists His mother solely for the reason He Himself gives, that His 'hour' has not yet come. From the rest of the Gospel we can see that the 'hour' is the hour when His enemies will be able to bring about His death (vii. 30; viii. 20; cf. vii. 6, 8; xiii. 1), but also the hour of His glorification by the Father (xii. 23; xvii. 1). Jesus, we are to understand, may at this point reveal the glory He already possesses, but there is a glory He cannot yet reveal. While His mother has in mind a glorification of Himself to be gained through the performance of a miracle, the heart of Jesus is set upon a kind of glorification which, He knows, only His passion can bring to Him.

Though the reader must wait until the Last Discourse to gain a full understanding of the 'hour' to which Jesus refers, he is given a clear clue in the following incident in the temple court. Jesus makes the prediction: 'Destroy this temple, and in three days I will raise it up' (ii. 19), and the Evangelist explains that He was speaking of the temple of His body. The hour will be the time when the Jews destroy the temple of His body; and this will be the occasion for the complete fulfilment of the promise to Nathanael. Now the disciples can see that for Jesus the heaven is already opened, that he lives in communion with God, as an only Son with His father. They then will come to see that He is also the means of establishing a like union with men, so that where He is they may be also (xiv. 3), so that they have the right 'to become children of God' (i. 13).

6

THE KINGDOM OF GOD

The episodes of chapter 2 have established three points in the Evangelist's presentation of the gospel: that in a series of significant acts or signs Jesus is revealing his glory, i.e. his close communion of being and purpose with the Father; that a fuller disclosure awaits a future 'hour', which the enigmatic saying about the temple identifies as the hour of His death and resurrection; and that men have responded to the initial revelation with varying degrees of belief, some with a faith which Jesus Himself recognises as too shallow to trust (ii. 23 f.), others with a deeper, though as yet imperfect, discernment (ii. 11). To these three a fourth point may now be added. We have already been told in the Prologue that the glory which men saw in Jesus Christ revealed to them and communicated to them a grace and truth lacking from the Law of Moses. This inadequacy of the Jewish religion is further illustrated by the transformation of the water at Cana, which stood for the purificatory rites of Judaism, into the wine of the gospel, and by the saying of Jesus about the destruction of the temple. It is true that in this second instance the Evangelist at once interprets the temple metaphorically, as symbolizing the body of Jesus; but, when we take account of the context in which the saying stands, it is clear that the metaphorical is not intended to exclude the literal. As we shall see again in a moment, the Evangelist is very fond of double meanings. The act by which the Jews are to destroy the temple of Jesus' body will also render the literal temple obsolete, to be superseded by the new temple which He will raise in three days.

The third chapter contains the first of the discourses of Jesus, which amplifies and expounds the first three themes. But it is introduced by a conversation which lays bare the reason why even a sympathetic representative of orthodox Judaism cannot as yet come to a genuine appreciation of Jesus. Impressed by signs being performed by Jesus, Nicodemus believes Him to be a teacher commissioned by God. He pays Him a friendly visit on that account. Jesus brings him at once to a matter of supreme moment to a devout Jew: how does a man 'see' the Kingdom of God? Only by being born 'over again' and born 'from above'. The Greek word *anothen* can carry either of these meanings, and in any other writing we should have to choose between them; but St. John habitually makes words do double service, and it is desirable to allow both senses to combine in a single usage, both here and at *v.* 7. Nicodemus takes the word in the first sense only and puts a literal interpretation on it. This gives Jesus the opportunity to draw his attention to the other meaning and to clarify it: no one can enter the Kingdom of God except by being born of water and spirit. The condition thus restated is necessary because by physical birth men are born of flesh and are flesh, whereas only those born of the Spirit are spirit—as to enter the Kingdom of God they must be. Nicodemus is being told by implication that he must abandon the postulate that entrance into the Kingdom is secured by obedience to the Scriptures as interpreted in Rabbinic Judaism (cf. v. 39-47). If he really understood the Scriptures, if he really merited the title 'Teacher of Israel', he would acknowledge the transcience and inadequacy of the realm of the flesh, to which all things human and earthly, including the old regime of Judaism, belong and the existence of a realm of the Spirit, as much beyond his own understanding and control as the coming and going of the wind. This being so, Nicodemus ought not to hear the words of Jesus with incredulous surprise. To be sure, he cannot himself bring about the new birth, or even know the manner of its coming; but he ought at least to know that without it those who are flesh cannot enter the Kingdom. His final question, 'How can these things be?', is a confession that such thoughts are hidden from the learned Judaism he represents, and accordingly he remains silent throughout the discourse that follows.

Jesus begins (*v.* 11) an explanatory and warning response to the question of Nicodemus with a solemn assurance that His words concerning birth from above had been a disclosure of what He knew, testimony borne to what He had 'seen', unacceptable though it was to Jews who interpreted the Scriptures as did Nicodemus. We are to understand that the possibility of a birth from above rests in the first instance on the ability of Jesus to testify out of His own experience. There must then have been in the experience of Jesus something analogous to the birth from above which He declares to be necessary for others, and this can only be His reception of the Spirit. We have already been told by the Baptist that the One on whom the Spirit descends and abides is He who baptizes with the Holy Spirit, i.e. He who makes possible for others the birth from above (i. 33). And we are going to be told that it is His unlimited endowment with the Spirit which makes Jesus able to speak the words of God (iii. 34), and that the words He speaks are themselves spirit and life (vi. 63). It follows therefore that the heavenly truths He is about to communicate (v. 12) include God's eschatological act in sending the Spirit to Him. The coming of the Spirit is not simply the precondition of His speaking the words of God, but an essential part of the content of the words.

We are now told (v. 13) that Jesus' ability to speak the words in which the Spirit will be active to bring about the birth from above is the result of His being the Son of Man who has ascended into heaven. We have already seen in the third chapter that this ascent cannot be the ascension which followed on the resurrection. Even at the moment when He is speaking to Nicodemus it can be said of Him that He 'is in heaven', just as in the Prologue it was said of the only Son that He 'is in the bosom of the Father'. Both these expressions apply to the earthly Jesus and indicate the closeness of His union with the Father. The ascent into heaven will thus be the process by which he entered into that union. The Son of Man descended from heaven when the Logos took flesh and established in the person of Jesus an objective union of manhood and Godhead. He ascended to heaven when Jesus attained to self-knowledge and accepted this union as willed by God.

Up to this point the discourse may be regarded as an expansion of the earlier statement that Jesus 'manifested his glory' (ii. 11). Now (v. 14) we are reminded that full belief in Jesus, without which there can be no birth from above, has a further condition, the arrival of the 'hour' which is the hour of His death. Here again we meet yet another example of St. John's liking for double meanings. For the lifting up of the Son of Man is both an act of human sin (viii. 28) and His exaltation by the vindicating power of God (xii. 31–32). The very event in which men finally reject the revelation of His glory is to be the event in which God finally makes possible their birth from above, which is also their entry into the Kingdom of God or into eternal life.

But how was it that those experiences of the Son of Man and their fruit for the believing could ever be? It was because of the love of God for the world. 'God loved the world so greatly that he gave his only Son, that no one who believed in him should perish but should have eternal life' (*v.* 16), having become, as a believer in Jesus, one born from above. Not even here is St. John carrying us back to the precosmic life of God. He believes, to be sure, that mutual love was characteristic of the pretemporal relationship of God and the Logos (xvii. 24). But here he is concerned with God's love for the *cosmos*; and *cosmos* in the Fourth Gospel regularly means, not simply 'the world as created by God', but 'the world organized in resistance to the Creator'. The heavenly truth that Jesus reveals is not that God is love, but the eschatological fact that the love of God for the *cosmos* has found expression in the manhood of Jesus and will come to fuller expression in the Cross. (For the use of the aorist tenses 'loved' and 'gave', when the action in question has still to be completed, cf. xiii. 31). It was true of the Logos that 'in him was life, and the life was the light of (i.e. intended for) men' (i. 4). But the truth of the gospel is that 'light has come into the world' (iii. 19), bringing with it both salvation and judgment, the one as the purpose, the other as a foreseen result of its coming.

The quest for the highest good of the soul through a rebirth to it was not an unfamiliar one outside Judaism.[1] It would seem to be a well-founded supposition that the Fourth Evangelist had this manner of aspiration in the pagan world within his purview in composing the Gospel, recognizing in it an indication of responsiveness to an activity of the Logos, and aware that he had a unique understanding to convey of how the rebirth came about, with a corresponding conviction of newness in the essential quality of the resulting felicity.

In the course of this one passage St. John has used four terms to designate different aspects of the one experience: to enter or see the Kingdom of God, to have eternal life, to be saved, and to come to the light. The last three are thoroughly Johannine, but the first occurs nowhere else in the Gospel (in xviii. 36 Jesus speaks of His own kingdom, not of the Kingdom of God). Christians who came to a reading of this passage after reflection on the

---

[1] See Dodd, *The Interpretation of the Fourth Gospel*, pp. 44–53, 303–5; *The Johannine Epistles*, pp. 67–9, 74–7.

material concerning the Kingdom of God in the Synoptic Gospels would not have found themselves on entirely unfamiliar ground. The question we must ask is how far this familiarity would carry them to an understanding of the Fourth Gospel.

Among the traditional utterances of Jesus which bear directly upon this question a leading place belongs to the two parables of the Lost Sheep and the Lost Coin (Luke xv. 3 ff.). They show that He was aware of the release of a new energy of the love of God set upon redeeming the 'lost'. It was not enough that He should say in effect: 'Seek ye the Lord while he may be found' (Isa. lv. 6). Such a passage as this, and the many others like it which might be cited from Israel's prophets, or from the literature of later Judaism and the Rabbis, do not disclose the full measure of the divine goodness lying open to the consciousness of Jesus. The two parables and His dealings with the 'lost' reveal that the Kingdom presented itself to Him as the exercise of a goodness in God which did not wait for the repentance of its objects, was not called forth by any deserving of their own, but, on the contrary, was conditioned on their side by the extremity of their situation (Luke vii. 40 ff.; cf. John iii. 16; xiv. 24; xv. 18, 19; xvii. 25).

However, if to the mind of Jesus it now counted for nothing that the objects of the divine action were unworthy of it, that did not mean that membership of the Kingdom was to be had for nothing. To the present Kingdom response had to be made. Hence the existence of an ethical teaching of Jesus—an ethic of the required response.

The evidence provided by the Synoptic Gospels for the ethic of response is not all of one sort. In some traditional sayings of Jesus certain inward qualities are extolled; in others a demand is made for unqualified obedience to the will of God and conformity with His goodness as known to Jesus Himself and manifested by Him. Thus (to notice first some instances of the former type of saying) a child's acceptance of the state of dependence in which it has to live, and its reliance upon the loving care of others, represent a necessary attitude towards the Kingdom of the present (Mark x. 13 ff.; Matt. xix. 13 ff.; Luke xviii. 15 ff.; cf. Matt. xviii. 1 ff.). Again, humility, contrition, and trust in God are responses proper to it and signs that the 'poor in spirit' are destined for the complete felicity of the divine community (Matt. v. 3). How happy is to be the lot of those who respond to the present Kingdom with 'hunger and thirst after righteousness'! (Matt. v. 6).

But besides approving and lauding the qualities concerned in such sayings as the foregoing, Jesus in other utterances about response demands from His hearers willingness to renounce the present order and the ethos which clings to it and to hold fast only and wholly to God now more wonderfully and yet more fatefully near to men than ever before. It was not that in His eyes the present age was evil through and through. In His task of awakening and intensifying response to the Kingdom as now come with Himself He was in the habit of using similes drawn from the realm of familiar human experience without any apparent misgiving. Nevertheless the present order was one which could not last on. Let anyone who had property (Matt. vi. 24; Luke xvi. 13; Mark x. 17–31; cf. Matt. xix. 16–30; Luke xviii. 18–30) or strong family ties (Matt. x. 37; Luke xiv. 26) be of an undivided will. In the parables of the Hid Treasure and the Costly Pearl (Matt. xiii. 44 ff.) the price to be paid for participation in the glory of life in the divine community is everything that a man has at his command. The requirement of a new ethos befitting the present Kingdom receives particularly radical expression in a series of utterances about anger, adultery, divorce, oaths, retaliation, loving enemies, and is summed up in a demand for a perfection like that of God (Matt. v. 21–48; cf. John iii. 3). This final demand is to be interpreted in the light of what precedes; and from this it appears that the term 'perfect', as applied to God, denotes the working—in Jesus and His ministry—of a goodness which was not deterred by the unworthiness of men; and that to be 'perfect' as God is 'perfect' means to display a goodness like His own in however unpromising circumstances. It is a summons to perfection in love, to the very perfection of God in love for the undeserving. The perfection of His love is seen in its refusal to acknowledge that it has any enemies so long as His offer of life in the future Kingdom is mercifully permitted to last and is not rejected. The sunshine and the rain are tokens of His undiscriminating goodness towards all men whilst He is making the offer (Matt. v. 45; Luke vi. 35). He leaves nothing undone to get the offer accepted, any more than a shepherd does to find a lost sheep, or a woman a lost coin. But He will not always be like that; He will judge and judge finally. Therefore whilst the offer still holds, close with it! How? On what terms?. Be as God is. How daunting! How impossible! 'Owe no man any thing, save to love one another' (Rom. xiii. 8). Never imagine, Paul means, that you can get quit of the debt of love; you cannot pay it off. No, the claims of love are always new and growing; you can never love enough.

As we cast about despairingly, we want to know whether an utterly radical demand is the last word of Jesus about response to the present Kingdom. Did He perhaps in some circumstances or in some moods accept the childlike state and disposition, or being 'poor in spirit', or 'hunger and thirst after righteousness', or contrition, as enough, and at other times summon to renunciation, the single will, and likeness to God in His own goodness? Was He of a varying mind about response? Or again, it is borne out by experience that when His moral absolute is accepted, and there is no wish for a mitigation and no wearying of it because it cannot be obeyed in full, the strength of self-confidence dies and pride is broken, and the childlike temper of soul is discovered without which no one could enter the divine community. Did Jesus notice this happening to hearers who really wanted to be His followers? Was that the reason why they were becoming childlike, poor in spirit, hungry and thirsty for righteousness? To whatever extent it may be possible to account in this way for the intermingling in the Synoptic Gospels of the two kinds of utterance concerning response, it remains that the absolute demand was put forward by Jesus with all seriousness; it was a true imperative. And it was not done with when His followers become childlike and so forth. The qualities which He welcomed in them were only the precious beginnings of response.

From various recorded sayings of His it appears that after a time, at all events, Jesus realised that His call for full response to the Kingdom present in His ministry would not be answered on a great scale. The parable of the Sower, for example, may be recalled in this connexion. It is altogether likely that it reflects the experiences and anticipations of Jesus as the One sent to be the organ of the present eschatological divine activity and to summon men to response. His work was not to be in vain; there would be a good result, a rich harvest; but much failure too is reckoned with. 'Broad is the way that leadeth to destruction, and many be they that enter in thereby. For narrow is the gate and straitened the way that leadeth unto life, and few be they that find it' (Matt. vii. 13 f.; Luke xiii. 23 f.). 'Woe unto thee, Chorazin! woe unto

thee, Bethsaida!' (Matt. xi. 20 ff.; Luke x. 13 ff.). The time was
fateful indeed. Life in the divine community depended upon total
response. It would not come from the people in the mass. Would
any ever yield it? Who could? 'It is easier for a camel to go
through a needle's eye, than for a rich man to enter into the
Kingdom of God' (Mark x. 25). 'Then who can be saved?'—a
question which applies to every man, not only to the rich. 'With
men it is impossible, but not with God: for all things are possible
with God.' Old guilt, guilt incurred before the coming of Jesus,
might count, did count, for nothing now that He, organ and very
presence of the Kingdom, was here; but His imperative and yet
impossible demand—what of the situation which that created for
His hearers?

It befits the nature of the present Kingdom as the outflowing
of the compassionate goodness of God upon the 'lost' that Jesus
should interpret it as offering occasion for the victory of divine
love. 'For verily the Son of Man came not to be ministered unto,
but to minister, and to give his life a ransom for many' (Mark
x. 45). In giving up His life He would be paying the price of life
in the divine community for the many. He would be dying in
order to get them into the still future Kingdom. They would
never get in unless He died; but as a fruit of His acceptance of the
Cross they would, or they could if they chose. To the full significance of the utterance, it would seem, belongs the thought that
the Son of Man in dying would accomplish for the many the
needful total response for which He had called. Between Jesus
and the many the same principle of solidarity applied as between
the Servant of the Lord and the many in the fourth Servant Song
in Isaiah lii. 13–liii. 12. His self-offering at the Cross s theirs
also and makes them acceptable to God. By this inclusive sacrifice
the situation which the impossible ethic of response had brought
to pass is dealt with; the response is yielded—by Him for the
many. This is not to say that men are relieved of the impossible
demand now that Jesus has acted as their representative. There
it is, embedded in the Gospels composed with His dying in
retrospect. His unlimited demand retains its authority, that by
acceptance of it with all that in them lies men may discover their
union with Him in what He did.

The Kingdom, understood in the sense of the eschatological
saving action of God, arrived in the work of Jesus. It came in

what He willed to do. He willed to die. He need not have remained
in Jerusalem to fall into the hands of His opponents. His dying
was the consummation of His work on earth, the coming of the
Kingdom in all its wonder. But this coming of the Kingdom and
the total response which Jesus yielded to it at the Cross constituted
the basis of the covenant of which He had spoken to His followers:
'This is my blood of the covenant, which is shed for many' (Mark
xiv. 24). This covenant, the new covenant of Jeremiah's prophecy,
was to be a new relationship between God and men, initiated by a
wholly divine work and sustained on man's side by submission to
the moral absolute of Jesus.

In the Synoptic tradition, then, the proclamation of the
Kingdom of God includes the demand for human response; and
the tension between the two types of required response—the
response of sheer receptivity and the response of absolute obedience—is resolved in the representative obedience of Jesus. When
we turn back to the Fourth Gospel, it is evident that at this stage
the emphasis is wholly on the response of receptive faith. When
in the Last Discourse Jesus begins to speak of the moral absolute
of His commandment of love, He can do so because this has now
been made possible by His own passion, regarded as an already
accomplished fact. The impossibility of entering the Kingdom by
human achievement, which in the Synoptic Gospels is expounded
only as an immediate prelude to the passion narrative in the story
of the rich man (Mark x. 17 ff. and parallels), is here enunciated
by St. John at a much earlier stage, and with a clear indication
that what is impossible for men will be made possible by God in
the lifting up of the Son of Man. We are thus led to expect that
the passion will have the same representative or inclusive character
as it does in the Synoptic tradition.

The chapter ends with a paragraph of comment on the divine
role of the Baptist in relation to the mission of Jesus, which is also
a summary and amplification of the discourse to Nicodemus. No
man, whether he be the Baptist or Jesus, can receive anything
unless it has been 'given him from heaven' (v. 27). To the Baptist
it has been given to be 'a man sent from God' (i. 6; cf. iii. 28).
Only to Jesus has it been granted to be the Messiah. In virtue of
this heavenly gift He can be described as the One who 'comes from
above' (v. 31). He who is of earthly, not of heavenly, origin belongs
not to heaven but to earth, and so do his utterances; that is to say,

so do the testimonies he bears to Jesus, which are 'of the earth' in
the same sense as the 'earthly things' spoken by Jesus Himself
(v. 12), preparing the hearers for the reception of the 'heavenly
things', which only Jesus can reveal. He who comes from heaven
bears witness to what He has seen and heard (v. 32). Thus it is
quite plain in this context that what He has seen and heard refers
not to the precosmic knowledge of the Logos, but to a knowledge
which has been given from above to the man Jesus. In using the
word 'from above' St. John is deliberately echoing the warning to
Nicodemus: only through Jesus is the new birth possible, because
whatever is to be granted to the believer in his birth from above
has already been granted to Jesus in the unique act of God that
made Him Messiah.

It may look as if an acknowledgment at this point that no one
was receiving the witness of Jesus is evidence for a misplacement
of vv. 31–36 in their present connection with vv. 22–30, where it is
said that everybody was coming to Jesus. But the appearance of
an incongruity may well be deceptive. Even if—and it is questionable—the phrase 'to come to Jesus' is here, as elsewhere in the
Gospel, the equivalent of 'to believe in Jesus' (cf. vii. 37 f.), it is
a quite evident Johannine conviction that there are beginnings of
belief in Jesus which never approach reception of His witness to
what He had seen and heard, and which in the end come to
nothing (ii. 23–25; vi. 66 f.; viii. 31).

He who received the witness of Jesus, as the Baptist did on the
showing of v. 29, thereby attested the truthfulness of God (v. 33).
This is so because, in spite of what a general refusal of the witness
of Jesus might appear to suggest, it is God who has sent Him, and
in His words of witness it is God Himself who is speaking; and
this in turn is possible because God gives Him the Spirit in full
measure (v. 34). We have already seen how important this verse
is for an understanding of St. John's Christology. Union with the
Logos—together with all that this implies in terms of life, light,
grace, truth, and glory—had already been imparted to the man
Jesus by the Incarnation. His reception of the Spirit is the occasion
on which he consciously receives and appropriates what had been
given to Him from above, His calling to be Messiah and mediator
of eternal life to men. It is also the occasion on which he became
aware of His unique Sonship (v. 35). For all eternity God and the
Logos had existed in a relationship of mutual love (xvii. 24). Now

the man Jesus has been taken up into that union of love, and this, we are to understand, is the first stage in the implementation of God's love for the world (v. 16). Through Him others are to be brought into the same union of love. Accordingly the Father has committed everything to Him, that is to say, as emerges in the following verse, everything to do with man's gaining or losing eternal life.

As we look back on this paragraph it is interesting to notice how close, in spite of obvious superficial differences, St. John is at this point to the Synoptic tradition of the Baptism. He himself does not actually record the Baptism, but he makes it unmistakably clear that Jesus' consciousness both of Messiahship and of Sonship was inseparably connected with His reception of the Spirit.

7

THE WORKING OF THE FATHER AND THE SON

The conversation of Jesus with the Samaritan woman in chapter 4 leads to a brief discourse in which the Evangelist introduces a quite new theme. 'My meat is to do the will of him that sent me, and to accomplish his work' (iv. 34). Hitherto the function of Jesus has been expounded almost wholly in terms of disclosure—the ascending and descending of the angels of God under an open heaven, the manifestation of glory, the speaking of heavenly things, the coming of light into the world; and to all of this the correct human response has been to see, to hear and to believe. Now we are told that Jesus has come not only to reveal but to accomplish, and that His close union with the Father, to which His words and signs have borne witness, is a union of will and purpose. The natural inference, which we shall find corroborated in subsequent chapters, is that what Jesus reveals is the purpose of God for humanity, and that He reveals it precisely because in Him it is fully achieved, first by the taking of His individual manhood into unity with the Logos, and later by the incorporation of others into that same unity. But the purpose which finds its full expression and accomplishment in Jesus is no new purpose. The harvest which He and His disciples must now reap has been prepared long since by other servants of God. 'Others have laboured, and you have entered into their labour' (iv. 38).

This theme is more thoroughly explored in the discourse which follows the healing of the cripple on the Sabbath. To his account of the incident the Evangelist adds the statement that the Jews persecuted the man's benefactor for disrespect of Israel's appointed day of rest. A saying of Jesus follows in defence of Himself. 'My Father worketh even until now, and I work' (v. 17). God's work of creation, providence, and redemption goes on seven days a week, and Jesus is co-operating with Him. The working of the Father of Jesus which is in question extends uninterrupted over the whole course of His activity in religion and history within and outside Israel, up to the ministry of Jesus; and to be the agent of God's own activity cannot be disobedience to Him. The Jews retort that Jesus has now added blasphemy to Sabbath-breaking, by claiming equality with God. Jesus does not repudiate the suggestion that He is equal with God, for more and more explicitly as the Gospel proceeds He will claim to be one with God, until in chapter x the idea that Jesus and His Father are one in being and action (x. 30), or that they are 'in' each other (x. 38), merges in that of Jesus' Sonship (x. 36). What Jesus does repudiate is the notion of His adversaries that this equality is something that He, acting on His own authority alone, has arrogated to Himself. His part has been simply to accept in humility and obedience a status which the Father has willed Him to have. It is the Father alone who can effect His decisively eschatological work of salvation, of which the healing of the cripple is an illustration; and, whilst this is in fact the work Jesus has been doing, He could not be doing anything of it unless He was able to watch the Father doing it. To be Son is to be in such unity with the Father that everything the Son does is also an act of the Father (v. 19).

The Son can and does do what the Father is doing because the Father loves Him and shows Him all that He, the Father, is doing (v. 20). The reason why the Father is said to love the Son is that, by His creation of Him within Himself—the Son being always the man Jesus in whom the Logos has acquired manhood—the reciprocal love which is constitutive in the Godhead became inclusive of Him and active in Him to communicate itself to men. All that the Father is doing He shows to the Son, so that—and this is the point of the saying—it is by means of the Son, by what the Son is and does, that He is doing it. Being in the Son and having the Son in Him (x. 38), the Father can show it to the Son and the Son can see it. As 'all things which the Father is doing' and the activity of Jesus in His ministry up to the present moment of its progress are one and the same, by the 'greater works than these' which the Father is to show Him—for Him to do—are meant more significant eschatological events of the ministry than those which have yet occurred. These 'greater works' are then specified in vv. 21 and 22 as the giving of life to men or their exclusion from it. The purposed end of the works of the Father which the Son sees and does is that through them men may have life or, from spiritual blindness to Him, remain in darkness, i.e. without life (ix. 39 ff.; xii. 35 f.). So far the ministry of Jesus was not decisive of either of its final consequences; His dying, and His dying alone, would make it so.

The 'greater works', then, which the Father would show to the Son would include His raising of the dead and giving them life, and this through the dying of the Son, who thus at the same time would Himself be doing them. 'For as the Father raiseth the dead and quickeneth them, even so the Son also quickeneth whom he will' (v. 21). All men were 'dead' in the sense intended here, being without the life which is communicable by the Logos (i. 4) and is to be communicated through His assumption of manhood in Jesus the Son, through the surrender and regaining thereof in His death and resurrection, and through the intervening ministry of utterance and sign by which these events are interpreted. Those who are raised and given life are such as hear the word of Jesus (v. 24), whether announced by Him before His dying or afterwards by His representative messengers (xvii. 18 ff.). Elsewhere in the Gospel they are variously described as 'of the truth', the 'sheep' of Jesus, etc., to whom also reference is made in the clause 'whom he will', which declares His oneness of will and action with the Father in raising the dead and imparting life to them. The rest of men are judged by the dying of the Son, that is, left without life. Thus, whether men are given life or denied it, whether they are saved or judged, this is to be seen as the outcome of a joint action of Father and Son. Without the Father the Son can do nothing. Without the Son the Father has determined to do nothing. 'Neither doth the Father judge any man, but he hath given all judgment unto the Son' (v. 22). From now on the only way to honour the Father is to honour the Son (v. 23).

The summarily expressed thought of vv. 20–23 is resumed in a more explanatory manner in vv. 24–27. The word of Jesus is a term which in St. John covers all that He reveals and therefore denotes the whole series of eschatological events which constitute the action of the Father in and through the Son. To trust in God as 'Him who sent me' is to accept the dependence of the events upon Him for their existence, when the word of Jesus disclosing them is being receptively heard, whether from Him or from bearers of it after His death (xvii. 8, 14, 18 ff.). One who so hears and so trusts will not appear—at the last day—for judgment, but through these obedient responses to that joint action of the Father and Jesus has already passed out of his condition of death to the possession of life.

The meaning of 'the voice of the Son of God' (*v.* 25) is to be understood from that of the word of Jesus in the previous verse. The dead are physically alive, but lack that life which can come to them only from the Logos, and therefore only through those eschatological events which constitute the burden of the word of Jesus. They are all to 'hear the voice' of Jesus, in the sense that they will have His word announced to them (cf. xii. 47); and from amongst the dead so addressed there will be those who will hear in the sense of hearkening responsively, and they will live, i.e. become sharers in the life of the Father and the Son. The time for this to happen is said to be both coming and present: His future missionary disciples would take to the dead the same word which He Himself was declaring in His ministry.

We have already seen how important *v.* 26 is for our understanding of the movement of St. John's thought. It was eternally true of the Logos that He had life in Himself, a life designed to be the light or blessing of men (i. 4). When it is said that the Father gave 'to the Son also to have life in himself', we are to understand that the life-giving faculty of the Logos has been imparted to the man Jesus. What He reveals, therefore, is not simply the character of this life, but the eschatological fact that in His manhood God has begun the process of communicating life to a dead world. The eschatological implications of the saying are clearly brought out in the following verse, which gives a further reason why the sovereign life-giving power granted by the Father to the Son includes the right to deliver judgment: He is Son of Man. The action of the Father from which comes judgment to some men as well as life to others functions in the person of Jesus whether He is called Son of Man or Son of God.

The universal scope of the authority of Jesus is seen in *vv.* 28–29. Here, as we shall see when we come to consider the Last Discourse, the coming hour is the last day, when those who did not in their lifetime hear and respond to the word of Jesus will be given the opportunity of doing so. (St. John uses the expression 'all that are in the tombs' to show that he has literal death in mind and not the figurative death of which he has just been speaking.) At the last day all who have not yet received it will be given the offer of life; but, as during the earthly ministry of Jesus (iii. 20), there will be those who refuse to come to the light because they cannot endure to have the worthlessness of their lives exposed by it.

This comprehensive activity of Jesus as judge is not, however, in any way at all independent of the Father (v. 30), as though the Father had handed over the reins of government and withdrawn from power. Jesus can judge only because He hears—because He understands the judging power inherent in the eschatological activity of the Father which is going on in Himself. But judge He does, which makes it so fateful for the judged that He cannot act thus without the Father; it shows that His judging work is right, seeking in it, as He does, the will of Him who sent Him, not His own will.

At v. 31 Jesus begins a defence—prolonged to the end of the present chapter—of the claims He has made for Himself. If it were true that He had been acting on His own authority, then His claims too would rest solely on His own testimony, and in that case they would admittedly be false. But in fact He has a witness whose evidence ought to be accepted without question. He could, of course, appeal to the testimony of the Baptist, but He is not prepared to rest His claims on the witness even of a man sent from God; the witness of such a man—one like a bright, shining lamp, in whose light the Jews had been willing for a time to exult —might lead others to believe in Him (i. 7) and so find salvation, but it could not substantiate the claims of Jesus to be one with God. But Jesus has a witness borne to Him which is greater than that provided by the Baptist, the witness of the works given to Him by the Father to bring to completion (v. 36). To anyone who is not wilfully blind it should be self-evident that these works have their origin in God, and that their human agent is sent by God. In them God is working out His own purpose, and therefore in them also God is bearing witness to the identification of Jesus with that purpose. At x. 36 the mission of Jesus from the Father to the world is made to rest upon the Father's consecration of Him; and we may thus with reason take it to be meant at v. 37a that action of the Father, by which He made the manhood of Jesus heavenly in origin and one with Himself, permanently attested the rightness of the claims He had been making for Himself in the present discourse.

The refusal of the Jews to accept the claims of Jesus merely proves their own total ignorance of God. For the voice and the presence of God are self-authenticating. If the Jews knew Him as well as they themselves supposed, they would unhesitatingly recognise His voice in the words of Jesus and His presence in the works of Jesus. Besides never having 'heard his voice' or 'seen his form', the Jews did not have His word dwelling in them (v. 38), as was evident from their rejection of Him whom the Father had sent. In itself the phrase 'His word' could have the same significance as the word which the Father had given to Jesus, in which case 'His word' would be the equivalent of 'my word' at v. 24. This sense of 'His word' can hardly however be right here; it would only turn the whole utterance into a tautologous verdict that the failure of the Jews to possess the word of God spoken by Jesus was due to their refusal to accept it from Him! Alternatively the phrase designates the self-revealing activity of the Father in manifestations of the pre-incarnate Logos, in Israel's recorded religion and history. Though they studied God's word, thinking by means of it to enjoy the possession of eternal life (cf. v. 39), the Jews did it undiscerningly and fruitlessly; their blindness to it at its present eschatological climax in the person and ministry of Jesus was proof that they had never grasped its meaning at earlier stages of unfolding.

The earlier work of the one Logos had foreshadowed His appearance in Jesus to give life to men; yet the Jews had not the will to come to Him, i.e. to believe in Him, and so to have life from Him (v. 40). Not to have the word of the Father dwelling in them is thus, it may be observed, an expression parallel in meaning with not being 'of the truth', not being 'of God', not belonging to 'the sheep' of Jesus, and other similar phrases used throughout the Gospel.

Jesus does not receive honour or glory from men (v. 41). What he does receive is 'the glory that cometh from the only God', which we have seen to be His union with the Father. To seek glory from men would be to advance Himself, and not to advance the purpose of God to which He is wholly subservient. His claims issue not from self-seeking, but from His acceptance of the status the Father has willed Him to have and of the works the Father has given Him to complete. This explains why the Jews fail to understand Jesus. They themselves are constantly looking for recognition from their fellows, and so are not open to receive the glory that comes from God and to be channels for His love. The only person they can understand and accept is one who comes 'in his own name' (v. 43), one who, like themselves, is bent on

G

self-advancement (*v.* 44). The truth about Jesus is the very opposite of what they have asserted. They have denounced Him for bearing witness to Himself, that is, for arrogating to Himself a dignity to which He has no right. If in fact He had done so, they would have acclaimed Him as one of themselves. But the glory which comes from Him who alone is God—a glory which is the oneness in love of the Father and the Son, or the life they possess together—is hidden from the Jews. They had not the love or the glory or the life of God in them, as their receiving of honour from one another showed—the ground of the honour in question being, in this context, the study of the Scriptures with the possession of eternal life as its end. For it was an illusion to think that there was any such honour worth having. The only true glory is that which comes from God through the eschatological events taking place in the person and ministry of Jesus and the appropriating response of believers. The God who reveals Himself thus in Jesus is the only God; and those who do not hear Him in the word of Jesus only prove themselves incapable of hearing Him speaking in the Scriptures. Thus Moses, so far from offering them life, actually becomes their accuser (*vv.* 45–47), because they have shown themselves unable to read the Scriptures with true comprehension and acceptance of their meaning. The writings of Moses, we have to keep in mind at this point, are being regarded as evidence for the activity in him of the eternal Logos seeking to attain the end of His creation of man by giving him life, an end ultimately to be achieved by His Incarnation. The Jews were making a fatefully wrong choice between themselves and the one Logos as interpreters of the significance of Moses.

8

THE BREAD OF LIFE

The first five chapters of the Gospel have set before us in a variety of ways the twofold mission of Jesus: He has come to reveal and to accomplish the redemptive purpose of God, to reveal it indeed in the very act of accomplishing it. Both the revelation and the accomplishment take place in two stages, one of which is at this period of the ministry a present fact, the other still in the future. Jesus can already reveal his glory, bear witness to the heavenly things He has seen and heard in the presence of His Father, shine as light in the world's darkness, do the works of the Father who sent Him (ii. 11; iii. 11 ff., 19; iv. 34; v. 17). But there is also for Him a future hour, which we have seen to be the hour of His Passion. By the Incarnation the individual manhood of Jesus has been created in unity with the Logos, so as to establish a community of being and purpose. At the Passion that manhood is to become inclusive of others, so that they too may be drawn into the same unity. In the sixth chapter, in the long discourse which follows and expounds the miraculous feeding, these themes, hitherto only suggested or adumbrated, are for the first time worked out in detail. The first part of the discourse (*vv.* 26–51b) is concerned with the claims of Jesus and the need for men to accept them. 'I am the bread of life' (*vv.* 35, 48). 'I have come down from heaven' (*vv.* 38, 42). 'I am the living bread which came down out of heaven' (*v.* 51; cf. *v.* 41). The second part (*vv.* 51c–65) is an answer to the question, 'How can men eat this bread and so receive the life it embodies?'

In interpreting the thought of the discourse as a whole it is important not to miss the significance of this twofold application of the figure of bread. From the one point of view Jesus is 'the bread of life', 'the living bread which came down out of heaven' (*vv.* 35, 48, 51), because with His presence in the human earthly order 'life' has now become accessible to men; from the other point of view He is the 'bread of life' because He chooses to die, in order that He may make the 'life' which is in Him the actual possession of many more as well. 'Except a grain of wheat fall into the earth

and die, it abideth by itself alone; but if it die, it beareth much
fruit' (xii. 24). 'Yes, and the bread which I will give is my flesh,
for the life of the world' (vi. 51). He already is the 'bread of life';
the giving is to take place in the future. Jesus had 'life' in Himself
(v. 26), but not yet could He give it to others, not before His
dying, not before His act of self-consecration at the Cross. The
Logos had life in Himself: life was eternally constitutive in the
Godhead (i. 4). Already, in willing the Incarnation, the Father
had granted to the Son to have life in Himself (v. 26). Only by
His death and the reception of its benefits by believers can this
life be extended to others. 'Except ye eat the flesh of the Son of
man and drink his blood, ye have not life in yourselves' (vi. 53).
And what is expressed here in terms of life could equally well be
expressed in the other Johannine Christological terms of love
(xvii. 24), glory (xvii. 5), or mutual indwelling (xiv. 19 f.). 'He
that eateth my flesh and drinketh my blood abideth in me and I
in him' (vi. 56).

It is important to distinguish the two phases of the discourse,
but equally important not to deal with either in isolation from the
other. The first phase, by itself, would be liable to two kinds of
misinterpretation. The statement, 'I have come down from
heaven', is clearly a claim to pre-existence. But does it mean that
Jesus pre-existed as heavenly manna (*vv.* 41, 51), or as heavenly
man (*v.* 62), or simply as Logos? Was it the intention of the
Evangelist that these words should be literally applicable to Jesus,
or was he using figurative language to assert the heavenly origin
and quality of the manhood of Jesus, manhood created within the
Godhead at the Incarnation, and thus the presence now on earth
in Him of the life which was eternally in the Logos (cf. v. 26)? We
might indeed be warned against literalism by observing that the
language of this passage develops out of a contrast between Jesus
and the manna in the wilderness, and, in particular, out of an Old
Testament quotation—'He gave them bread out of heaven to eat'
(*v.* 31). If the manna came down out of heaven, all the more
certainly must the true bread, the bread which gives 'life', come
down out of heaven. And if Jesus is Himself this bread, then in a
theme developed within a framework of reference to the manna, no
other phrasing could have been so appropriate as 'I have come
down from heaven'. It is interesting to note in corroboration that
when in *v.* 46 the thought expressed by this phrase is wanted

again, but for the moment the manna is not under allusion, this form of expression is dropped and we have 'he who is from God'. But all these queries are decisively resolved when we reach the transition to the second phase of the discourse. For now we are told that the bread in question is 'the flesh' of Jesus (v. 51). A little further on in the discourse we find the phrases 'he who eats me' and 'he who eats my flesh' appearing as equivalents. 'He that eateth my flesh and drinketh my blood hath eternal life' (v. 54). 'He that eateth my flesh and drinketh my blood abideth in me, and I in Him' (v. 56). 'As the living Father sent me, and I live because of the Father, so he that eateth me, he also shall live because of me' (v. 57). Later we shall have to consider in greater detail why St. John considers it necessary to introduce a reference to blood into a comparison between the manna and the person of Jesus. For the moment it is enough that 'flesh' is a clear cross-reference to the Prologue (i. 14), and that He who claims to have come down from heaven and to be the real bread from heaven is the Jesus of flesh and blood. And it is not to be supposed that the human flesh of Jesus literally came down from heaven.

The second possible misapprehension concerns men's appropriation of the bread of life. This bread is twice contrasted with the manna. 'What then doest thou for a sign, that we may see, and believe thee? What workest thou? Our fathers ate the manna in the wilderness: as it is written, He gave them bread out of heaven to eat. Jesus therefore said unto them, . . . It was not Moses that gave you the bread out of heaven; but my Father giveth you the true bread out of heaven. For the bread of God is that which comes down out of heaven and gives life to the world' (vv. 30–33). 'Your fathers did eat manna in the wilderness, and they died. This is the bread which cometh down out of heaven, that a man may eat thereof, and not die. I am the living bread which came down out of heaven: if any man eat of this bread, he shall live for ever' (vv. 48–51). The bread which is thus contrasted with the manna was now in the world, and therefore presumably available to men. But how were they to eat of it? In the first part of the discourse the question is indeed raised, but only to be answered in a deceptively summary manner. 'I am the bread of life: he that cometh to me shall not hunger, and he that believeth on me shall never thirst' (v. 35). 'He that believeth hath eternal life' (v. 47). To 'come to me' and 'to believe in me' or simply 'to believe' are equivalent expressions for appropriating response to the 'life' which was in Jesus. As the term is used here, to 'believe' means primarily to grasp and to accept Jesus' revelation of Himself as 'the bread of life', to know why He makes this claim, and to be of the trustful persuasion that the claim is a true one. And it might almost look as if the believer could of himself render response enough. If it seems so in this first phase of the discourse, we must make our own correction of the impression from the second. Only from within the union of believers with Jesus which is the fruit of His dying, and by the operation of the then indwelling Paraclete, will the full measure of response be possible. There are indeed beginnings of belief in Jesus, and these beginnings are accepted as preparations for the union with Him brought to pass by His death (vi. 37, 44, 45, 65); but these beginnings cannot come to maturity unless men are drawn by the Father into union with Jesus, and this, as we shall see (xii. 32) can happen only through the Cross.

The scene of the discourse is laid in Capernaum, where the people had come seeking Jesus (vv. 22–25). They are curious to know when He had arrived there, but He turns the question aside and rebukes them for seeking Him because they had been provided with a meal the day before. They ought now to be seeking Him on account of the 'signs' which they had seen, i.e. on account of what the signs, and in particular the sign of the Feeding, had revealed about Himself. They had seen 'signs' in the sense that they had been made witnesses of the outward events, yet not seen them in the sense of having grasped what the signs revealed.

A 'sign' in St. John is a sensible act of a miraculous character which is held to be a conveying medium of a self-revelation of Jesus. What had He revealed about Himself in this one? In the discourse the revelation is given in the medium of words. It is worthy of notice that in this Johannine version of the Feeding of the people it is Jesus himself who distributes the food—a variation from Mark vi. 41 and viii. 6 which, in view of the representation of the discourse that Jesus both is and gives the bread of life, is hardly without symbolic significance. However, as soon as the sign has been wrought, the people in the story conclude that Jesus is the eschatological prophet. 'When therefore the people saw the sign which he did, they said, This is of a truth the prophet that cometh into the world. Jesus therefore perceiving that they were about to come and take him by force to make him king, withdrew again into the mountain alone' (*vv.* 14, 15). The reader is meant to understood that they had seen in the provision by Jesus of the wonderful meal a renewal of the gift of the manna in the wilderness. In Rabbinic sources (cf. Strack-Billerbeck, II, p. 481) the expectation appears that the last deliverer (the Messiah), like the first (Moses), would cause manna to descend from heaven. The people associate 'the prophet' with the liberation of Israel (ibid. p. 479 f.), and Jesus anticipates that they will now try to make Him the Messiah-king, the earthly deliverer of the Jews. Although, as the subsequent discourse shows, they are right in interpreting the Feeding as a sign having eschatological significance, He will not allow their intention to be carried out (cf. xviii. 36 f.). The proper eschatological meaning of the sign was other than the people imagined. 'Ye seek me, not because ye saw signs, but because ye ate of the loaves, and were filled. Work not for the meat which perisheth, but for the meat which abideth unto eternal life, which the Son of man shall give you: for him the Father, even God, hath sealed. They said therefore unto him, What must we do, that we may work the works of God? Jesus answered and said unto them, This is the work of God, that ye believe on him whom he hath sent' (*vv.* 26–29).

The RV rendering, 'work not for the meat that perisheth', rather obscures the connexion between *v.* 26 and *v.* 27, which becomes straightforward when the prohibition is given conative force: 'Do not try to obtain the food which perishes.' The reference is not a general one to toil for food, working for a living, but a particular one to the food which the people had eaten the day before. They ought not to be seeking Jesus now in order to be fed again with food which wastes away, always losing its power to sustain the life of man; they should be seeking Him to get the food which His action of yesterday had revealed that He could give them, the food which lasts on, never losing its own nourishing property, to issue in eternal life for those who secure it. He would give it to those who sought Him in order to get it from Him. In support of the promise it is added that the Father, God, had 'sealed' Him, i.e. had accredited Him to the people as His own emissary by giving Him the power to perform this sign. They ought to have recognized in it one of the works which the Father had given Him to do, and therefore the Father's seal on His activity (v. 36; cf. ix. 3; x. 25, 37 f.; xiv. 10 f.). However, this further appeal to the sign is of no avail. They can even say: 'What doest thou for a sign, that we may see, and believe thee?' (v. 30). Still, they do want to know (v. 28) what they must do in order to work the works of God, thereby so far rightly understanding that they must yield obedience to God's will, if they are ever to receive the food. But they are thinking in terms of obedience to the commandments of the Jewish Law, and Jesus in reply points to the one work of God. This work of God—by which is meant at once His own work and His demand—consists in 'believing in him whom God has sent', but, as we have already noticed, this recurring formula in John holds more meaning than is immediately obvious. Here it applies to the recognition that the sign of the Feeding is a revelation that Jesus both is and gives the bread of life. On hearing what they must do if they are to obtain this bread, the people remain critical of the claim that God has willed their dependence for it upon Jesus and not upon the Law of Moses. Their questioning attitude finds expression in a demand that Jesus should justify His words by performing a sign, and in an appeal to the divine attestation of Moses' authority provided by the giving of the manna in the wilderness. 'They said therefore unto him, What then doest thou for a sign, that we may see, and believe thee? What workest thou? Our fathers ate manna in the wilderness, as it is written, He gave them bread out of heaven to eat' (vv. 30–31). It would hardly be right to suppose that they are requiring Jesus to repeat the miracle of the manna; for it would appear from the episode related in vv. 14–15 that the day before they had thought they had seen Him performing this sign. Rather, they want a sign which would show that He had divine authority to say: 'This is the work of God, that ye believe on him whom he hath sent.' But in fact, of such a sign they had already been the undiscerning witnesses. 'But I said unto you, that ye have seen me, and yet believe not' (v. 36). Jesus therefore does not resort again to symbolic action, but responds with a declaration (vv. 37–40) that all who were already partakers of the Logos, by the predisposing gift of the Father, at the time of their encounter with Him as incarnate, would believe in Him; and none of them would ever be rejected by Him, His heavenly origin ensuring that His ministry was not a self-appointed one—and therefore not a futility—but a working of the will of Him who had

sent Him—the Father, whose will it was that everyone who saw the
Son and believed in Him should possess eternal life and be raised
up by Him at the last day. The Jews can still only say: 'Is not this
Jesus, the son of Joseph, whose father and mother we know?'
(v. 41); and a little later they regard the utterance about his flesh
as incomprehensible.

We have noticed that the thought of the discourse takes a new
turn at v. 51c. How can Jesus make the 'life' He has in Him the
possession of others too? He can and will do so by giving them
the 'bread' which is His flesh. What have they to do who would
eat this bread? In v. 53 it is asserted with all emphasis that in
order to eat the bread which Jesus is because of the 'life' He has
in Him they must eat the bread He will come to be on account of
His Passion. 'Except ye eat the flesh of the Son of man and drink
his blood, ye have not life in yourselves.'

After reception of 'life' had been made dependent upon 'eating'
His 'flesh', the assurance is given that he who thus shares in the
self-consecration of Jesus at His crucifixion has eternal life, and
will be raised up by Him at the last day (v. 54). In support of this
assurance appeal is then made to the ability of His 'flesh' to
produce 'life' in those who 'eat' it. 'For my flesh is meat indeed'
(v. 55). There is an allusion here to the manna eaten in the
wilderness and an implication that the 'flesh' of Jesus alone was
real food, and not the manna, since this did not give 'life'. The
next saying begins as a repetition of v. 54, but ends with an
explanatory change of terminology: 'He that eateth my flesh and
drinketh my blood abideth in me and I in him' (='hath eternal
life', v. 54). This variation of phrasing is significant; it throws
light on what in the discourse and elsewhere in the Fourth Gospel is
meant by eternal life; and it seems intended to do so. Eternal life
is now seen to consist in a reciprocal indwelling between Jesus and
him who 'eats' His 'flesh'. This relationship of reciprocal indwelling is then declared to be modelled on, and dependent on, the
analogous relationship already subsisting between Jesus and the
Father. 'As the living Father sent me, and I live because of the
Father; so he that eateth me, he also shall live because of me'
(v. 57). We are reminded that the language of mutual in-being,
used in the previous verse to describe the union between Jesus
and believers achieved by His death and their acceptance of it, is
used elsewhere in the Gospel of the unity existing between the

Father and Jesus (x. 38; xiv. 10–11; xvii. 21); and we are thus entitled to interpret *v.* 57 in the light of these passages. When Jesus here says, 'I live', He is laying claim to possession of a life which is His in virtue of His being 'in the Father'; and in adding, 'he that eateth me, he also shall live', He is promising participation in the same relationship. Finally, we are told that '*this* (the manhood of Jesus taken up into union with the Logos, and so furnished with eternal life) is the bread which came down out of heaven' (*v.* 58).

We have not yet given consideration to the repeated allusions to the 'blood' of Jesus in this part of the discourse. He has eternal life who not only eats the flesh of Jesus but drinks His blood. 'My flesh is meat indeed (or real meat), and my blood is drink indeed (or real drink)' (*v.* 55). Two distinct proceedings are here being contemplated. Are we to suppose then that in these verses the significance of eating the flesh of Jesus is being distinguished from that of drinking His blood? Should we take the sayings to mean that besides eating the flesh of Jesus one must drink His blood in order to have eternal life, as if the eating did not suffice, but had to have added to it the drinking, to which some further significance attached? If it were so, we should have to say that the usage of the expression 'my flesh' is now being modified by comparison with that of *v.* 51, where the flesh only was mentioned. But there is no need to think so. It is much more likely that 'flesh' and 'blood' are here employed as equivalents. But if that is so, why should a drinking of blood be mentioned at all? There appear to be two reasons. If St. John had used only the word 'flesh' in this context, it would naturally have been taken to refer to the incarnate life of Jesus, what we have been calling His individual manhood. The additional mention of 'blood' puts it beyond doubt that he intends a further reference to the life of Jesus as voluntarily laid down, His manhood as consecrated by Him in dying (xvii. 19); and it justifies us in assuming that this forward look to the Passion is intended also by the use of the word 'flesh'. The second reason is that it was barely possible at the end of the first century A.D. for one Christian to write or for others to read a description of Jesus as the bread of life without some echoes of the Eucharist. An intention to allude to the Eucharist in *vv.* 53 ff. as a means of 'eating' the 'flesh' of Jesus would necessitate the shaping of the sayings in such a way as would make them applicable to the two elements of the observance. In the background of these verses is the question: How does one eat the flesh of Jesus? The answer being given is that the Eucharist is a means of doing so. Not of course the only means; for earlier in the discourse stand the sayings about belief and the possession of life. But the allusion to the Eucharist at least emphasizes the point we have already made, that life cannot be given even to a believer apart from the death of Jesus. In this way the mention of the drinking of the blood in addition to the eating of the flesh can be explained; it was required by the fact of there having been two Eucharistic elements.

There seems indeed to be rather more concern in these verses (vv. 53–58) to insist on the principle that one must eat the flesh of Jesus, feed on His self-consecrated manhood, in order to have eternal life, than there is with the way to do so. Still, the principle is being given an application to the Eucharist, with the result that, to the exclusion of an account of it on the night before the Crucifixion, the rite becomes the subject of interpretative allusion in the course of the public ministry. The fact that the Eucharist is being contemplated in a discourse purporting to have been uttered in close connection with the miracle of the Feeding leaves unaffected the Synoptic and Pauline tradition about the origin of the observance on the night of the betrayal of Jesus. As we have seen, His 'flesh' would not be available for 'eating' until He had consecrated it at the Cross. How is it then that the rite is brought to view in advance of any possibility of observing it? There is no intention to disturb the tradition which carried back its origin to the night preceding the death of Jesus; the reference to it occurs at this point for a reason which has nothing to do with regard for sequence of events in His ministry, the desire being to point to a means by which that 'eating' of His 'flesh', upon which depended the possession of eternal life, may take place. 'How can he give us his flesh to eat?' the Jews ask in v. 52. The question is approved, though not in the sense that the words bear for them.

Many disciples, it is now represented (vv. 60 f.), could not accept the discourse, putting in question the whole of it, but especially the harsh, concluding stage. Their reaction to His words draws from Jesus utterances which are hard to interpret. First a question is put to them. 'Doth this cause you to stumble?

What then if ye should behold the Son of man ascending where he was before?' (*v*. 62). There is allusion here to some occurrence by which a revelation of high importance concerning the Son of Man would be given; and correspondingly the seeing that is spoken of is not simply a matter of eyesight, but of discernment of whatever the occurrence in question was to reveal. It is not said expressly how the many disciples' perplexity would be affected, if they did see the Son of Man ascending where He was before. How much more disconcerted they would be? If we are proceeding rightly so far, this is not the intended inference. Rather the point is that if they perceived the true significance of the coming event, if they discerned in it the ascending of the Son of Man, they would no longer be baffled by the discourse; the meaning of its contents would be apparent to them and joyfully acceptable. What revelation, then, concerning the Son of Man were they to have the opportunity of grasping?

The saying must not be seen in isolation, but as a member of a series of utterances in which the dying of Jesus is described as His going to His Father (vii. 33; viii. 14; viii. 21 f.; xiii. 1, 3; xiv. 28; xvi. 5, 28). To these utterances are to be added, for interpretation in common, the passages in which the lifting up of Jesus is spoken of with a double meaning, applied in a literal sense to the crucifying of Jesus regarded as the sinful act of the Jews (viii. 28), and at the same time in a figurative sense to His crucifixion regarded as His exaltation through the voluntary acceptance of death. From a comparison with these other passages we can see that the ascending of the Son of Man where He was before is to be no mere restoration of the *status quo*. The Logos has taken manhood, and it is as man that He will ascend where He was before. It is to be added that just as in dying He would be consecrating both His own manhood and those who believed in Him (xvii. 19), so in dying He would be ascending together with His own to where the Logos had previously existed alone with God. The place metaphor is best understood from the utterances in the prayer of Jesus. 'And now, O Father, glorify thou me with thine own self with the glory which I had with thee before the world was' (xvii. 5). 'Father, that which thou hast given me, I will that, where I am, they also may be with me; that they may behold my glory which thou hast given me: for thou lovedst me before the foundation of the world' (xvii. 24). Into the always-existing glory or love within the Godhead the manhood of Jesus would go at the Crucifixion; and with Him would go His own, who would know what had happened to them when they received the Spirit (xiv. 20). To be sure the manhood of Jesus did not first come to be in the Godhead when He died; no, but the accomplishment of His will to die, in order that the life which was in Him might be given to the world, would make the participation of His manhood in the love and glory of God complete.

It appears then that the ascension of the Son of Man is at once an allusion to the Crucifixion and a disclosure of its true meaning. 'What then if ye should behold the Son of man ascending where he was before?' What, that is to say, if they should discern in the dying of Jesus His passage and their own into the heavenly glory, the love-union of God and the Logos, as they would come to do, if they received the discourse believingly now? They would know then as a matter of fact experienced—what they could not know in that way for the present—that He was Himself the bread of life, and that in dying He had been giving it to them, as He had promised.

It may be observed here that in xx. 17 Mary Magdalene is charged with a message for the disciples ('I am ascending to my Father and your Father, to my God and your God'), which, coming from the risen Jesus at His first appearance, is meant to point to His resurrection as the sign revealing the factual character of His ascending at the Crucifixion, spoken of at vi. 62. This ascending is halting short of completeness ('I am not yet ascended unto the Father'), so that proofs of it may be given by His risen physical presence. Once these are offered, and He has sent the enabling Paraclete (xiv. 26; xvi. 13), He will accept from His own on earth not only such love as Mary now displays, but love for Him as He is in the perfection of His union with the Father. Underlying the expressions 'my Father and your Father', 'my God and your God', 'my brethren', is the thought of a joint ascending together with those who now share His life.

With *v.* 63 we come to a new problem. 'It is the spirit that quickeneth; the flesh profiteth nothing: the words that I have spoken unto you are spirit, and are life.' In the discourse hitherto it is the manhood of Jesus, the bread of life, that quickens or gives life. Men live, have eternal life, when by believing in Him they accept the bread of His dying manhood. Why then is it now said that it is the Spirit that gives life? Clearly the whole process by which Jesus offers Himself to men and is accepted by them as bread of life is here being ascribed to the work of the Spirit. The Spirit has not yet been given to believers, and cannot be given apart from the Passion of Jesus (vii. 39; xiv. 16, etc.). Up to that time the Spirit works upon them, not by indwelling, but by operation through the words of Jesus. 'The words that I have spoken unto you are spirit.' God is Spirit (iv. 24); and the whole discourse of Jesus is being treated as a mode of activity of God, just as in the previous chapter the miracles were said to be works which the Father was constantly doing and showing to the Son. As a phase of this action of God, the words of Jesus had power in them to call forth belief in Him from all whom the Father was drawing or giving to Him (*vv.* 37, 43–45, 65).

What then are we to make of the remaining utterance in *v.* 63: 'the flesh profiteth nothing'? On the face of it, the teaching in the second part of the discourse is now being contradicted: 'Yea, and the bread which I will give is my flesh, for the life of the world. . . . He that eateth my flesh and drinketh my blood hath eternal life. . . . For my flesh is meat indeed' (*vv.* 51–55). It cannot however be the intention to say that the flesh of Jesus, the manhood which has been taken into unity with the Logos, is of no avail for giving life. What is meant is that, for undiscerning Jews (*v.* 52) and for shocked disciples (*v.* 60), not responsive to the Spirit active in the words of Jesus, not drawn to Jesus by the Father, as they have just shown themselves to be, even His physical existence is not the life-imparting miracle that it should be. In Jesus the Logos has become flesh. But His words, unless they are recognized to be spirit, utterances given to Him by God, in which God Himself is active, and His works, unless they are seen to be signs of His status as the emissary of God's redemptive purpose, do not for those who hear and see them carry the life-giving efficacy of the Logos.

In the first part of the discourse, as we have observed, Jesus is represented to be the bread of life because, as having come down from heaven, He has life in Himself to impart to all who believe in Him. Yes, but it is not apart from His own utter obedience to His knowledge of the Father's will for Him that He has it. In the discourse itself this thought does not lie on the surface, but it is presupposed, because it has been one of the themes of the previous chapter and is to be the theme of the two succeeding chapters. 'He that sent me is with me; he hath not left me alone; for I do always the things that are pleasing to him' (viii. 29). 'He is with me,' 'He hath not left me alone': the phrases are meant to carry no less a weight of meaning than the reciprocal 'in-being' formula itself, which defines the life that is in Jesus (x. 38). 'My meat is to do the will of him that sent me and to accomplish his work' (iv. 34). 'My meat' means that by which Jesus lives, lives in the sense that He Himself has eternal life. And if it is His obedience to the Father's will which is a condition of His being the bread of life in the earlier usage of the figure of bread, so it is in the later when it is applied to His flesh. Thus we find it said in xiv. 30–31, with reference to His acceptance of the Cross: 'I will no more speak much with you, for the prince of this world cometh: and he hath nothing in me; but that the world may know that I love the Father, and as the Father gave me commandment, even so I do.' Again at x. 17–18: 'Therefore doth the Father love me, because I lay down my life. . . . No one taketh it from me, but I lay it down of myself. This commandment received I from my Father.'

We have been reserving consideration of the utterance in *v.* 46: 'Not that any man hath seen the Father, save he which is from God, he hath seen the Father.' We are meant to understand that Jesus utters the discourse in this chapter, makes the revelation which it conveys about the significance of His person and Passion, about believing in Him and about the Eucharist, as One who has 'seen the Father', and that He has seen the Father because He is 'from God'. Earlier we have given reasons for believing that this saying, along with others which speak of Jesus as having seen God, refers not to the precosmic experience of the Logos, but to the earthly experience of the man Jesus; and this is the thesis which we must now test by examining the utterance in its context.

The announcement that no man has seen the Father has far-reaching implications. In the previous verse it had been said: 'It is written in the prophets, And they shall all be taught of God. Everyone that hath heard from the Father, and hath learned, cometh unto me.' Then follow the words, 'Not that any man hath seen the Father,' i.e. not that anyone who has heard and learned from the Father has on that account 'seen' Him. What is this hearing and learning from the Father which ensures that a man will 'come to' Jesus, i.e. believe in Him, receive what He reveals about Himself, but which must not be regarded in itself as a 'seeing' of the Father? The immediate reference is to the discernment and acceptance of the Father's testimony to Jesus in the Scriptures, as may be seen from the parallel passage in an earlier chapter. 'And the Father which sent me, he hath borne witness of me. Ye have neither heard His voice at any time, nor seen his form. And ye have not his word abiding in you: for whom he sent, him ye believe not. Ye search the scriptures, because ye think that in them ye have eternal life; and these are they which bear witness of me; and ye will not come to me, that ye may have life' (v. 37–40). The threefold denial in this attack on the Jewish opponents of Jesus must not lead us to suppose that men who were taught by God through the Scriptures had therefore been enabled to 'see' Him. No, only Jesus had 'seen' Him, and this because He was 'from Him'. Nevertheless, a right reading of the Scripture was a vital matter for Jews, a *sine qua non* of believing in Jesus and so of seeing the Father (xii. 45; xiv. 9), as appears from *vv.* 44–45, where one drawn by the Father, when the Jews are in question, is one who had been taught by Him, one who has heard and learned from Him in the Scriptures. Believing in Jesus required, then, a readiness for it wrought in a man by God beforehand.

Guided by the utterance in *vv.* 44–45, we can the more easily understand that the following descriptive expressions which occur in the Gospel relate to those who have been prepared by God to believe in Jesus. Thus, they were men who were 'of the truth'.: 'Everyone that is of the truth heareth my voice' (xviii. 37). A similar turn of phrase is found at viii. 47: 'He that is of God heareth the words of God', where the intended sense is the same. Correspondingly, to be 'not of God' had the result for a man that he could not hear God's words in the words of Jesus (viii. 43, 47). They were the doers of good: 'all that are in the tombs shall hear his voice, and shall come forth; they that have done good, unto the resurrection of life. . . .' (v. 29). They were men who 'do the truth': 'He that doeth the truth cometh to the light, that his works may be made manifest, that they have been wrought in God' (iii. 21). It is said of them that they were 'thine' (xvii. 6). They were those whom the Father had given to Jesus (vi. 37, 19; x.29; xvii. 2, 6, 24; xviii. 9). And besides these there were the 'other sheep' (x. 16), who, since they would hear the voice of Jesus, had been prepared by God by some means other than the Scriptures.

How great a divine preparatory work is conceived in St. John to have gone on in men thus variously described is strikingly suggested in iv. 35–38. It makes them like fields ready not for sowing but for harvesting, as ready to be given eternal life as ripe grain is to be reaped. The giving of it, to which the reaping corresponds, is the completing divine action which takes place in Jesus.

We must now resume consideration of the statement, 'Not that any man hath seen the Father' (vi. 46). We have been drawing a parallel with v. 37–40; but it is a mistake to press the parallel too closely. The seeing spoken of in v. 37 is different from the seeing which is in question in vi. 46 (and again at i. 18); for in the latter case not only has no one hitherto seen God, but in the intended sense of seeing Him no one could have seen Him, the possibility of doing so being first provided in Jesus. But while v. 37 does not go together with vi. 46 and i. 18, each of these latter pronouncements helps out the interpretation of the other. 'No man hath seen God at any time; the only begotten Son, which is in the bosom of the Father, he hath declared him.' The kind of seeing of God which is here in view is not physical seeing; it is not a question of eyesight. So much is evident from the term 'declared' in the second part of the verse. There is no doubt that this second half implies the possibility now of just that kind of seeing of God which the first half asserts that no one has ever experienced. Further, in i. 18 and vi. 46 the kind of seeing intended is the same, but in the latter verse the verb is used twice, without change of meaning, the second time of Jesus and His seeing the Father. The thought of physical vision is as remote here and i. 18 as it is in xiv. 9, where 'to see the Father' is indistinguishable from 'to know the Father' two verses earlier. Here knowledge of Jesus is discernment of the relationship of 'in-being' between Himself and the Father, and knowledge of the Father is the recognition that He is accomplishing His eschatological saving action in Jesus. The Father was only to be seen or known in Jesus, the Logos incarnate, crucified, and victorious over death. 'The only begotten Son, which is in the bosom of the Father, he hath declared him.'

But from all this there follows an obvious conclusion. If only Jesus has seen the Father, and only through Him is it subsequently possible for others to see the Father, then the word 'see' must mean the same in each case. That is to say, Jesus' ability to see

H

the Father must be as much a consequence of the Incarnation as the ability He communicates to others. There can be no reference to the seeing of God by the pre-incarnate Logos.

9

THE TIME OF JESUS

The discourse on the bread of life produced a crisis in the ministry of Jesus. Up to this point, we have been told, in the person of Jesus the light of the eternal Logos has been in the world, and with it has come judgment. Mankind has been divided into two groups, according as they have or have not responded to the light. On the one side there have been the disciples, those who have believed in Jesus; on the other have been the Jews, the representatives of the unreceptive world. But now the vast crowd of disciples withdraws its allegiance and returns to the world of darkness from which it came (vi. 66). This is the second in a series of warnings that the first stirrings of belief in Jesus may come to nothing (cf. ii. 23 ff.; viii. 31 ff). Jesus is left alone with the Twelve and elicits from their spokesman Peter a clear statement of their conviction that He has 'the words of eternal life' and is 'the Holy One of God'. Yet not even this faith is above suspicion. Neither the preparatory work of the Father nor the choice of Jesus Himself is any guarantee that faith is genuine. 'Did I not choose you the twelve, and one of you is a devil?' (vi. 70).

In the following two chapters St. John turns to explore more fully the nature of this crisis. His brothers propose to Jesus that He should go up to Jerusalem to celebrate the Feast of Tabernacles. If the claims He has been making in Galilee are true, they deserve a wider publicity. 'Manifest thyself to the world' (vii. 4). But Jesus, as we have already seen in v. 41 ff., is not prepared to rest His case on popular acclaim. 'My time (*kairos*) is not yet come: but your time is alway ready. The world cannot hate you; but me it hateth, because I testify of it that its works are evil. Go ye up to the feast: I go not unto this feast; because my time is not yet fulfilled' (vii. 6-8). Like so many utterances of Jesus in the Fourth Gospel, this could be taken simply at its face value, as a refusal to do as His brothers desire and to go up to Jerusalem for a mission of the kind they recommend. 'To go up' (ἀναβαίνω) is the natural and topographically accurate word for a Jew to use of his pilgrimage to Jerusalem. But it is also the word which St. John has just used (vi. 62) to refer to the coming ascension of the Son of Man. Knowing St. John's fondness for double meanings, we shall probably be right to suspect that one is intended here: 'I do not ascend at this feast.'[1] Without some such double meaning we should be left with the uncomfortable fact that Jesus first denies that He is going up for the feast, and then goes. It is even more obvious that the *kairos* to which Jesus twice refers is something more than the right time for a visit to Jerusalem. It must be related to the 'hour', which in this Gospel is the word more commonly used to denote the critical period of the ministry (ii. 4; iv. 21, 23; v. 25; vii. 30; viii. 20; xii. 23; xiii. 1; xvi. 32).

Before we proceed further, we must pause to ask whether the Evangelist meant *v*. 8 ('my time is not yet fulfilled') to be an exact repetition of *v*. 6 ('my time is not yet come'), or whether the use of two different verbs indicates a progress of thought from one verse to the other. In favour of exact repetition it may be urged that St. John had a way of using pairs of synonyms interchangeably (compare iii. 35 with v. 20); though this point is considerably weakened when we observe that, if he only wished to avoid a repetition of the same verb, he had in ἥκω (ii. 4) or in ἔρχομαι (vii. 30; viii. 20; xvi. 21, 32; xvii. 1) the suitable word for his purpose. On the other hand it is not his practice, within a single brief context, to repeat an utterance without some real advance of meaning (compare iii. 3 with iii. 5). We have also to reckon with the normal usage of the verb πληρόω (fulfil) in expressions connected with time. It is regularly used in classical Greek, the Septuagint, the papyri, the New Testament, and elsewhere to denote the completion or expiration of the period of time in question. We ought not to adopt a special, biblical meaning in any passage where the normal meaning would make sense. It may be observed that, if this verb is so understood in Mark i. 15, then the perfect tense there can be given its proper force: 'The time of crisis is over, and so the Kingdom of God has arrived.' The time of crisis must then be understood as the struggle with Satan mentioned in i. 13. The Evangelist does not make this explicit in his description of the Temptation, but it appears from the Parable of the Strong Man in iii. 27, where the strong man is of course Satan, that he can be read as saying that Jesus had first to conquer Satan if the Kingdom of God was to come, and did conquer him

---

[1] For εἰς 'at (the time of)' cf. II Maccabees vi. 7.

in forty days of struggle with him before the ministry began. In the Fourth Gospel there is no initial Temptation, and the struggle with Satan is mentioned only in the later discourses (xii. 31; xiv. 30; xvi. 11, 33). But Satan, when he does appear, is called 'the prince of this world', and there is no doubt that Jesus already felt Himself to be in conflict with the world. Already the world hated him (v. 7), as it could not hate His brothers. We need not then hesitate to give the verb πληρόω its normal sense in v. 8: 'I do not go up to (or ascend at) this feast, for my time (of conflict with the world and with Satan, its ruler) is not yet finished (and will not be finished at this feast).' It is to be understood in reading these utterances that the decisive victory of Jesus over Satan and the world, as well as His ascending, was to take place at the Crucifixion (xvi. 33).

It need not disturb us that, according to this interpretation the time of crisis (*kairos*) is both future and also present but incomplete. It is characteristic of St. John's thought about time that 'the hour is coming and now is'. From one point of view the crisis is the moment of the Crucifixion and has not yet come; from another point of view the crisis is already present, but will not have run its course until the world's hostility reaches its climax. Hitherto, when St. John has in any way alluded to the coming hour of crisis, he has seen it as a necessary part of the divine economy of salvation. But it also has its human causes; and from now on he will be more and more concerned with the part played by Jewish hostility in the realisation of the purposes of God (vii. 19, 23, 25, 30, 32, 44; viii. 59; x. 39).

The interpretation we have given to the time of Jesus has one further corollary. When Jesus says to His brothers, 'Your time is alway ready', He must be taken to mean more than that for them a pilgrimage to Jerusalem is always opportune. We have been told that they did not believe in Jesus, and this means that they are to be regarded as part of the unbelieving world. The world cannot hate them, because, whether they admit it or not, they actually belong to it. What we are being told, then, is that, although Jesus' *kairos* has not yet arrived, or has not yet reached its climax, the *kairos* of the world is already fully present. What this means is explained in the following sentence (v. 7). The world hates Jesus because He testifies of it 'that its works are evil', both by the shining of the true light which draws attention to the

darkness (iii. 19 f.; cf. viii. 12), and also by direct indictment
(vii. 28; viii. 19, 31–59). In iii. 19–21, to do works which are evil
is the opposite of doing the truth—one of several modes of
expression used in the Septuagint to denote fidelity to the covenant
and the revealed will of God for Israel. Jesus, then, has drawn
upon Himself the hostility of the Jews by exposing their unfaith-
fulness to God as revealed in Israel's religion and also in His own
teaching (cf. vii. 17); and it is in this sense that the *kairos* is always
present for His brothers and for all other Jews who are on too
good terms with the world.

Underlying the veiled utterances about the time of Jesus lies
yet another Johannine theme which will emerge more clearly in
the course of the chapter. In *v*. 39 we are told that 'the Spirit was
not yet given, because Jesus was not yet glorified.' The 'not yet'
of *v*. 39 is clearly the same as the 'not yet' of *vv*. 6 and 8. One
reason why the brothers of Jesus belong to the world is because
they hold worldly ideas of glory and are anxious that Jesus should
prove His case by winning public acclamation. As in the Synoptic
Gospels, the brothers of Jesus, like their mother (cf. ii. 3), misunderstand Him. We have already seen that the Evangelist
intended readers of the Cana story to understand that Jesus was
moved to say, 'My hour has not yet come,' by a realisation that
His mother had seen in the shortage of wine a possible opportunity
for her Son to win glory for Himself by producing a supply; but
a glory which He could not accept (cf. *v*. 41; vii. 18; viii. 50), and
this because His own heart was set upon gaining a glory which only
His dying could bring Him. He would seek the glory He desired
by obedience to the redemptive purposes of the Father and by
victory over the ruler of this world (xii. 31; xvi. 11, 33); and He
would find it in His resulting love-union with all believers, His
own life shared with them for ever.

But why is it that the Jews, for all their elaborate preparation
for the coming of God's Messiah, do not believe in Him now that
He has come? When the feast is already half over, Jesus goes up
to the Temple and teaches. The Jews are surprised that He can
teach as He does, when He has not been given rabbinical instruction. Jesus tells them that His teaching is not His; it is the teaching
of the One who had sent Him, as anyone who resolved to do God's
will could know for himself (*vv*. 14–17). What is meant by doing
the will of God is however left unexplained. With help from the

saying in vi. 40 readers of the Gospel could have understood that
the will of the Father was of a twofold character: that there
should be men who possessed eternal life, and they they should
possess it through their seeing the Son—seeing Him with the eye
of understanding—and believing in Him. Men's part was to
render to the Son the required response. Whoever was resolved
on that would come to know whether the teaching of Jesus was
from God or simply from Himself. It is not said why. In Johannine thought elsewhere however the response in question has to
spring from a predisposing divine work wrought in those who
yielded it (cf. vi. 44-45). Anyone who had been taught by God
and had learned in some measure to know and to love Him, and
so had resolved to do His will, would recognise the authentic
notes of His voice as He spoke through the words and works of
Jesus. St. John provides many witnesses to attest the truth of the
claims of Jesus, but in the last resort he offers his readers no other
verification than this. The failure of the Jews to believe in Jesus
merely proves that they have not even that elementary, preparatory
knowledge of God which comes to those who are ready to obey
Him.

The reason why obedience to the will of God is the one
qualification for the understanding of the teaching of Jesus is that
He Himself is totally subservient to the will of His Father. 'He
that speaketh from himself seeketh his own glory: but he that
seeketh the glory of him that sent him, the same is true, and no
unrighteousness is in him' (v. 18). Humanly speaking, the union
between the Logos and manhood in Jesus, which the Father has
willed in the Incarnation, is possible because Jesus has recognised
and accepted that will with utter obedience. Only to one who has
some experience of obedience, then, can such a union of will and
purpose be intelligible or credible. But in place of obedience the
Jews have only self-seeking. They seek honour for themselves
from men (cf. v. 44) and cannot understand One who is wholly
devoid of such ambition, who seeks only 'the glory of him that
sent him'. This last phrase is ambiguous, and it is likely that the
ambiguity is deliberate. It could mean that Jesus, instead of
seeking human recognition for Himself, seeks honour from men
for the Father who sent Him, tries to impart to men that truth
which will lead them to honour God. But it could also means
that Jesus, instead of looking to men for honour, looks only to

God and to that glory which God has willed to impart to Him through His union with the Logos (cf. v. 44, where the phrase used is unambiguous—'the glory that cometh from the only God'). He possesses a glory which He has already manifested, and will possess a greater glory when the Passion establishes a love-union between Him and believers; but both forms of glory are His, not by His own self-assertion or by public acclaim, but only because He has obediently submitted to the divine will that the glory of the Logos should be communicated first to Him and through Him to others. To deny the glory would be 'unrighteousness', a sin against what He knows to be God's will.

We have been treating this argument as a resumption of the one which followed the healing of the cripple in chapter 5, and the justification for this is that Jesus now openly alludes to that episode. 'Did not Moses give you the law, and yet none of you doeth the law? Why seek ye to kill me? The multitude answered, Thou hast a devil: who seeketh to kill thee? Jesus answered and said unto them, I did one work, and ye all marvel. For this cause hath Moses given you circumcision (not that it is of Moses, but of the fathers); and on the sabbath ye circumcise a man. If a man receiveth circumcision on the sabbath, that the law of Moses may not be broken; are ye wroth with me, because I made a man every whit whole on the sabbath? Judge not according to appearance, but judge righteous judgement' (vv. 19–24). The assertion that 'none of you keeps the law' and the question, 'Why are you seeking to kill me?', make an intelligible sequence of thought if it is understood, as seemingly it should be, that Jews who do not do the will of God, and therefore do not believe in Jesus, thereby fail to keep the law. Their hostility to Jesus and His ministry shows that they are not true followers of Moses. On the contrary, Moses is ranged on the side of Jesus. Moses had laid down that circumcision should take place on the eighth day; and, if the eighth day after the birth of a boy fell on a Sabbath, it was understood that circumcision constituted no violation of the Sabbath Law. The Jews ought to understand all the more readily that Jesus and Moses were in accord about the Sabbath; for the restoration of a man's whole body must *a fortiori* be no violation of the Sabbath Law. This was a point on which Jesus would have had the support of Rabbi Eleazar ben Azariah (early second century), who said: 'If circumcision, which concerns one of the two hundred and forty-eight members of a man's body, sets aside the Sabbath, how much more must his whole body (if he is in danger of dying) set it aside' (b. Yoma 85ᵇ).

The Jewish authorities do nothing to prevent Jesus from speaking openly in the Temple. Some of the people of Jerusalem who, unlike the crowd (v. 20), know about the intention of their leaders to kill Jesus (cf. v. 18) ask themselves whether therefore these leaders have in fact come to believe that Jesus is the Messiah. No, they reflect, He cannot be, for they know where He has come from, whereas no one knows where the Messiah will come from when he appears (v. 27). They are not saying that no one was thought to know the parentage and birthplace of the Messiah (see v. 42; cf. Psalms of Solomon xvii. 21); they are following a Jewish belief (cf. Justin, *Dial.* viii. 4; cx. 1) that before he came forward publicly the Messiah would live in concealment at some place unknown. (The supposition that they may have been expecting the Messiah to come from heaven suits neither their plain, matter-of-fact statement that they know where Jesus has come from nor their belief that 'no one knows where he is to come from'.) Jesus confirms them in the knowledge they had of Him that He had not been living in concealment, and that He had come to Jerusalem from Galilee, but declares that their knowledge of Him was no basis for an inference that His mission had been undertaken on His own authority. 'Ye both know me, and know whence I am; and I am not come of myself, but he that sent me is true, whom ye know not. I know him; because I am from him, and he sent me' (vv. 28–29).

Here is a passage which may be regarded as a test case for the main thesis of this work. We argued in the first chapter that the content of the revelation given by Jesus was not some changeless truth which the Logos had known from all eternity in His life of union with God, but rather the redemptive purpose of God which the incarnate Logos, the man Jesus, was led by the Spirit to recognise, to obey, and to consummate. We must ask, therefore, whether the knowledge which Jesus here claims is derived from His pre-existence as Logos or from the intimate relationship with the Father which He enjoyed during His earthly life (cf. i. 18; iii. 13), and whether the sending here twice referred to is the sending of the Logos into the world at the Incarnation or the sending of the man Jesus on His mission to the world. The context is decisively against any reference to the pre-existence of the Logos. The opposition has suggested that, since the local origin of Jesus is known, He is disqualified from being Messiah and is therefore an upstart. Jesus denies that His Galilean origin settles the question of His credentials. He did not leave his Galilean home to embark on a nationwide mission on His own authority. He did so not because He chose, but because He was sent, and sent by One whom He knew with an intimate personal knowledge.[2]

These sayings of Jesus rouse the anger of the hearers, but a move to seize Him comes to nothing; His destiny is in divine control (v. 30). From among the crowd nevertheless many believe in Him, thinking of the signs that He had performed and questioning whether more could be expected of the Messiah. The authorities hear of it and send Temple police to arrest Him. Jesus then utters some dark sayings which the hearers are at present totally unable to comprehend, and which will ultimately be repeated and elucidated in the Last Discourse. 'Yet a little while am I with you, and I go unto him that sent me. Ye shall seek me, and shall not find me: and where I am, ye cannot come' (vv. 33–34). These sayings are, as we shall see, laden with the meaning that Jesus would die when His hour came, and that His dying would be the conquest of death for Himself and for His believing followers by such a triumph over it as would retain for Himself and secure for them life in the Godhead, and yet also bring to pass the irretrievable ruin of the unresponsive to His word, judgment then coming to them in the form of an anguish of longing for One they could not find, and without whom they could only die in their sins (viii. 21); and this on account of their inherent incapacity to believe in Him when He was with them.

The argument now reaches its climax in a saying which raises some acute critical difficulties. There are three possible punctuations of vv. 37–38.

(a) 'If any man thirst, let him come unto me, and let him that believeth on me drink, as the scripture hath said. Out of his belly shall flow rivers of living water.'

(b) 'If any man thirst, let him come unto me, and let him that believeth on me drink. As the scripture hath said, Out of his belly shall flow rivers of living water.'

---

[2] The reading παρ' αὐτῷ expresses the idea of the reciprocal in-being between Jesus and the Father without significantly affecting the sense of the probably original παρ' αὐτοῦ.

(c) 'If any man thirst, let him come unto me and drink. He that believeth on me, as the scripture hath said, Out of his belly shall flow rivers of living water.'

There are three points to be decided. Does Jesus invite the thirsty to come and drink at once, as in (c); or are the coming and the drinking two separate phases of response, as in (a) and (b)? Are we to take the reference to Scripture with what precedes, as in (a), or with what follows, as in (b) and (c)? And is the living water said to flow from the body of the believer, as in (a) and (c), or from the body of Jesus, as is the most natural interpretation of (b)?[3] Let us deal with each of these questions in turn.

Jesus claims to be able to supply the thirsty with living water, i.e., the water which gives life (cf. 'bread of life' = 'living bread', vi. 48, 50). But the Evangelist explains (v. 39) that by life-giving water Jesus had meant the Spirit, and he adds that Jesus was not promising to give believers the Spirit to drink then and there, during His public ministry ('for the Spirit was not yet'); He would do it when, by His dying, He had won for Himself the glory of having included them in His own union with the Father, fit recipients then of the same Spirit once given to Him (i. 32–33; iii. 34). In the Last Discourse, as we shall see, the Spirit is the interpreter of the completed divine action achieved in the words and works of Jesus (xiv. 26; xv. 26; xvi. 13). It is clear, therefore, that according to the theology of the Evangelist, the thirsty man could not drink the living water before Jesus died; but he could and should come to Him at once. At v. 40, where the Jews are told that they have not the will to come to Jesus that they may have life, to come to Him must be variant phrasing for to believe in Him, to account for what they lose in not coming to Him (cf. v. 44). At vi. 35, the synonymous clauses ('He that cometh to me shall not hunger, and he that believeth on me shall never thirst') show that to come to Jesus and to believe in Him are equivalent expressions (cf. vi. 37, 44, 45, 65). We should then take the invitation of vii. 37–39 to mean that the thirsty man must come to Jesus at once, and having thus become a believer, must drink the living water of the Spirit, when the death of Jesus has made it available for men. 'If any man thirsts (for living water), let him come to me (to get it); let him who believes in me drink (as drink he will, though not forthwith, of the living water he thirsts for).'

[3] See Dodd, *The Interpretation of the Fourth Gospel*, p. 349.

The first impression left by the singular ('the scripture') in *v.* 38 is that the reference is to a particular Old Testament passage, that the clause should be constructed with the words which follow it and held to make them an obscure, unidentifiable Old Testament quotation. We avoid this difficulty if we adopt the punctuation of (a) and suppose that the Evangelist intended no difference between the singular used here and the plural used in v. 39–40, where too an appeal is made to Scripture as a whole to witness that Jesus is the giver of life. This appears the more probable from the use of the singular a few verses farther on (vii. 42), where material from several Old Testament books concerning the coming of the Messiah is gathered together in a composite allusion; and from ii. 22 and xx. 9, where it is not clear that any one Old Testament passage is meant.

The only other passage in which St. John uses the phrase 'living water' is iv. 10–14, and this will provide the best commentary on the promise, 'Out of his belly shall flow rivers of living water'. We know from the comment of the Evangelist at vii. 39 that the water which Jesus offered the Samaritan woman cannot be the life-giving word of Jesus to the exclusion of the action of the enlightening Spirit. When it is said (iv. 14) that the water which Jesus could give would become in him who drank it a spring bubbling up for eternal life, the meaning will be that the Spirit would become ever active in a recipient thereof for the production in him of eternal life. We conclude, therefore, that the punctuation of (a) is to be preferred.

The Feast of Tabernacles would have provided an occasion for the words ascribed to Jesus in *vv.* 37–38. At the libation ceremony observed during the feast, when water drawn from the pool of Siloam was borne into the Temple and poured over the altar of burnt offering, use was made, according to rabbinic interpretations of Tabernacles, especially of Isaiah xii. 3 ('Therefore with joy shall ye draw water out of the wells of salvation'), Zechariah xiv. 8 ff ('And it shall come to pass in that day that living waters shall go out from Jerusalem. . . . And the Lord shall be king over all the earth'), and Ezekiel xlvii. 1–12 (where waters issue forth from the Temple). It may be that the sayings ascribed to Jesus in *vv.* 37–38 aim especially at winning response from minds familiar with this eschatological water-symbolism; and it is worthy of notice that the Evangelist's equation of the living water offered by Jesus and the Spirit should correspond with rabbinic interpretation of the water at Tabernacles (see Strack-Billerbeck, II 434 f.).

10

THE CLAIMS OF JESUS

The eighth chapter opens with a new claim of Jesus. 'I am the light of the world: he that followeth me shall not walk in the darkness, but shall have the light of life' (viii. 12). Up to this point the secret of Jesus' person and mission has been expounded mainly in terms of life and glory. It was said of the precosmic Logos that 'in him was life' (i. 4); and this life has been communicated to the Son (v. 26), in order that, at the appointed 'hour', He might draw others into union with this eternal life (iii. 16). The glory which the Logos had with God before the world was (xvii. 5) has been manifested in the life (i. 14), and especially in the signs of Jesus (ii. 11), in such a way that those who had the eyes of faith might see in Him 'the only begotten from the Father'; and there have been dark hints of a future glory to be won when others can be given 'the right to become children of God' (i. 13). We shall expect to find, therefore, that the new claim in terms of light is a variation on the same theme, whatever fresh nuances it may add. The life which was the eternal possession of the Logos was also the light by which, and by which alone, men could be rescued from the all-embracing darkness (i. 4); and this light had come into the world in the person of Jesus (xii. 46) in order that it might become the possession of men.

In a previous chapter we raised the question whether in the Prologue the shining of the light in the darkness (i. 5) was a reference to the pre-incarnate activity of the Logos or to the Incarnation. We concluded that the reference was to the Incarnation, partly because the shining of the light was said to be the theme of the Baptist's testimony (i. 6–8), and partly because subsequently (iii. 19) the coming of the light into the world was clearly to be identified with the sending of God's Son. We may now add a further weighty argument in favour of this conclusion. The claim of Jesus to be the light of the world is taken up and developed in two further passages. In the story of the blind man Jesus says to His disciples, 'When I am in the world, I am the light of the world' (ix. 5). The implication is that the time for the shining of the light is limited. 'We must work the works of him that sent me, while it is day; the night cometh, when no man can work' (ix. 4). The same point is made more fully in the second passage. 'Yet a little while is the light among you. Walk while ye have the light, that darkness overtake you not: and he that walketh in the darkness knoweth not whither he goeth. While ye have the light, believe on the light, that ye may become sons of light' (xii. 35–36). If the light of the Logos had always been shining in the dark world, even before the arrival of Jesus, it is difficult to see why it should be totally withdrawn by His departure. It need hardly be added that, when Jesus was no longer in the world, but had gone to the Father, He would still be the light of all who believed in Him through the apostolic preaching contemplated in the Last Discourse and Prayer (e.g. xv. 20; xvii. 20). The point is that, during His ministry, for those to whom He was revealing Himself by His utterances and signs, there was only a limited amount of time in which to find that He was the light of the world; and if they failed to use that limited time, they would have none at all after His death.

The figure of daylight turning before long to darkness is used to hasten believing response to Jesus and recognition of what the alternative to it is. Darkness, when a man cannot see where he is going, when he stumbles (xi. 10), is the alternative to daylight; and correspondingly the alternative to accepting the self-revealing activity of Jesus is the impossibility of finding a way to God. It is clear that amongst benefits coming to man from sunlight or daylight one in particular is held in the series of light-utterances of Jesus to illustrate something to do with man's relation to God, and that is the benefit of being able to see where he is going. By Jesus, as the world's light, the world may see its way to God.

In answer to the utterance at viii. 12 the Pharisees revert to an earlier saying of Jesus that a claim which rests on a man's own unsupported testimony may be dismissed as false (v. 31). But they misrepresent Jesus by citing only the first half of His announcement there, and by omitting His assurance that His testimony was validated by the testimony of His Father (v. 33). The testimony borne by the Father concerning Jesus was the work being done by Jesus, a work which was at the same time the Father's and His own. Here the argument of Jesus is restated to accommodate it to the theme of light. His testimony is true because it is based on His knowledge of His own heavenly origin and heavenly destiny. 'I know whence I came and whither I go' (*v.* 14). A man who possesses light can see where he is going (cf. xii. 35). Jesus knows that He not only has such light, but can supply it to others, because He knows where He comes from. He knows that He has come from God and is going to God (xiii. 3). It would, however, be a serious mistake to suppose that in all this the Evangelist was thinking simply of the eternal Logos, leaving the presence of God and returning to it, and thus restoring a heavenly *status quo*. If men are to find their way to God, it is because Jesus, as man, has already done so, has gone to prepare a place for them (xiv. 3). It is therefore the manhood of Jesus which is here said to have its source and destiny in God.

The judgment which the Pharisees are said to form about Jesus is 'after the flesh', i.e. based on their own worldly standards, unlike the divine judgment which belongs to the complex of eschatological events being accomplished in the ministry of Jesus. When He thinks of Himself out of relation to these events Jesus can say, 'I judge no man'; but, as being in His own person the field in which these events occur, He in fact becomes judge of those who are blind to them (*v.* 16; cf. xii. 48–49; iii. 19 ff.; ix. 39 ff.), judging in a valid manner because He does not act alone in His ministry, but in conjunction with Him who had sent Him. Not only in judgment, but in all His activity, it can be said that Jesus is never alone; for everything He says or does is at the same time the word or deed of the Father. 'I am not alone, but I and the Father that sent me' (*v.* 16).

In support of His argument Jesus cites the Jewish law (Deut. xvii. 16) that in serious charges the matter might not be established on the testimony of one, but only at least of two witnesses; His own testimony is confirmed by that of His Father (*vv.* 17–18). Not wanting to have it represented that the Law could be turned against them over their intention to kill Him (vii. 1, 19, 25, 32, 45; viii. 37, 45), the Jewish opponents of Jesus see their way, they think to refute Him. If He is going to rely on the testimony of a witness, that witness must appear and give his evidence; 'Where is thy Father?' (*v.* 19). The answer is that they could only know the Father of Jesus if they knew Jesus Himself. To know Jesus is to know that in Him the Logos has taken flesh, that in Him manhood has been brought into unity of love and purpose with the Father;

and apart from this self-revealing activity of the Logos, the Father
remains unknown by men. Only by believing in Jesus could
anyone know what was the testimony borne to Him by His Father
and recognise its truth.

Jesus now makes one of those veiled allusions to His coming
death which the Jews so consistently misunderstand. 'I go away,
and ye shall seek me, and shall die in your sin: whither I go, ye
cannot come' (v. 21). When they make nothing of His words and
reply with a sarcastic comment, Jesus adds: 'Ye are from beneath;
I am from above: ye are of this world; I am not of this world. I
said therefore unto you, that ye shall die in your sins: for except
ye believe that I am (he), ye shall die in your sins' (vv. 23–34). It
is important for us to recognise what sort of a distinction is here
being made. Is it a metaphysical distinction between the heavenly,
uncreated nature of the Logos and the lower, earthly, created
nature of men, or a moral distinction between Him who is identified
with the saving purpose of God and those who are not? Clearly it
is a moral distinction. The implication is that, if the Jews were
able now to believe in Jesus and subsequently to find Him and go
where He had gone, they would not die in their sins; they would
have been transferred out of the category of those who are 'from
beneath' and 'of this world' into the category of those who are
'from above' and 'not of this world'. And this inference is fully
borne out at a later stage when Jesus says of the disciples: 'They
are not of the world even as I am not of the world' (xvii. 14). The
disciples are 'not of the world' because Jesus has chosen them
(xv. 19). By the same token Jesus is 'from above' because His
human life is wholly derived from and dependent on the will of
His Father. When He speaks, He speaks not out of memories of
a premundane existence, but 'as the Father taught me' (v. 28).
Even when He uses the absolute claim, 'I am', He can still add,
'I do nothing of myself' (v. 28). Everything that He does and
speaks, even the knowledge that He has of His own union with
God, is derived from His human experience of being instructed
by the Father, and from His own willingness to do what pleases
the Father (v. 29).

At v. 31 Jesus turns to address those Jews who had believed in
Him, though obviously with a tenuous faith. 'If ye abide in my
word, then ye are truly my disciples; and ye shall know the truth,
and the truth shall make you free.' The word of Jesus is at the

same time the word of the Father (cf. xiv. 24), of which it is said that it is truth or reality (xvii. 17). Accordingly any who held fast to the word of Jesus would come to know reality, and—so it is promised them—they would be made free by the reality which they would know. The allusion to the Son in *v.* 36 shows that the reality by which they would be made free is reality in the sense the term bears in xiv. 6, where Jesus declares that He is Himself reality. They are not told that they would be made free simply by knowledge of reality; knowledge of it would qualify them to be made free by the reality itself, that is, by Him who is the embodiment of that reality. But how would He make them free? Jesus answers in a parable. 'Everyone that committeth sin is the bondservant (of sin). And the bondservant abideth not in the house for ever: the son abideth for ever. If therefore the Son shall make you free, ye shall be free indeed' (*vv.* 34–36).[1] The point taken for comparison between a man who commits sin and a domestic slave is the insecurity of a slave's position in a household: the one may no more expect to belong permanently to the household of God than the other may count upon remaining in the household of his owner. Correspondingly the point about freedom is that a man who gains it comes to belong securely to the household; and if One whose position in the household of God is secure, and that One is His Son, makes free others in it, then their position in the household of God will also be secure. Sin is committed when the word of Jesus is not clung to wholly for security in the household of God, but is allowed to have a place only beside reliance for it on the Abrahamic covenant. By the household of God implied throughout *vv.* 31–36 is meant God and a world made up of 'slaves', with the exception of the Son of God who is in it to set it free, that is, to liberate it from the insecurity in which it exists in relation to God. Beyond that however the instructed reader of St. John will understand that he is being left for enlightment to his insights into the meaning of the Sonship and the dying of Jesus in this Gospel.

Offspring of Abraham, members of the Abrahamic covenant, who cannot believe in Jesus to the point of learning from Him

---

[1] The reading 'is a slave' (D b sy^s Cl Cypr) is to be preferred to the reading 'is a slave of sin'. For the latter reading makes sin the master of the household; whereas already in *v.* 35 by secondary allusion, and then in *v.* 36 by primary reference, the son of the master of the household is Jesus, the master himself being therefore God.

I

that the divine end in the institution of the covenant is the freedom
to be gained by means of His word, are left by the encounter in
deadly hostility to Him, and unaware that they are preparing their
own ruin (*v.* 37). But they must not suppose that their opposition
renders the authority of the word of Jesus groundless. On the
contrary, He drew its content from what He had seen in the
presence of His Father; and it followed from their attitude towards
His word and Himself that they were accepting promptings from
their father concerning Him (*v.* 38). Abraham, they retort, was
their father; they were acting out of loyalty to him. But no, they
were ceasing to be children of Abraham, i.e. they were forfeiting
their status within the covenant; otherwise their response to Jesus
and His ministry would be Abrahamic in character (*v.* 39),
whereas in fact, although He had spoken the truth, which He had
heard from God, they were seeking to kill Him. 'This did not
Abraham' (*v.* 40); Abraham had not been deaf and disbelieving
when God had been speaking to him, as they were now when God
was speaking to them through His Son. In their behaviour with
Jesus they were, then, obeying not Abraham but their father. The
opponents of Jesus hold their ground: it was a calumny to attribute
illegitimacy in the sight of God to a people convinced that He was
their only Father (*v.* 41). The reproach leads to a denial by Jesus of
the rightness of its premise: God is not the Father of those who do
not love Jesus, who do not receive His word. In one Johannine sense
of the term, God becomes Father to those who receive Him as He
comes to them in the eschatological events which make up the content of the word of Jesus. In another sense, which is short of the
first, He is the Father of all who have been predisposed by Him to
receive His word as it is spoken by Jesus, and so given the assurance
of His becoming their Father in the final measure. From their company the Jews of the passage are excluded by their absence of love
for Jesus—a ground of disqualification which is then made more
specific as their failure to recognise the heavenly origin of Himself
and His mission (*v.* 42). They have shown that they have not
understood what Jesus has said. Why was that? The question
serves to prepare the way for an announcement of their incapacity
to hear responsively the word of Jesus and to carry further the
sombre theme of vi. 44–45 concerning men whom God has
abandoned: those who refuse the word of Jesus thereby make it
evident that the springs of belief and action within them have

their origin in the devil. 'Ye are of your father the devil, and the lusts of your father it is your will to do. He was a murderer from the beginning, and stood not in the truth, because there is no truth in him. When he speaketh a lie, he speaketh of his own: for he is a liar, and the father thereof' (v. 44).

In the words 'he was a murderer from the beginning' there is explanatory reference to the resolve of the Jews to kill Jesus, but also and mainly to the reason for their deprivation of eternal life in common with all others since the creation of man ('from the beginning') whose works had been evil. It is nowhere said or implied in the Gospel that the devil was already there 'in the beginning', as it is said of the Logos in i. 1. Before the creation of 'all things' by the Logos nothing existed, in the thought of St. John, but the divine eternal order. The devil, then, had no pre-temporal existence. He came to be as in some sense a consequence —divinely foreseen and accepted—of the creative work of the Logos, offering resistance 'from the beginning' to the end purposed in man's creation. The world brought into being by the Logos was created other than Himself, not a reproduction of His own eternal perfection, though designed ultimately to share it; and in so far as it was not perfect, there was room in it from the first for the possibility that the spiritual failures and losses which are associated in St. John with ideas of a personal devil and his activity would take place. It is certain that the fulfilment of the divine intention for man in his creation is held in the Gospel to be dependent upon the occurrence of what 'in the beginning' were far-off divine events, and there are no evident indications in it of a belief that the accomplishment of these events was a subsequently designed remedy for a thwarted first attempt to impart life to man without them.

The devil did not come into being within the truth or reality of the Godhead, and he had remained all along outside it ('stood not in the truth')—witness the use he was making of the Jews in their attitude to Jesus Himself. When he utters 'the lie', as now in their hostility to Him, he does it out of regard for his own business, for he is a liar and he propagates the lie, which is the negation of the truth, the divine reality manifested in Jesus.

It was because Jesus, in contrast to the devil, spoke the truth that the Jews, organs as they were of the lie, did not believe Him (v. 45). Who of them—in their corrupt spiritual condition—could claim the right to convict Him of being mistaken about God and therefore misguided in His mission (*v.* 46)?. The reason why they did not believe Jesus was that they were not 'of God', not God's children (in the second of the senses mentioned above). For the man whose father is God hears responsively in the words of Jesus the words of God, and this they were not doing (*v.* 47).

In the early third century Rabbi Jannai gave the name of 'Samaritan' to a Jew who studied the Scriptures and the Mishnah but had not been of service to disciples (Strack-Billerbeck, II 524 f). Perhaps then from this use of the word as a term of abuse, if it went back far enough, we may understand the reply of the Jews to Jesus in *v.* 48 ('thou art a Samaritan') as a contemptuous dismissal of His case.[2] In addition they suggest that He was possessed by an evil spirit and thus out of His mind (cf. x. 20 and *Corpus Hermeticum* IX 4). Jesus answers with an assertion of His faithfulness to His Father (*v.* 49). In protesting that the Jews were insulting Him He was not aiming at self-glorification, as they might be supposing. He had no need to seek His own glory, since there was One (namely, His Father) who sought through His ministry the glory for Him of having believers in love-union with Him, and who at the same time was passing judgment on the Jews for their rejection of His mission (*v.* 50). Confirmation of the use of 'glory' here in two senses, first of the rejected idea of self-glorification and then of the glory desired for Jesus by the Father, comes from the corresponding uses of the cognate verb, 'glorify' in *v.* 54. Once it is recognised that the glory which the Father seeks for Jesus is His union with believers, which will also bring them into union with the Father and so give them life, *vv.* 50 and 51 can be seen to be in an appropriate connexion: the fact that God seeks the glory of Jesus is in itself a guarantee for any man who keeps the word of Jesus that he will not by dying forfeit his true life. The Jewish opponents, incapable of grasping the word of Jesus, could not therefore understand the destiny to which it pointed. They wrongly supposed that He had just given His followers a promise of exemption from the dying of their bodies, which in face of the fact that Abraham and the prophets were dead only one possessed would do. Did He in His madness think that He disposed of a power over death which Abraham did not have (*v.* 53)? What claim was He making for Himself (cf. v. 18; x. 33; xix. 7)? The

[2] For other proposed interpretations see Bultmann, p. 225, note 6.

first utterance of Jesus in *v.* 54 allows that the verdict of the Jews
on Him would be a sensible one, if he were engaged in self-
glorification, for then His glory would be an illusion. But the
verdict is wrong, for reasons offered as the verse goes on. Thus,
the declaration that it is His Father who gives glory to Jesus means
that He brings to pass between Jesus and believers the love
relationship which is life; and it covers in its range of reference the
assumption of manhood by the Logos, His will that His acquired
manhood should be laid down in death and taken back again in
resurrection (x. 17 f.), God's granting to Jesus the words He utters
(iii. 34; xvii. 8) and the signs He performs in the Gospel (v. 17;
ix. 3; x. 32, 37 f.; xiv. 10), His sending of the Spirit for the further
enlightenment of believers in respect of the significance of the
whole complex of divine events (xvi. 14)—for from these events
comes the life of believers, the glory which the Father had
given to Jesus (xvii. 22).

The case against the false verdict proceeds. Although they
(rightly) call Him who is the Father of Jesus their God, the Jews,
not knowing Him through the word of Jesus, do not in fact know
Him at all. Jesus knows Him, and being, unlike them, no liar, He
must be true to that knowledge (*v.* 55). By the 'day' of Jesus (*v.*
56) is meant the time charged with the significance of the divine
eschatological actions which make up the content of His word. To
the arrival of His day, i.e. to the presence in Jesus of these divine
activities, life-giving to man or judging him, the Jews were blind,
whereas Abraham, whose children they wrongly thought they
were, had joyfully welcomed it. Through Abraham came a
revelation and through Jesus the consummation of the one agelong
purpose of God to deliver man from evil and give him life; and
the Abrahamic covenant had been brought by Him to its fulfilment in the 'day' of Jesus. 'Your father Abraham rejoiced to see
my day; and he saw it, and was glad' (*v.* 56). There are evident
affinities of thought in this utterance with the late Jewish belief
that God had granted to Abraham a vision of the age to come (cf.
IV Ezra iii. 14), which also suggests that 'rejoiced to see my day'
means 'exulted at seeing—then and there—my day', and not
'exulted that he was to see my day—when it came'. The Jews,
ignorant of what Jesus had meant by His 'day', appear again in
defence of their verdict on Him: some wild fancy about a joyful
relationship between Himself and Abraham held His mind. Not

yet fifty years old, He imagined that He had lived from the time of
the dead patriarch, and He had come to know from him then and
knew now how Abraham regarded Him (*v.* 57)! By this argued
incredulity of theirs the Jews spoke more rightly than they could
know: Jesus, they are scandalized to hear it said, had existed
before Abraham was born (*v.* 58). In their presence was the Logos,
precosmic (i. 1), creative (i. 3), self-revealing, who had taken to
Himself manhood in Jesus, who would give it up in death, regain
it in resurrection and 'ascension'; and by these events make known
and give to men the divine life or love, as those of them who obeyed
His word would assuredly discover and others never.

11

THE GOOD SHEPHERD

A parable or figurative discourse in x. 1–5, addressed by Jesus to uncomprehending Pharisees (x. 6; cf. ix. 40 f.), is followed in *vv.* 7–18 by reflections from Him bearing on the intended applied meanings of the terms 'door' and 'shepherd'. The man who does not go through the door of a sheepfold, but climbs over the wall to get to the sheep, is contrasted with the man who approaches the sheep by way of the door and is let in by their guardian; the one is a thief or robber on his business and the other is the shepherd. The sheep recognise the voice of their shepherd and are themselves known to him individually. Trustfully the sheep let him lead them out of the fold and go in front of them to their pasture; but from a stranger they run away.

Jesus first claims to be the door for the sheep (*v.* 7). He is so —the reader is to understand—on the ground of the occurrence of those eschatological events which were constitutive of His word. Just as the light which was eternally in the Logos was the light for men (i. 4), and became available to them in the divine-human person of Jesus (viii. 12; ix. 5), so in Jesus the means of entrance to the presence of God has become available to men. It may be inferred from *v.* 16 that by 'the sheep' are meant those amongst the people of Israel and in the Gentile world who in consequence of a divine preparatory work in them could steadfastly await Him under the trial and then, when He came, hear His voice, i.e. respond to His word with understanding and acceptance.

We have argued in an earlier chapter that there are no grounds in the Fourth Gospel for taking the words of the Prologue, 'the light shineth in the darkness', to be a reference to preincarnate activities of the Logos. We have also recognised that St. John uses a great variety of expressions to indicate that some men have been predisposed by God to accept the word of Jesus; and we shall find later in this chapter that he regarded this predisposing activity as in some sense a presence of the Logos. It is possible, however, to accept both these conclusions without self-contradiction. The present passage provides the full justification for this distinction between the preparatory work of God or the Logos and the shining of the light which brings salvation and life. Both inside and outside Israel Jesus has 'sheep', men who have been so prepared by God that when the 'shepherd' came they were able to recognise his voice, and when others came they were able to turn a deaf ear to them (*v.* 8). But all who before the ministry of Jesus had made claims to being themselves the door of access to the fold were thieves and robbers. It was Jesus alone who was the door; whoever entered the fold through Him, i.e. by receiving His word, as all His sheep would do, would be safe there under attack from thieves and robbers, and so in a secure position to obtain that pasture which is eternal life. Whilst the thief only comes to steal and kill and destroy the sheep, Jesus came that they might have life and have it in abundant measure.

The claim that Jesus is the door might leave His hearers with the impression that then and there, during His ministry, He could open up for them access to God and to abundant life. This impression needs to be corrected by the second application of the parable. 'I am the good shepherd: the good shepherd layeth down his life for the sheep' (*v.* 11). It is this that distinguishes Him from the hireling shepherd and proves that the sheep belong to Him. It is by His death that He protects them and makes perfect the kinship between Him and them. The nature of this kinship is now developed in terms of mutual knowledge. 'I know mine own, and mine own know me, even as the Father knoweth me, and I know the Father; and I lay down my life for the sheep' (*vv.* 14–15). Jesus and the Father are united in the intimate bond of mutual knowledge: the Father knows Jesus as the One in whom the self-revealing Logos has taken flesh, and Jesus knows the Father as the One who abides in Him, speaking His own words and accomplishing His own works. In a similar union the shepherd and the sheep are to be linked: Jesus knows His sheep to be those whom His Father has given Him out of the world, and the sheep know Him as the One through whose voice they hear and receive the word of the Father. But this union can be achieved only when the shepherd lays down His life for the sheep, and so gives life to them.

The corporate character of the shepherd is further brought out when Jesus adds: 'Other sheep I have which are not of this fold: them also I must bring, and they shall hear my voice' (*v.* 16).

His activity as shepherd is now being thought of as covering His missionary disciples after His death, men who by His dying He would have made so much one with Himself (xiv. 20) that in receiving them the 'other sheep' would be receiving Him and hearing His voice (cf. xiii. 20). The 'other sheep' are those who will hear the voice of Jesus through those whom He consecrates to go to them after His death (xvii. 18 ff; cf. xiii. 20; xv. 8, 16). The fold is not to be regarded as a particularly Jewish fold; in its intended figurative sense it stands for the full security, in respect of the possession of eternal life, which believers can find in Jesus, even during His ministry. The future mission to the 'other sheep' will not bring them into 'this fold', but will make of all the sheep one flock—one in the unity of mutual knowledge described in *vv.* 14–15—owned, protected, guided, and died for by Jesus their one shepherd.

This unifying power of the death of Jesus is the reason why[1] the Father loves Jesus and holds Him in union with Himself (*v.* 17); God loves the world with a love which is directed at the world's redemption. But the first stage in the implementation of this love is that it is bestowed upon Jesus (iii. 35; v. 20), so that in Him manhood is taken up into union with God. Divine love requires a human response, and the response of Jesus is not simply a reciprocal love, but obedience to the redemptive purpose of the Father. He can say, 'I lay down my life, that I may take it again'. But, as we shall see more fully in the Last Discourse, the life which He takes again is infinitely richer than that which He lays down. In the process of being laid down it is transformed from an individual manhood to a corporate manhood in which others can be included. His dying could be charged with this meaning because, though caused by the Jews, it was the expression, not of their opinion and will concerning Him, but of His acceptance of the commandment He had received from His Father, with whom it rested to determine the significance of the event (*v.* 18).

The Jews urge Jesus not to keep them in suspense, but if He is the Messiah to tell them so plainly (*v.* 24). Yes, He is the Messiah, though not in the sense of their question, or in a sense that they could grasp. He was the One who had come in the name of His Father to bring the final salvation, as His public ministry of utterance and sign attested; but they were unresponsive to the

[1] On διὰ τοῦτο see Abbot, *Johannine Grammar*, 2391.

witness thus borne to Him (*vv.* 25–26). To explain this lack of response Jesus reverts to the imagery of the sheep and the shepherd. Because they are not His sheep, they lack the needful divinely implanted capability of recognising the fact of His Messiahship, when revelation of its nature takes place in His works, or of accepting what He does for those who possess such a capability: His sheep hear His voice, He knows them and they follow Him, He gives them eternal life, and they will never perish; no one shall rob Him of the sheep He brings into the fold, because, being the sheep of Jesus, they are also the sheep of the Father, and Jesus and the Father are one (*vv.* 26–30). (In *v.* 29a there is a complex set of textual variants, which fortunately make no substantial difference to the sense. Whichever text we adopt, the point is that the sheep of Jesus belong to Him because they have been given Him by His Father, so that the security of belonging to Jesus is reinforced by the greater security of belonging to the Father.)

The Jews now prepare to stone Jesus for blasphemy, on the ground that to claim unity with God is tantamount to claiming to be God (*v.* 33). By way of rebuttal Jesus quotes the Old Testament 'Is it not written in your law, I said, Ye are gods? If he called them gods, unto whom the word of God came (and the scripture cannot be broken), say ye of him, whom the Father sanctified and sent into the world, Thou blasphemest; because I said, I am the Son of God?' (*vv.* 34–36). Jesus assumes that the words of Psalm lxxxii. 6 were addressed to inspired prophets and leaders of the psalmist's own day, and makes use of an *argumentum a minori ad maius*. If those to whom the Logos of God came by way of occasional inspiration can for that reason be called gods, how much more does He have the right to be called Son of God who has been consecrated and sent into the world by God. The logic of the argument requires that the consecration of Jesus should be identified with the coming of the Logos to Him for lasting union. This passage is important for us, because it shows that St. John was prepared to attribute the divine preparation of the Old Testament to the pre-incarnate activity of the Logos, but not therefore to put this on a level with the full revelation of the incarnate Logos in Jesus. He can say of an Old Testament prophet that to Him the Logos of God came, but not that in Him the light of the Logos so shone as to lead men to a saving knowledge of God or to give them the right to become children of God. It also demonstrates something we have taken for granted from the start—the interchangeability of the Christological terms in this Gospel. Jesus has not in this debate said in so many words, 'I am the Son of God'. He has said, 'I and the Father are one'; and we are to understand that the one claim is synonymous with the other.

The debate closes with a final appeal: 'If I do not the works of my Father, believe me not. But if I do them, though ye believe not me, believe the works: that ye may know and understand that the Father is in me, and I in the Father' (vv. 37–38). The works of His Father which Jesus does are His public utterances and signs, but they are also the eschatological events, the accomplishment of the Father's purpose of love, culminating in His own self-determined dying and resurrection (x. 17–18), which those utterances and signs announce and interpret. If the events of which they tell were illusory, the Jews would rightly believe that Jesus was not God's Son; but if they are factual, and the Jews reject the argued claim of Jesus that He is indeed God's Son, let them accept the testimony of the works, for from believing them sets in and endures knowledge of the reciprocal 'in-being' of the Father and Himself, which is the inner meaning of His Sonship. But the Jews only try again to seize Him, thus showing themselves not to be of those who are made ready by God beforehand to respond to the announced reality of the events and to perceive their meaning.

12

THE RAISING OF LAZARUS

Our concern is with what may be learnt from this chapter about the content of the Johannine belief in Jesus as the revealer of God. The questions for primary consideration are: (a) the meaning of the terms 'glory' and 'glorify' in xi. 4 and 40 and of the clauses in which they are used; (b) the interpretation of the saying, 'I am the resurrection and the life' in *v.* 25.

In the story the illness, death and raising of Lazarus are brought into connexion with the death of Jesus. In *v.* 4 the illness of Lazarus is said to be 'for the glory of God, that the Son of God may be glorified thereby'; and we have already seen that St. John reserves the verb 'glorify' for references to the death of Jesus (vii. 39). In *vv.* 7–8 we read that the disciples have forebodings about a journey to Bethany, which are subsequently given more forceful expression by Thomas: 'Let us also go, that we may die with Him' (*v.* 16). And it is after the raising of Lazarus that the Sanhedrin resolves to kill Jesus (*vv.* 47–53).

We turn first to *v.* 4. The illness of Lazarus, it is explained here, was not 'unto death'; death was not all that would come of it, no, the illness had to do with 'the glory of God' and the 'glorification' of His Son, and we have to determine what these phrases mean. 'For the glory of God': are we intended to understand that the sense of this clause is 'to reveal the glory of God' or 'to give God glory' (cf. vi. 51, where 'for the life of the world'='to provide the world with life')? And what here is glory? We shall be in a better position to answer these questions if we try first to interpret the second of the two explanatory clauses.

The illness was to lead to the 'glorification' of the Son of God. Yes, for His raising of Lazarus from the dead would bring Him to the Cross, and at and because of the Crucifixion He would be 'glorified', i.e. would win glory for Himself. Thus, on this point of Crucifixion and glorification, we may turn to the utterance in xvii. 1: 'Father, the hour is come; glorify Thy Son (give glory to Thy Son), that the Son may glorify thee (may give glory to thee).' Compare xii. 23–24: 'The hour is come, that the Son of man should be glorified (win glory for Himself). . . . Except a grain of wheat fall into the earth and die, it abideth by itself alone, but if it die it beareth much fruit.'

Glory in what sense? In xvii. 22 the gift made by Jesus to believers, by which they are bound together in union with one another and become sharers in His own union with the Father, is called His glory. In xvii. 5 glory is the term used to designate that relation between the Logos and God of which the first two verses of the Prologue are an attempt at description; and love is substituted for it in xvii. 24–26. In x. 38 the utterance, 'the Father is in me and I am in the Father,' is a form of description of what in St. John is revealed by the works of Jesus; but the works of Jesus include His signs, and the signs are held in St. John to be revelations of His glory (ii. 11). Taken together, these sayings throw light on what can be meant in this Gospel by the glory of Jesus, showing that the word can relate to the community of being between the Father and Himself. Just as glory is a Johannine term for the love relation between God and the Logos in the beginning, so it is for the union in love of the Father and the Logos incarnate. His glory in this sense Jesus revealed in His public ministry. 'We beheld His glory' (i. 14).

We have been trying to get into position to interpret the second explanatory clause in *v.* 4. In that verse however it is a question not of a revealing of His glory by Jesus, but of His winning glory for Himself. That is so; but when we find the noun 'glory' used of His union with the Father, it is rather to be expected that the verb 'glorify' will relate to the union between Jesus and those who believe in Him, into which His dying draws them according to Johannine teaching. Observe, for example, how the formula used in x. 38 and xiv. 10–11, where the death of Jesus is still in prospect, is 'the Father is in me and I am in the Father'; but in xiv. 20, where His death is contemplated in retrospect, it is: 'In that day ye shall know that I am in my Father, and ye in me, and I in you.'

It appears then that, as the glory which Jesus already possesses and in His public ministry reveals is His union with the Father, so the glory which He is to win for Himself at the Crucifixion is His union with all who believe in Him. To His gaining of glory in this sense the illness of Lazarus would be made by Jesus to minister. But the illness was also 'for the sake of the glory of God'.

What is meant? Still bearing in mind the second explanatory clause, we may once more appeal to xvii. 1 for light on the sense of the words in question. 'Glorify thy Son, that the Son may glorify thee'. The glorifying of the Son by the Father would be at the same time the glorifying of the Father by the Son. For were they not one (x. 30)? Was not the Father in the Son and the Son in the Father (x. 38; xiv. 10; xvii. 21)? And so, it would seem, the words 'for the sake of the glory of God' will mean 'to serve the end of the glorification of God. But what would be the glory which would come to God, the glory which the Passion of His Son would bring Him? It would not be a glory conceived differently from that which the Passion would bring to Jesus. If the Passion established a community of being between believers and Jesus, so would it also between believers and God.

Instead of responding at once to the message of the sisters of Lazarus, Jesus stays where He is for two days (v. 6). There is an implication in the second half of v. 4 that He must allow Lazarus to die; for it is represented there that He would go to His glorification through the raising of Lazarus from the dead. Moreover, in allowing Lazarus to die, He was providing occasion for the revelation of Himself as 'the resurrection and the life' (v. 25). The waiting for two days is left for readers to understand from these ruling interests of the whole story.

In furtherance of the end of His own and His Father's glorification Jesus—aware supernaturally that Lazarus had died—next proposes to go to Judea, where mortal Jewish enmity awaited Him (v. 7). His disciples show by their attempt to dissuade Him that they have no understanding of the more deeply significant parts of the saying in v. 4. The response of Jesus to their protesting fears for Him (vv. 9–10) is a rebuke of their undiscerning attitude towards His death, which is represented as making them like men who, when they could have the light of a whole day for a journey in safety, try at night and come to grief. 'Are there not twelve hours in the day? If a man walk in the day, he stumbleth not, because he seeth the light of this world. But if a man walk in the night, he stumbleth, because the light is not in him.' To the full measure of sunlight in the figurative utterance corresponds the work of Jesus in revelation, from which His disciples ought, they are being told, to arrive at a new mind about His death and see in it the glorifying of Himself and the Father.

It has often been thought that these two verses are meant to apply to Jesus Himself: as sunlight allows a man to move about securely for the twelve hours of a day, so Jesus is under divine protection until the time allotted to Him for His work is over; and that is not yet; He can go safely to Judaea. This understanding of the verses however does not fit in well with the direct connexion set up in the chapter between the miracle wrought upon Lazarus by Jesus and His own death; nor with the saying of Thomas in *v.* 16, 'Let us also go, that we may die with him'. According to Bultmann (op. cit., p. 304), who rejects the interpretation just described, but holds that the verses are meant to apply to Jesus Himself, the observation, 'Are there not twelve hours in the day?' is to be taken to suggest that a day lasts only for a limited amount of time; and the point of the whole utterance is that Jesus must use the little that still remains to Him on earth. This seems very doubtful. The thought of only a brief period of activity left to Jesus is hardly to be conveyed by an allusion to what was in Jewish reckoning a full day's sunshine. If the verses had to be held to refer to Jesus Himself rather than to the disciples, it would be better to consider whether they might mean that for Him to go to Judaea to perform a great act of self-revelation, and one which would lead Him to His glorification, would be to see His way, by the light of His knowledge of the Father; not to go would be to lose it. But this too is an unlikely interpretation. Never elsewhere in the Gospel does a saying in which the figures of 'day' or 'light', of 'night' or 'darkness' are used (iii. 19–21; viii. 12; ix. 4–5; xii. 35–36, 46) have to do in the first place with the obedience of Jesus to the Father.

Jesus now explains to the disciples, first in ambiguous language and then, when that is misunderstood, in plain speech, the purpose of His journey to Judaea (*vv.* 11–14). Lazarus is dead; and Jesus rejoices for their sakes that He was not at Bethany before he died (*v.* 15). He rejoices because He will now be able to offer them for their acceptance and their infinite gain the revelation of Himself as 'the resurrection and the life' which He will accomplish by raising Lazarus from the dead. Then at last the reply of Thomas shows that the figurative language has not been wholly lost on them (*v.* 16).

When Jesus comes to Bethany He finds that the dead Lazarus had been in the grave for four days (*v.* 17). The custom of burying on the day of death (cf. Acts v. 6, 10) indicates that he had died four days previously. But it need not be inferred that his death had taken place on the day when Jesus received the news of his illness; it is not said how long He was on the journey. The four days are mentioned with allusion to Jewish belief that the soul still remained in the neighbourhood of the dead body for three days (Strack-Billerbeck II, p. 544); by the fourth day therefore all hope of a revival had gone. In *v.* 18 a point is made of the nearness of Bethany to Jerusalem; how natural it was that many Jews should be there (*v.* 19). They had come to console the sisters; but no doubt, in the intention of the Evangelist, their presence also serves as testimony to the performance of the miracle. In *v.* 20 we reach the beginning of the crucial stage in the development of the story. At the knowledge that He is coming Martha goes to meet Jesus. Her words in *v.* 21 ('lord, if thou hadst been here, my brother had not died'), spoken in sorrowful regret that He had not journeyed to Bethany as soon as He had received the news, express trust in Him as a healer of the sick. But she goes on (*v.* 22) to make a confession of faith in Jesus as One to whom God grants any prayer that He offers to Him. Martha is now petitioning Jesus indirectly that Lazarus be given his life again. The response of Jesus is ambiguous ('Thy brother shall rise again'), and Martha takes it with resignation to refer to resurrection at the last day. However, the two verses (*vv.* 23–24) are meant to prepare the way for the self-revealing utterance to come.

'I am the resurrection and the life' (*v.* 25). We have to perceive beneath the surface of the words the two Johannine conceptions regarding the person of Jesus which we have repeatedly seen to be formative of the thought of the Gospel as a whole: that Jesus, as man, was in the Father and the Father in Him, and that His manhood had a prospective inclusiveness in regard to believers. Because of the relationship between Jesus Himself and the Father and because of the solidarity to be established between Jesus and others if they believe in Him, He is their *anastasis*, their rising from the dead. There is an implication that apart from the Incarnation, by which one amongst men participated in the life of God, there was nothing in prospect for the world but its darkness and death. 'I am the *anastasis*, I alone.' There was no other way to eternal life but by His divine-human person crucified and risen. What a claim indeed it is! And how greatly Judaism and religion beyond its borders are affected by it! 'Ye search the scriptures, because ye think that in them ye have eternal life . . . .' (v. 39). As for the old pagan world, there was a great deal of pessimism in it over the order of things in which the lot of man was cast, and hope was concentrated on various means of release from it, some of them crude enough, others rising to a high spiritual level, but all springing from the desire to find divine helpers stronger than fate or evil demons or death. Thus there was the way of deliverance offered by the Mystery-cults. After the observance of preparatory rites which appear to have differed among these religious societies, a devotee was admitted to a ceremony of initiation under a vow of secrecy as to what was said and done. Everything conspired to secure for him an intense emotional experience of nearness to the cult-god, with an epiphany of the deity as its crown. The words of Lucius (Apuleius, *Metamorphoses* xi) refer to this experience: 'I drew nigh to the confines of death, I trod the threshold of Proserpine, I was borne through all the elements and returned to earth again. I saw the sun gleaming with bright splendour at dead of night, I approached the gods above and the gods below, and worshipped them face to face.'[1] Once he was in communion with the deity of a Mystery, a votary was believed to be exalted above the sphere of *Heimarmene* (Fate), and although his body might still remain under the domination of this evil planetary influence, his soul even in this life was now free, and after death would rise safely through the spheres to the divine world above.

Another mode of deliverance was that of the 'knowledge of God' (*Gnosis*), the goal being still the same—the ascent of the soul beyond *Heimarmene* and evil demons, beyond the tyranny of the material, beyond change, decay and death. To know God, it was held, was to be united with Him, and being in union with Him, the soul was raised out of the present evil. It was to be sure the 'knowledge of God' that the Mystery-religions claimed to bestow; but some minds gave the conception a richer content and did not care for the externalism of the Mysteries. Numerous sects came to be founded on some form of the 'knowledge of God'. Lofty expression is given to the idea of salvation attained along this path in the *Corpus Hermeticum*. Here God is found by the aspirant, not in a ceremony of initiation, as in the Mystery-cults, but in

---

[1] From the translation by H. E. Butler.

K

right thought about Him and in mortification of the flesh.[2] In
the first of the tractates in the collection it is told how Poimandres
—the Supreme Being—granted to his prophet in ecstasy a revelation of the divine origin of the universe and of man. Such knowledge was believed to be the knowledge of God and the possession
of it to bring men to immortality. 'This is the happy end for
those who possess knowledge: to be deified' (*Poim.* 26). 'The God
and Father of whom man came is life and light. If therefore you
learn to know that he is of life and light, and that you are of these,
you will return to life' (ibid. 21).

Mystery-religions, Hermeticism, and the Fourth Gospel are on
common ground in making eternal life depend upon the knowledge of God, though they all mean something different by it. But
when we put the question by what means the saving knowledge of
God is to be obtained, then how the difference between these
pagan cults and the Fourth Gospel appears! In the one case an
elaborate ritual of initiation and gods who were mythological
beings, personifications of the forces of Nature; or again, cosmo-
logical speculation, and self-knowledge, knowledge of one's
origin and destiny. (Compare the beliefs of the Valentinian
Gnostics in the *Excerpta ex Theodoto*, lxxviii. 27—'But it is not
only the washing [in baptism] that is liberating, but the knowledge
of who we were, and what we have become, where we were or
where we were placed, whither we hasten, from what we are
released, what birth is and what rebirth.') But as for the Gospel:
'If ye had known *me*, ye would have known my Father also: from
henceforth ye know him and have seen him. . . . He that hath seen
me hath seen the Father' (xiv. 7, 9). '*I* am the resurrection and the
life.' He that believeth on me, though he die, yet shall he live.'

We have been saying that it is on account of His union with
the Father and the union in which by His dying He enables others
to be included that Jesus makes the declaration in *v.* 25a. How, it
has still to be asked further, does He do that for them? By His
whole ministry: by utterances which, if we do not allow their
significance to escape us, reveal both His union with the Father
and what that fact means in possibility for men; by signs, which
are held in St. John to convey the same revelation in another way;
but also, and indispensably, by the victorious Passion and resurrection. It is by virtue of all these activities that He is the *anastasis*.

---

[2] For details see Dodd, op. cit., pp. 10–53.

Lazarus is raised from the dead before Jesus dies, but the Evangelist does not wish his readers to understand that to mean that Jesus was, in the full sense of the claim, the *anastasis* of believers independently of His own dying. Lazarus was a believer, and had therefore already come into a union with Jesus which death could not destroy, as the miracle is intended, for one thing, to show. But we are not expected to imagine that he was brought back from the dead into the perfection of union between Jesus and himself, or that the physical life to which he was restored would not in the end be subject to physical death. Full union could be achieved only by the dying and resurrection of Jesus, the subsequent intensifying of the apprehension of His self-revelation by the work of the Spirit, and finally the melting away of all remaining unlikeness of the believer to Jesus (cf. I John iii. 2) through whatever divine action may be contemplated in connexion with the 'last day' and the coming again of Jesus. The claim of Jesus to be the *anastasis* has all this future, as well as the present, reference in it.

The words that follow explain what it means to a believer that Jesus should be 'the resurrection and the life'. 'He that believeth on me, though he die, yet shall he live: and whoever liveth and believeth on me shall never die' (*vv.* 25–26). But how do these two explanatory declarations differ from each other? Does the first give an assurance that the believer who dies will rise again? Does the second teach the indestructibility of his resurrection life? So it has sometimes been thought. But it would appear more likely that the same thing is being said in both, first of the believer who has died, and then of the believer who is alive. In the former of the utterances, the verb 'live' has that Johannine sense according to which it designates the participation of the believer in the union of Jesus and the Father; and the verb 'die' has its everyday meaning. A believer's physical death would not deprive him of a share in this union. In the second, 'live' has only its everyday meaning; but by the 'dying' which the believer is never to know is to be understood the loss through death of the life which is union with God.

It should be noticed that this is one of the most useful passages in the Gospel for determining the properly Johannine significance of the formula 'believe in me', for here it occurs in a really illuminating setting. This is often not the case. For instance, in ii. 11, where it is said that Jesus 'manifested his glory' and his disciples 'believed in him', it is implied that believing in Jesus is begin used of seeing the glory of Jesus, so that the content of the belief here will depend upon that of the glory in the passage, for which however we have to seek help elsewhere in the Gospel. The same is true of the sayings at iii. 16 and iii. 18. In xi. 25–26 however we have a passage which contains its own clue to the usage of the formula. 'I am the resurrection and the life. He that believes in me. . .'; to the content of 'me' belongs that of the immediately preceding self-revelation of Jesus, that it is His sharing in the life of the Father, together with His dying in order to share it with others, that makes Him the *anastasis* of the believer. To believe in Jesus is to discern the significance of His person and of His dying, and since we must not overlook the element of trust inherent in the phrase, it is also a trustful persuasion about the truth of His claims.

Martha is now asked if she believes what has just been said to her. Her answer is, 'Yea, Lord: I have believed that thou art the Christ, the Son of God, even he that cometh into the world' (*v.* 27). Comment is often to be met with somewhat to the effect that Martha does not understand the words of Jesus in their depth of meaning, but that nevertheless she holds fast to Him. But it is questionable whether the Evangelist desired his readers to receive the impression that this is a puzzled, or a not very comprehending response. Martha is represented as being of a settled belief (note the perfect tense of the verb). The designations of Jesus which appear on her lips express the Johannine faith in Him as significantly as could be. 'The Christ' brings the eschatological salvation. 'The Son of God' is in union with the Father. The point of the combination of the two designations should not be overlooked: it is in the fact of the union that His ability to bring the salvation consists. 'He who was to come into the world' is a designation not found in xx. 31, where the other two terms are again combined, nor in the confessions of faith mentioned in i. 49; iv. 42; and vi. 69. But it is important here, for it has attaching to it the same thought about Jesus as is conveyed by sayings which describe Him as coming from God (viii. 42; xiii. 3; xvi. 27, 28, 30; xvii. 8) or coming down from heaven (vi. 33, 35, 38, 41 f., 50 f., 58). We are expected to read the last part of the answer of Martha in the light of these and other kindred passages. The confession as a whole cannot be an uncomprehending or half-comprehending response. There is no hint that enough has not been said. The Evangelist however had no wish that his readers should be so curious about Martha as to ask how much she has understood or how far she has got. His purpose will have been to indicate that anyone who with trusting conviction makes this confession about Jesus will find that He is the resurrection; he will pass from death to life.

The story moves now to its climax. 'Jesus saith, Take ye away the stone. Martha, the sister of him that was dead, saith unto him, Lord, by this time he stinketh: for he hath been dead four days. Jesus saith unto her, Said I not unto thee that, if thou believest, thou shouldest see the glory of God?' (*vv*. 39-40). Where in the story had Jesus promised Martha that she should see the glory of God? Nowhere had He promised it in just those words. He had given her the assurance that her brother would rise again (*v*. 23), and we are expected to understand that the reference is to that. In the miracle of the raising of Lazarus the glory of God would be revealed. But it is not said that the performance of the miracle itself depends on the faith of Martha. Martha must believe, and on her faith depends her own ability to see in the miracle a revelation of the glory of God. Only because she has the faith in Jesus which she has just expressed will she be able to see it; not otherwise, nor would anyone else, though all present would see Lazarus come forth from the tomb. What then was the glory of God which the miracle was to reveal and the believing Martha to see? The glory of God has already been spoken of at *v*. 4, but we may not at *v*. 40 allow interpretation to follow in all respects the same course as at the earlier verse. It is not now a question of a glory of God which the dying of Jesus brings to Him, but of a glory already belonging to Him, to be revealed by Jesus in His act of raising Lazarus. Jesus can make the claim to be the resurrection and the life only because, through the Incarnation, He has had imparted to Him that glory which the Logos had with the Father before the world was (xvii. 5). To see the glory of the Son is at the same time to see the glory of the Father, to see the union of love which subsists between them. If the sister of Lazarus has a discernment and trustful acceptance of this, in the raising of her dead brother she would have it granted to her—as representative of all bereft believers in Jesus, present and to come—to perceive an attesting revelation of the union, and in it the ground of assurance that all the believing dead would live. The glory is called 'the glory of God' here because the love-union is being thought of from His side, while in ii. 11 it is thought of from the side of Jesus.

13

THE WASHING OF THE DISCIPLES' FEET

On the face of it the story of the washing of the disciples' feet by Jesus appears to be offered as an object lesson in humility. 'I have given you an example, that ye also should do as I have done to you' (xiii. 15). But we must take proper account of several other features of the story, which show that it is intended also to be a symbolic representation and interpretation of the Passion.

There is first the comment made on it in advance in xiii. 1. 'Having loved his own which were in the world, he loved εἰς τέλος.' In itself εἰς τέλος either means 'to the end' in a temporal sense or 'to the uttermost' in a qualitative sense. The resulting thought here is hardly fine enough for the mind of the Evangelist when the expression is taken with temporal force only. Of course Jesus loved His own to the end! But it may well be that the Evangelist was combining both meanings (see Abbott, op. cit., 2319-2323): Jesus loved His own to the last and then He showed them the perfection of love. This supreme act of love was not to be found in the footwashing itself, but in His voluntary dying (xv. 13; cf. x. 18). It was by this that the disciples were both made 'clean' (v. 10) and given their lesson in humility; by the washing its twofold significance for them was being set forth. The general impression on the reader is that it depended on their letting Jesus wash them, whether Peter and the other disciples became fit to 'have part with' Him; but this figure is applied in two different ways. On the one hand in v. 7 Jesus speaks of the washing as if it could become intelligible to them only at a later date, the time when after His death and resurrection the Spirit would come to aid their understanding. Yet in vv. 12-17 Jesus speaks to them about the meaning of what He has done. The story has thus indications that there was something in the washing for which the disciples would have to await enlightenment from the Spirit later on, and something else in it which was not altogether beyond their comprehension at once. In the one case it was the character of His action as a revelation of the efficacy of His death for their purification, necessary if they were to 'have part with' Him; in the other case it was its character as a lesson in the further requirement demanded of those who would be so enabled to 'have part with' Him—a life lived together in imitation of Him in His humility and His love.

What is meant by 'having part with' Jesus is well illustrated by Matthew xxiv. 51, where 'appoint his portion with the hypocrites' means 'make him share the fate of hypocrites'. Peter is being promised that, if Jesus is allowed to wash him, he will not be separated from Him when He goes from the world to the Father (*v.* 1), that, although he cannot follow Him now, he will follow Him afterwards (*v.* 36), that he is to be with Him where He is (xiv. 3); in short, that he is to be taken up into the relationship of love already subsisting between the Father and Jesus (xvii. 26), and so to have eternal life.

Small divergencies being left out of account, there are three forms of the saying in *v.* 10 to be found in the manuscripts.

(a) 'A man who has bathed does not need to wash, except for his feet, but is altogether clean; and you are clean. . .'

(b) 'A man who has bathed does not need to wash, but is altogether clean; and you are clean. . . .'

(c) 'A man who has bathed has no need (i.e. of what Peter has begged for), but is altogether clean; and you are clean. . . .'

The words 'except for his feet' look like a correction intended to remove what was mistakenly felt to be a difficulty that Jesus should say that washing was not necessary, when He Himself had washed the disciples's feet and had told them that they ought to wash one another's feet. It is arguable that reading (c) is primitive (so Boismard); but the choice between (b) and (c) involves no substantial difference in sense. If we adopt one of these as the unrevised saying, then the words 'altogether clean' appear on the surface to be a simple truism about ritual purity; but in the intended applied sense the saying is a cryptic utterance which would become intelligible to the disciples later on, when they would understand that Jesus had been speaking about a purity which He would obtain for them by His death, a purity rendering them fit to 'have part with' Him and leaving them in no need of ablutions to make them so. Jesus can already say to the disciples 'you are clean', because—as is true of so many of the sayings in this part of the Gospel—the purging away of their impurity by the dying of Jesus is seen as already achieved and permanent (cf. xvi. 33).

It has often been thought that the disciples are said at xiii. 10 to be 'clean' for the same reason as at xv. 3. But in fact the word is used in distinguishable senses in the two verses. At xv. 3 the disciples are pronounced clean as being fit for 'fruit-bearing', i.e. for making converts to Christianity, and this they were because of the word which Jesus had spoken to them. At xiii. 10 they are said to be clean as being fit to 'have part with' Jesus, and this they were because He had just washed their feet, an act which set forth the cleaning efficacy which His approaching death would have for them.

After the washing Jesus, at His place again, asks the disciples if they understand what He has done for them, and they silently leave it to Him to enlighten them about it. If the preceding comments on the first half of the story are not at fault, the intended range of reference of the question is restricted: do they understand (not the full significance of the washing but) the instruction which His action has conveyed of the manner of living required of them if they were to have part with Him—a living with one another in a humility and a love corresponding to His own? They are not expected to understand that such conduct is a necessary qualification for their having part with Him, which only His death can achieve; but rather that it is a necessary consequence, an indispensable quality of that life which they are to receive as a gift at His hands.

A slave is not a greater person in a household than the owner, whose conduct of affairs in it, it is not for him to know (v. 16; cf. xv. 15). The disciples of Jesus will only show that they are still like slaves, that they still do not know the Master they serve and are still not in close association with Him in His work, if they do not act towards one another with a humility and a love like His own; whereas if they do, they will show that they have ceased to be slaves any longer and become instead His friends, to whom He makes known all that He has heard from His Father (cf. xv. 12–15). The saying of Jesus which follows, reminding the disciples that a messenger is not of more account in any business than the one who makes him his representative for the transaction, conveys a warning to them against acting for Him on their own authority and thus only in self-glorification (cf. vii. 18). By being linked with the slave metaphor this second one shows that the whole utterance is a teaching about graces needful in missionary bearers of the message of Jesus. The blessing of union with Jesus comes to those who not only believe but are prepared to live by their belief. 'If ye know these things, blessed are ye if ye do them' (*v.* 17).

What Jesus has been saying does not apply to all those who have heard it, for one of them is to be a traitor. All of them have been chosen by Him (cf. vi. 70), and His betrayal by a close associate might therefore seem to cast doubt on His ability to read the character of men. The others are to be assured that Jesus knows them all, and that Judas is there only because of a divine necessity, ordained in Scripture (Psalm xli. 9). The fact that Scripture had decreed that the initial blow against Him should come from one who shared His table and the fact that He had been able to warn them of this in advance should convince them, once the blow fell, that He had gone to His Passion aware that it would come and taking it upon Himself (cf. x. 17 f), and might help them still to believe that He was the One He had revealed Himself to be in His ministry of utterance and sign.

Judas is pronounced 'unclean' ('and you are clean, but not all', *v.* 11) after it has been said of him that the Devil had put it into his mind to betray Jesus (*v.* 2). Over the power of the Devil to infect with 'uncleanness' Jesus triumphs in His death. 'Now is the judgment of this world; now shall the prince of this world be cast out' (xii. 31). 'I have overcome the world' (xvi. 31). The Spirit would convict the world in the matter of judgment, because the prince of this world had been judged (xvi. 11). The washing of the disciples, which enables them to have part with Him, also delivers them from the world and from the Devil's power to defile them. This is possible, according to the Johannine teaching, because the dying of Jesus takes up the disciples into union with Himself, and He is One on whom the Devil has no legal claim (xiv. 30).

Once the traitor has been excluded from the group of disciples chosen for the mission to the world, Jesus assures the others that anyone in the world who receives those whom He sends to it will be receiving Him, and in receiving Him they will be receiving the One who had sent Him (*v.* 20). Those who receive Jesus before His death do so in the sense that they believe in Him, believe in His claims and accept His promises; after it however they do so in the further sense that they come to be in union with Him and

so with the Father. The 'sending' of Jesus by the Father and of
the disciples by Jesus must thus be added to the rich stock of
terms by which the Evangelist has sought to express that unity of
being and purpose which God has willed to establish, first with
Jesus by the Incarnation, then with the inner circle of disciples
through the Crucifixion, and finally with the world at large
through the mission of the disciples.[1]

With the departure of Judas Jesus begins to speak as though
His Passion were an already completed fact. Now is the Son of
man glorified, and God is glorified in him; and God shall glorify
him in himself, and straightway shall he glorify him' (*vv.* 31–32).
Jesus had known the mind of Judas (vi. 64, 70; xiii. 10 f, 21 ff),
and He has appealed to him in the loving act of washing his feet
and again giving him the morsel (*v.* 26). He now allows him to
go out, yielding Himself finally at that moment to His coming
death, and immediately interprets His choice of it. The Son of
man turns the betrayal of Him into His own glorification and the
glorification of God. In one of the uses of the Hebrew perfect, a
coming event, believed by the announcer of it to be divinely
ordained, was represented as already having taken place. One
way of rendering such a perfect in the Greek of the LXX was by an
aorist (e.g. Isa. lii. 9), a usage which has influenced the choice of the
aorist here in St. John; the glorification of the Son of Man was
now as certain as was His dying, for from His dying it was to come.
We have already been given a hint of this in the story of the washing of the disciples' feet, which was intended in the first place as a
revelation of the effect of the death of Jesus: by His dying Jesus
would cleanse the disciples, thus making them fit to have part
with Him. But the cleansing was even at that point so certain that
it could be said, 'you are clean'. So now, with His last choice of
the Passion made effective by His letting Judas go, Jesus had
already entered into it, so that their cleansing was already a fact.
'Now'—that is, His passion being upon Him, and His disciples
being cleansed so as to have part with Him, to share with Him in
His own union with the Father—the Son of Man has won glory for
Himself. We have already seen, both in the first chapter and in
the story of Lazarus, what glory in such a context must mean. It
is a term used to designate the relationship of the pretemporal

---

[1] For the connexion of this saying with its verbal counterpart in Matt. x. 40
see Dodd, *Historical Tradition in the Fourth Gospel*, pp. 343 ff.

Logos and God (xvii. 5), which can equally be called love (xvii.
24–26); the relation of mutual indwelling with the Father into
which the manhood of Jesus was taken at the Incarnation of the
Logos, and to which His signs and works bore witness (i. 14;
ii. 11; cf. x. 38); and the gift made by Jesus to believers, which
united them with Him and so with the Father (xvii. 22).

What then can it mean that the Son of Man should be glorified?
Does it mean that now, at the time of His Passion and on account
of it, the Son of Man will pass into the glory-relationship between
Himself and the Father, to which we have just referred?   No,
clearly not; the relationship was there already.   Since the glory
which He bestows on His disciples consists in their being in Him
and He in them, the glory which He wins for Himself must be the
other side of this relationship.   He will now win for Himself glory
in the sense that He will come to be in the disciples and they will
come to be in Him.   His glorification is the establishment between
Himself and them of a relationship corresponding to that existing
between Himself and the Father.

What then are we to make of the second part of the announcement of Jesus, that God will glorify the Son of Man in Himself?
Bernard, commenting on the clause, wrote: 'This goes beyond the
'glorification' of Christ *in* His passion (*v.* 31); it is the 'glorification'
which succeeded it, God the Father 'glorifying' Him in Himself,
by taking up the humanity of Christ into the Godhead, after the
Passion.'   But the humanity of Jesus was already in the Godhead.
'The Father is in me, and I am in the Father' (x. 37 f.; xiv. 11).
Yes, and yet, what more, if it may be so put, what more, in the
thought of the Gospel, was His humanity than His own when He
died?   What more than His own did He in dying cause His humanity to be?   He then became in the disciples and they in Him; or,
as we may say, His humanity became inclusive of them.   A prospect
of understanding the clause now opens out: God will glorify in
Himself the One whose humanity has become inclusive of His
disciples.   Although the very fact that He had come to be in them
and they in Him was a glorification of Him, yet there remained for
Him, as being bound together in the union with His disciples, a
still fuller, a complete and final, glorification, for which He is later
to pray at xvii. 5.   He is to carry the disciples with Him into the
glory which He enjoyed in the presence of the Father before the
world was.   It is of God's granting to Jesus glory in this sense, it

appears, that the two clauses of *v.* 32 speak. Yet when all this has
been said, the word 'straightway' shows that the reference is still to
the Passion.

The glorification of Jesus by God involves His departure from
the disciples. He warns them of it with tender solicitude. 'Little
children, yet a little while I am with you. Ye shall seek me: and
as I said unto the Jews, Whither I go ye cannot come; so I now
say unto you' (*v.* 33). Two occasions are mentioned in the Gospel
on which Jesus had uttered similar words to hostile Jews. 'Yet a
little while am I with you, and I go unto him that sent me. Ye
shall seek me, and shall not find me: and where I am ye cannot
come' (vii. 33). 'I go away, and ye shall seek me, and ye shall die
in your sin: whither I go, ye cannot come' (viii. 21). As addressed
to the disciples the words lose all their once calamitous significance.
The Jews would not find Jesus, but the disciples are not told this.
It is said to them indeed, 'Whither I go, ye cannot come'; but He
and they were not to be separated for ever. As the immediate
sequel shows, we are expected to add in thought a qualifying
'now' or 'at once' (cf. *v.* 36).

'Whither I go'; the simple-sounding phrase is nevertheless of a
deliberately mysterious character. It is in fact laden with all the
significance attaching to the announcement of the glorification of
Jesus by God in the previous verse. He goes, goes by dying, to the
glory which the Logos had before the world was created; and He
does not go alone, but takes the disciples with Him, for they and
He are now made one. Yet He tells them that they cannot go
where He goes; not now, though later they would. For though
they are really in Him and therefore sharers with Him in the
eternal glory of the Logos, this is so in a manner yet hidden from
them. But it would become a manifest fact, a matter of their full
experience. So they hear Peter being told that he will be able to
follow Jesus afterwards. This simple-looking language is again
pregnant with undetected and unexplained meaning as to what
awaits them. Later in the discourse the mysterious promise will be
expanded into the thought of what the Spirit must and would do
for them to unfold in them, to their very knowledge, the glory
which Jesus had bestowed upon them, and the further thought of
that future conclusive coming again of Jesus with which would
coincide their complete realization of what He had imparted to
them in the hour of His dying.

Instead of speaking about these themes at once, Jesus lays upon them a new commandment. 'A new commandment I give unto you, that ye love one another; even as I have loved you, that ye also love one another. By this shall all men know that ye are my disciples, if ye have love one to another' (vv. 34–35). What may be the reason for the appearance of the commandment just at this point? Jesus had told them He would only be with them a little longer, and they would seek Him but not be able to come where He was to be. The sudden reference to a new commandment might not appear especially relevant to this. Of course, it is in view of His departure, for the time of separation, that He gives the commandment; but why should it stand here in particular? There is significance indeed in the fact that it does, and we may draw it out in this way. 'I shall only be with you a little longer; you will seek me and not be able to come to me at once; but I tell you that your loving of one another, as I have loved you, will be the true seeking of me. Seek me by such love; for seek me thus you must, if you are to find me.' Earlier in the chapter we noticed teaching to the effect that, if Jesus' cleansing of the disciples, that is to say, His self-sacrificing love of them in dying for them, was to be effectual, was to make them fit to have part with Him, His love must be accepted as the pattern for theirs. 'I have given you an example, that ye also should do as I have done to you' (v. 15). 'If ye know these things, blessed are ye if ye do them' (v. 17). This teaching that such love of the disciples of Jesus for one another has a meaning for them beyond what might appear, being in fact an appropriating to themselves of the cleansing efficacy of the Cross, is picked up and developed in the new commandment. The Son of Man wins glory for Himself, and so for those who come to be united with Him. Yes, but they have to love one another, as Jesus has loved them, if their glorified state is not to remain in abeyance, hidden both from themselves and from the world.

It is instructive in another way that the new commandment should be associated with pronouncements about the glorification of the Son of Man, or rather, as we have decided, about the joint glorification of the Son of Man and His disciples. It suggests that the hidden glorified state of believers in becoming manifest does so as love, as love in the manner of the love of Jesus; so that glory, whether used with reference to God, or to the Logos, or to the Son of Man, or to believers, designates a relationship and activity of love.

We have been trying to bring to light a not obvious, yet it would appear an intended, connexion of thought between the commandment of love (*v.* 34) and the three preceding verses; and in so doing we have anticipated the next step in the argument. 'By this shall all men know that ye are my disciples, if ye have love one to another' (*v.* 35). The love of believers for one another would reveal the fact of their union with Jesus, and it would thus constitute a further stage in the revealing of Jesus Himself to the world.

The commandment is characterized as a new one, the newness consisting partly in the utterly radical nature of the demand, partly in the qualifying clause. The old precept in the Pentateuch was, 'thou shalt love thy neighbour as thyself' (Lev. xix. 18), but the disciples are to love one another 'as I have loved you'. The words are uttered with the Passion in view. His love for them then exhibited—love to the uttermost—was to be the measure of theirs—an impossible demand, were we not to understand that His love would be the source of their own. If there could be any serious doubt that the qualifying clause refers to the dying of Jesus for His own, it would be removed by the terms in which Peter expresses his devotion to Him: 'Lord, why cannot I follow thee even now? I will lay down my life for thee' (*v.* 37). The Evangelist brings a Peter before us who has not an inkling of what the utterances in *vv.* 31–33 had meant; but he will not allow the words 'as I have loved you' to be wholly lost on him.

We can understand best what is here meant by love, if we recall the interpretation already given to the footwashing. The act of the washing had exhibited to the disciples in symbol a meaning of the Passion: that by dying Jesus would remove all defilement from them, to the end that they might have part with Him. But once they were cleansed, as cleansed they were when Jesus died, they were not simply in a state of preparation for this relationship to set in later; it set in at once, though indeed hiddenly, and awaiting for its complete unfolding or manifestation the action of the Spirit and the final coming again of Jesus. The love which Jesus had shown them was not merely the emotion, desire, and will which find expression in the Cross; it was the self-giving, the veritable self-communication of Jesus. 'As I have loved you' means 'as I have given myself, not simply for you (though that is true), but to you'. In so loving them He was establishing between

Himself and them that union which was implied in the glorification of the Son of Man. So too the disciples, in loving one another, were to be in one another, one with each other, as He was in them and one with them. They must let the oneness of Jesus and the Father be reproduced in themselves, become one as He and the Father were one. 'And the glory which thou hast given me I have given unto them; that they may be one, even as we are one' (xvii. 22). It was only because He Himself, by His dying, had given His glory to the disciples, that, as we are to understand, the new commandment could be addressed to them.

14

DEPARTURE AND RETURN

Jesus has announced His imminent departure and has plunged His disciples into bewilderment and dismay. The earlier sayings in chapter xiv are addressed to the anxiety evident in Peter's question, 'Whither goest thou?' They are meant to remove the disciples' disquietude on this score; hence the opening words, 'Let not your hearts be troubled.'

How ought πιστεύετε to be rendered in each of the instances here in v. 1? The choice lies between two imperatives, two indicatives, or an indicative and an imperative:

(a) 'Believe in God and believe also in me.'

(b) 'Ye believe in God and ye also believe in me.'

(c) 'Ye believe in God, believe also in me.'

As the discourse proceeds, sayings occur which tell rather in favour of indicatives being intended in both cases. Thus, the disciples are said in v. 4 to know the way to where Jesus is going; that is to say, they are being told that they know how to get to His destination, how to get there themselves. Jesus was going to His Father's house (v. 2), or, as is implied in v. 6, He was going to the Father. They are being told then in v. 4 that they know how to get to His Father's house, how to come to the Father. But this is only another way of saying that they believe in God, that they believe in Jesus. Again, it is said in v. 7b that already at the present time they know and have seen the Father. This shows how v. 7a should be taken: 'If you knew me (as you do), that would mean that you knew my Father also.' There is a parallel to this at v. 9b: 'He that hath seen me hath seen the Father.' Jesus does not doubt that Philip has seen and known Him, and therefore has believed in Him; on the contrary He finds it incredible that this should not be so. What Philip has not recognised is that the fact of his seeing and knowing Jesus carries with it a further fact, that he has at the same time seen and known the Father. From these several indications the inference seems a likely one that both instances of πιστεύετε in v. 1 are indicatives.

We may now try to follow the thought in *v.* 1. 'Let not your heart be troubled: ye believe in God, and ye also believe in me.' They ought not to be so anxiously wondering where Jesus is going, for their belief in God and in Him should give them an answer to their question. We have noticed on earlier occasions in the Gospel that to believe in Jesus is the equivalent of seeing His glory, recognising His union with the Father (ii. 11; x. 38), and this equation should be allowed a place in an interpretation of the present passage. 'Let not your heart be troubled over where I am going, for you know—I have taught you in utterance and sign— that I and my Father are one, that I am in Him and He is in me.' The relationship between the Father and Jesus which is the content of faith in St. John is contemplated first from the side of the Father and then from the side of Jesus; and it is driven home to them by the very fact that to believe in the one is to believe in the other also. The twofold utterance thus reminds the disciples that they have received Jesus' revelation of the union of the Father and Himself. In that fact lay the sure relief from their distress, if only they could understand its full implications. Presently—in *v.* 4—Jesus is to carry them one stage further: 'You know the way to where I am going, you know how to reach my destination yourselves.' The knowledge that is implied in *v.* 1, their knowledge of the union of the Father and Jesus, is a knowledge which ensures their being where Jesus would be! But in the meanwhile He had already given them a new description of His own destination: He was going to His 'Father's house' (*v.* 2). By the use of this simple, figurative phraseology an attempt is being made to assist the disciples' understanding of the idea which has been more elaborately conveyed in xiii. 32 ('God shall glorify him in himself, and straightway shall he glorify him'). His Father's house serves as a description of the relationship of glory or love, in which the Logos existed with the Father before the foundation of the world (xvii. 5, 24), and in which Jesus has hitherto lived his individual human life. His going is His dying, by which He receives this glory and love inclusively of the disciples and of all believers. Accordingly we read that He goes to prepare a place for them in His Father's house: He is to die, and in dying He is to receive for them the glory of the Logos that they may participate in it. 'In my Father's house are many mansions (μοναί)': it was the will of God that a great company should share in the glory of the Logos. Jesus'

glorification by God at and because of the Passion would be itself
His preparation of a place for these few disciples immediately in
question, but what would be true of them would be true also of the
many other believers, present and to come.

The word μονή occurs again in *v.* 23, but nowhere else in the
New Testament. In itself it can mean a temporary stopping place
on a journey. The A.V. and R.V. rendering, 'mansion', goes back
by way of Tyndale to the Vulgate and Old Latin *mansio*, a place
where a traveller halts and rests upon his journey.[1] But μονή can
also be used of an abode or permanent habitation.[2] The latter is
the sense which Bernard himself adopted here. 'The idea,' he
concluded, 'conveyed by the saying, "In my Father's are many
μοναί", is that of a hospitable palace with many chambers, rather
than of a journey with many stages.' On the other hand Temple
gave to μοναί the other sense of 'resting-places', shelters for the
disciples at stages on their pilgrim way to the Father's house.[3]
It will be obvious that there is something at fault in this way of
approaching our verse, some distortion of the intended sense of its
imagery. For the μοναί are not said to be on the road to the
Father's house, but in it. And it is in His Father's house that Jesus
prepares a place for the disciples, not on the way to it. 'My
Father's house': the picture which the expression is meant to
raise up in the mind is that of a great palace with the Presence
Chamber of God in it, and near by this many other chambers.
Jesus goes to prepare a place for His disciples amongst these other
chambers. His Passion, His dying, the readers of the Gospel are
meant to understand, constituted the preparation of it. These
disciples, believers though they were, had to have a place prepared
for them, and prepared for them by Jesus in dying. Once again
we have occasion to realize that it is not alone the facts of the
Incarnation and of faith which ensure a man's possession of eternal
life according to St. John. The implication of the verse is clear
that there would be no place for the disciples in the Father's house
without that preparation of it there which was to be made by the
dying of Jesus, just as in xiii. 8 they could have no part with Him,
or, to use the language of the present verse, they could not be with
Him where He is, they could not join Him in His Father's house,
unless He washed them, cleansed them by His death.

[1] Swete, *The Last Discourse and Prayer of the Lord*, p. 6.
[2] Cf. Bernard, *The Gospel according to St. John*, pp. 531 ff.
[3] *Readings in St. John's Gospel*, p. 266.

Are the μοναί in the passage temporary stopping-places or permanent abodes? In the latter case the disciples, and all believers, were to be brought by the death of Jesus near to God, near to Him for ever. In the former case more even than that awaited them; they were to be in the end in the Presence Chamber itself. Which of these two interpretations are we then to choose? The next verse yields us something to go on. 'And if I go and prepare (when I have gone and prepared) a place for you, I come again, and will receive you unto myself; that where I am ye may be also' (v. 3). 'I will take you to myself': it is not said that He will take them to the place where He goes to make ready for them amongst the many mansions. He will take them to Himself, and they will be with Him where He is? And where is that? Is He in a mansion near the Presence Chamber? Or is He in the Presence Chamber itself, that is (to drop the metaphor), is He in the perfection of union with the Father? In the latter case, v. 3 contains a promise that not even a place near the Presence Chamber was all that lay ahead of the disciples; they were to be with Jesus in the Presence Chamber, sharing with Him His most complete union with the Father. If the phrase, 'where I am', should be understood to refer to the Presence Chamber, and not to a nearby mansion, then the disciples were not always to be in a place prepared for them amongst the many mansions; and the word μονή here will after all have the sense of a temporary dwelling-place, though not on the way to the Father's house, as Temple conceived, but in it. As to whether the phrase should be held to refer to the Presence Chamber, is not Jesus in the Father and the Father in Him (x. 38; xiv. 10 f., 20)? Are they not one (x. 30; xvii. 11, 22)? Does not the Father love the Son and show Him all that He Himself is doing (v. 20)? Does He not know Jesus and Jesus know Him (x. 15)? The phrase itself occurs elsewhere in the Gospel several times, but only one of the instances is of use in deciding whether in the present verse it points to such relatively incomplete union with the Father as His being in a μονή would imply, or to the complete union of the Presence Chamber. 'Father, that which thou hast given me, I will that, where I am, they also may be with me; that they may behold my glory, which thou hast given me: for thou lovedst me before the foundation of the world' (xvii. 24). Here the phrase refers to the state of glory (cf. xvii. 5), or to the relationship of love in which the Logos dwelt with God before the Creation.

There can be no doubt then that the reference of 'where I am' in both passages (xiv. 3 and xvii. 24) is to the Presence Chamber itself; and it is to take the disciples to be with Him there that Jesus is to come again.

We are now in a position to elucidate *vv.* 2–3. According to *v.* 2 Jesus goes to prepare for the disciples a place among the mansions. It might appear that the coming again of Jesus in *v.* 3 must surely be for the purpose of taking them to the prepared place. But, for the reasons we have mentioned, it appears that He is to come again to take them to Himself in the Presence Chamber of God. How then may the assurance about the preparing of a place for them be understood? It was not made ready only to be left empty. It would accord with the thought of the Fourth Gospel about the death of Jesus to reflect that in dying He not only made ready a place for the disciples, but also took them into it. There, from the moment of His dying, they were to be, within His Father's house. He would leave them behind in the world, and be withdrawn from their outward sight; nevertheless He and they alike would be in His Father's house, He in the Presence Chamber and they not far away from, but all in the one house. Then in *v.* 3 He gives to the disciples the assurance of their final beatitude: from where He is He will come to them again where they are to take them to Himself, that they may be where He is.

It is hardly necessary to dwell on the point that it would be agreeable to Johannine thought about the death of Christ to hold that it not only prepared a place for the disciples, but also brought them into it. His dying unites believers with Himself (xii. 32), but the union has still to come to its full fruition as an experienced fact. And there has been more than one hint in the earlier chapters of the Gospel that even this personal appropriation of the benefits of Christ's death would not be the full consummation of His saving work (v. 28–29; vi. 39, 40, 44, 54; cf. xii. 48). Similarly here, we are expected to infer that, although the death of Jesus brings His disciples at once into His Father's house, His coming again is His coming at the last day to take them into the state of final blessedness. We should not allow ourselves to be driven from this conclusion when, as the Last Discourse proceeds, we meet recurring promises of another coming of Jesus which cannot be regarded as repetitions in varying phraseology of the sense we have given to the first one in xiv. 3, since they manifestly refer to

the period of the church's life between the departure of Jesus and
His coming again at the last day (xiv. 18, 21, 23, 28; xvi. 16, 22).
It is characteristic of the eschatology of St. John, as it is of the
eschatology of the New Testament as a whole, that the final consummation of the purposes of God, having been fully and
definitively anticipated in the person and work of Jesus, should
also be in a different way anticipated in the experience of believers.

In *v.* 4, as we have already seen, the disciples are being told in
effect that their belief in God and in Jesus is knowledge on the
ground of which they will themselves arrive at His own destination. Thomas reacts to the words in a manner characteristic of
the Evangelist's method when a hard saying has been uttered by
Jesus and it is the intention to pursue its theme. His troubled
response ('Lord, we know not whither thou goest; how know we
the way?') provides occasion for the greater and harder pronouncement: 'I am the way, and the truth, and the life' (*v.* 6).

To begin with the first part of the utterance: 'I am the way.'
Jesus is the way, the way to the Father, as the second part of the
verse indicates; 'no one cometh unto the Father, but by me'. He
Himself is the way to the Father, or, in the language of *v.* 2, to His
Father's house. But how is He the way? We remember the
moment at which the words are spoken and its significance. He is
entering upon His Passion, and the Passion unites believers with
Himself, where He is in the bosom of the Father (i. 18), in heaven
(iii. 13), in the Father (x. 38), in His Father's house (xiv. 2), so
that believers, being made one with Him when He dies, come to be
there too. If this is so, we should read this first part of the saying
as if it read—'I by my dying am the way'. Yet not only because
He dies is He the way, but also because He is the One He is, the
One whom the Father had willed to be in Himself, as the first of
many more. He is the way because He is the Logos incarnate who
united believers with Himself by His Passion.

But the saying does not stop at this point. 'I am the way, *and*
the truth, *and* the life.' What sort of logical link is intended by the
connecting 'and'? Swete thought that it should be regarded as
explicative, indicating more clearly the significance of the pronouncement, 'I am the way'. ' "The Truth" and "the Life" are
. . . but other aspects of "the Way", bringing out its meaning more
clearly' (op. cit., p. 15). Or we may, he wrote, reverse the order of
the threefold saying: 'He is the Life which is the Truth, and being

the Life and the Truth He is also the Way' (ibid. p. 17). Others
besides Swete have wanted to explain the connexion between
the three terms in some such way as this.[4] Others again have
supposed that a Hebrew idiom is being employed, the sense being
'the true and living way' (cf. Jer. xxix. 1, where 'a latter end and
a hope'='a hoped for latter end'). But if this is what the Evangelist
had desired to say, we might have expected him to use here the
two adjectives of which He was so fond: ἀληθινός (true) and ζῶν
(living). We must in any case continue to be critical of suggestions
which do not leave us in a very good position to interpret the
threefold utterance. To Bernard it appeared that the words 'the
truth and the life' are 'not directly involved in the context, but are
added to complete the great declaration'. The central thought is
'I am the way'. The juxtaposition of 'way' and 'truth' will have
been due, it seemed to him, to a reminiscence of the Old Testament
(cf. in particular Psalms lxxxvi. 11; cxix. 30). With regard to 'I
am the life', Bernard wrote that the declaration 'could not be out of
place at any point of the Gospel; but nevertheless it does not help
the exposition at this point, where the thought is specially of
Christ as the Way'. He evidently found the second and third
terms of the trio a difficulty, and he left a misleading impression on
the minds of his readers that the direction in which to look for
help was the Old Testament. But as in the case of 'the way', the
facts of the Incarnation and the Passion must be allowed a con-
trolling influence in the determination of the intended significance
of 'the truth'. It is His union with the Father, and His choosing to
die in fulfilment of His Father's will, that make Jesus 'the truth'.
When it is asked what in fact is meant by the Greek ἀλήθεια in
this verse, a satisfying answer is not to be expected, if the supposition is that the usage rests on that of the Hebrew ʿmeth, which, as
applied to a divine attribute in the Old Testament, is funda-
mentally a designation of the faithfulness of God to His word. On
the other hand, a properly Greek usage, according to which
ἀλήθεια is that which alone is real, always-existing, divine, gives
an intelligible and satisfactory sense in xiv. 6, though to be sure
only as laden with all the newness in the Johannine conception of
what the divine reality is.

[4] Hort, The Way, the Truth, the Life, pp. 11, 56; Huby, Le Discours de
Jésus après la Cène, pp. 46 ff.; Shaefer in Z.N.W, 1933, p. 215; Barrett, p. 382.

A Greek philosophical term is being employed in a highly distinctive Johannine way. But we have still two questions before us: what does St. John mean by 'the truth', and what is the connexion between this word and the rest of the utterance in which it stands? The bewildered Thomas had addressed a double question to Jesus, namely, how could He assure His disciples that they knew the way to where He was going (and thus that they knew how to get there themselves), when in fact they were ignorant of His destination? Accordingly, we should expect to find Jesus speaking of the destination as well as of the way to it. Is not this what we do find? He is the way. The way to where? To the truth, to the divine reality, to the heavenly order, to God as He is in His true being. Jesus is declaring Himself to be the embodiment of God as He really is; He includes in Himself that heavenly order which consisted, before the world was made, in the glory or reciprocal love of God and Logos; and at the same time He is announcing that, being what He is, He is Himself the destination or goal of the disciples. He is their way, and, let them now understand, it leads to Himself. Thus the words 'I am the truth' express in the most summary manner possible the content of that self-revelation which Jesus had been conveying in utterance and signs throughout His ministry. As the discourse continues, we shall find that it requires to be amplified only at one further point: the way not only leads to Jesus Himself, but leads to union with Him, and so to participation in His own union with the Father.

We turn now to the third part of the utterance: 'I am the life.' In a comment on this verse Temple understood the sense to be 'the vitalizing energy of all that lives' (op. cit., p. 231). In the Prologue 'life' has often been so interpreted, and we have seen earlier how questionable this meaning is even there. Here it gives an even more questionable turn to the argument. 'Life' in fact is not here anything different from that 'life' which Jesus is said to have in Him: 'For as the Father hath life in himself, even so gave he to the Son also to have life in himself' (v. 26). Because by the Incarnation Jesus possesses in Himself that life which was the eternal possession of the Logos, and because by His Passion He is able to bring believers into union with Himself and therefore into touch with this eternal life, he can claim to be 'the life' for them, just as He is also for them 'the way' and 'the truth'. Life then is simply another, and more familiar, term for that destination which

has already been described as 'truth'. To pass into the heavenly
order of reality, to attain to eternal life, to reach the Father's
house—all these are alternative descriptions of the one experience
of salvation, which can only be achieved through Jesus. 'No one
cometh to the Father, but by me.' The many mansions of the
Father's house would have remained without occupants if the
crucial events of Incarnation and Passion had not taken place.

What then of saints and good men of the generations before
Jesus came? And of those of His own time who were dying
in ignorance of Him? What would the Evangelist have said
about the famous passage in Justin Martyr: 'Men who lived in
company with the Logos are Christians, even if they were accounted
atheists; and such among the Greeks were Socrates and Hera-
clitus' (*Apol.* i.46.3)? Is all connexion between Christianity and
religious thought and culture in pre-Christian times and in the
contemporary world being severed? For an answer to these
questions we must turn back to an earlier part of the Gospel. 'The
hour cometh in which all that are in the tombs shall hear his voice,
and shall come forth; they that have done good, unto the resurrection of life; and they that have done ill, unto the resurrection of
judgment' (v. 28–29). We have seen in a previous chapter that 'all
who are in the tombs' is not figurative language, denoting all the
living who are without 'life', because the revelation of Jesus has
still to be conveyed to them. Doers of good who have died without
the opportunity of believing in Jesus are being contemplated.
They are to rise to 'life' at the last day. But the passage should not
be taken to mean that those who had done good would just on that
account rise to life, as if Johannine faith in Jesus, and therefore the
Incarnation and the Passion and Resurrection, were not really
crucial after all. Men of the past, so we should understand, who
had done good, were men who would have received the revelation
of Jesus if it had come to them. Yes, but it is still not on that
account that they are to rise to life. The decisive significance of
Jesus Himself for them is being preserved. For the passage contains the noteworthy teaching that at the last day Jesus would
reveal Himself to them. Then would be their opportunity for
hearing His voice, seeing His glory, accepting the truth embodied
in Him. Jesus can say: 'Everyone that is of the truth heareth my
voice' (xviii. 37); and this is true whether the opportunity of
hearing it comes through the lips of the earthly Jesus Himself,

through the preaching of His disciples after His death, or through His final act of grace at the rending of the tombs. By this means St. John is able to maintain the absolute nature of the claim that no one comes to the Father except through the mediation of Jesus. 'No one cometh unto the Father, but by me': to the apparent exclusiveness of these words we must add the comprehensiveness of outlook which we find in those passages which speak of Jesus' activity at the last day.

We have seen that by the coming again of Jesus spoken of in xiv. 3 such a coming is meant as would bring His disciples into the perfection of His own union with the Father. We may now adduce one further reason for believing that this coming was to take place at the last day. In the discourse on the bread of life the believer has been four times assured that he is not only to receive the gift of eternal life, but also to be raised by Jesus at the last day. From v. 28–29 something more has now emerged: doers of good who have not previously had the chance of believing in Jesus will at the last day emerge from the tomb into the resurrection of life. Clearly for each the same ultimate destiny is in view; and clearly for neither is that destiny to be reached before this culminating act of Jesus. His coming again at the last day will thus not only complete the union of the disciples with Himself and therefore with the Father; it will also draw all doers of good, all who have ever been in any degree partakers of the Logos, into the same union.

We pass on to v. 7a, and are confronted with a variation of reading:

    (a) 'If ye knew me, ye would know my Father also.'[5]
    (b) 'If ye know me, ye will know my Father also.

The (a) reading presents the appearance of an unfulfilled condition, with an implied reproach to the disciples for not possessing the required knowledge of Jesus; and it seems strangely at odds with the assurance given in the second half of the verse that from now on they do in fact possess it. On the other hand this obvious difficulty would in itself have been enough to account for the emergence of the variant reading. The (b) reading, though fairly often adopted, cannot be original, since it implies that there can be

[5] The R.V. rendering, 'If ye had known me, ye would have known my Father also,' exacerbates the difficulty of the verse by treating the verbs as true pluperfects, when in fact ἔγνωκα as well as οἶδα is perfect in form but present in meaning, as can be seen from v. 9a.

a present knowledge of Jesus which is not at one and the same time a knowledge of the Father, but only a guarantee of a future knowledge of the Father; whereas the whole logic of the passage demands that to know Jesus is to know the Father too, so close is their union. We must therefore accept the (a) reading, and try to see how the two halves of the verse fit together. Jesus has assured the disciples that they already know the way to where He is going (v. 4). Thomas, spokesman for the rest, has protested that they know neither His way nor His destination (v. 5). Jesus in response has declared that He is both the way and the destination; those who travel by the way will find that it leads to that truth and life which are embodied in His own person, but also that it leads to the Father (v. 6). It would be quite out of place at this point for Jesus, who has just asserted that Thomas knows the way, to suggest, even by an unfulfilled condition, that after all he cannot know the way since he does not know Jesus. The unfulfilled condition must accordingly be taken in a slightly different fashion: 'If it should prove to be the case that you know me, then it would also prove to be the case that you know my Father.' Thomas is being gently rebuked, not for lacking a knowledge of Jesus, and therefore of the Father, which he ought to have had, but for failing to apply correctly such knowledge as he actually possessed. He had not adequately appreciated that, in knowing Jesus, he knew the Father also; and that this knowledge provided the answer to his perplexity about the way and the destination of Jesus. It was strictly true that he knew the way, even if he was unaware of the extent of his own knowledge.

Whatever may have been the ambiguities of Thomas' knowledge, they are now to be once and for all resolved: 'henceforth ye know him, and have seen him'. In committing Himself to His imminent death, Jesus has completed his self-disclosures, and in revealing Himself has revealed the Father also. But more than that, He has come to the point where He is to impart Himself to the disciples, so that they may be drawn into union with Him. Especially by this act of love to the uttermost (xiii. 1), which is also an act of the Father's love, the Father is to be known and seen. In the full sense of firmly grasping the revelation of the Father, they have of course not yet seen and known Him, as the sequel is to show; only the revelation has been implanted in them, the seed is in the ground. It is hardly surprising therefore that the so positive-sounding assurance of Jesus becomes, as it was intended to become, the occasion of further perplexity on the part of a new spokesman, Philip, and thus an opportunity for Jesus further to expound His theme.

'Have I been so long with you, and dost thou not know me, Philip? He that hath seen me hath seen the Father' (v. 9). Philip and the others have had the opportunity to know Jesus, and therefore to see and to know the Father. They ought to have recognised in His ministry of discourse and sign a self-revelation, which was also a revelation of the Father. Once again, however, it would be wrong to conclude from the gentle reproach in His words that the revelation had come to them quite unavailingly. This is certainly not the point of view of the Evangelist. After the great discourse in chapter 6, did he not make Peter say, 'Thou hast the words of eternal life' (vi. 68)? The conviction which he attributes to Jesus is to be given unambiguous expression in the prayer of chapter 17: 'The words which thou gavest me I have given unto them; and they received them, and knew of a truth that I came forth from thee, and they believed that thou didst send me' (xvii. 8). From start to finish it is Jesus who affirms that the disciples have the requisite knowledge of Himself and the Father and the disciples who profess ignorance. It would be quite a false resolution of this tension to say that St. John is making Jesus speak from the point of view of the later church of his own day. It would be truer to say that, from the moment of Judas' defection, Jesus speaks as though the Passion were an already accomplished fact. But the simple explanation is that the perplexity of Philip serves to prepare the way for a further development of the theme of the discourse, and also to point to the fact that it is to the greatest need of men and its only satisfaction that Jesus is addressing Himself. 'Lord, reveal to us the Father, and that is enough for us.'

'He that hath seen me hath seen the Father.' There is no question here of a merely physical vision. Throughout this chapter, and indeed throughout the Gospel, the terms 'see' and 'know' are used interchangeably. In the case of Jesus Himself to have seen the Father is the same thing as to know Him (vi. 46; viii. 55; x. 15; xvii. 25). So too in the case of the disciples to see Jesus means to see Him as He really is. He who has seen Jesus, that is, he who has grasped and received His revelation of Himself, has had revealed to him the true nature of God and of His purpose for mankind. To see Jesus is to see Him in the facts of His Incarnation and Passion, the one fact uniting Him with His Father, the other giving effect to the purpose of the Incarnation by incorporating men of faith into the same union; and in these facts the Father is seen. To see the Father is to recognise in these facts His own self-disclosure. The Scriptures bore testimony to Jesus (v. 39), but until He to whom they bore their testimony had come and died and risen, men could not have life (v. 40; xiv. 6); they have it in consequence of seeing the Father as revealed in Jesus, Logos incarnate and crucified.

Jesus now explains why it is that to see or to know Him is also to see and know the Father 'Believest thou not that I am in the Father, and the Father in me? the words that I say unto you I speak not from myself: but the Father abiding in me doeth his works' (v. 10). Their reciprocal immanence is not merely the means by which the Father has enabled Himself to be seen and known; it is the very content of the revelation. Philip, then, and the others ought not to be longing to have Jesus reveal the Father to them, for the revelation of Him was there already. But the important point is that He is now said to be revealed, not simply in His eternal and changeless character, but in His 'works'; and the first and definitive one among these works is the taking of the manhood of Jesus into the relationship of mutual indwelling with Himself. Even this, however, does not exhaust the meaning of the verse: the situation of Jesus from within which the words are spoken must not be lost sight of; He has finally accepted His Passion and has now virtually entered into it. In x. 38 hostile Jews are bidden to believe the works of Jesus; if they did, i.e., if they perceived and acknowledged that which the works revealed, they would possess the knowledge that the Father was in Jesus and Jesus in the Father. What was not evident in connexion with this earlier passage comes into the foreground now: it is a reciprocal immanence which continues in the Passion. Beginning as an immanence peculiar to Jesus and the Father, it is now being enlarged by the Passion to include all who see the Father in the person of Jesus, all who discern and own the fact and purpose of the Incarnation. The works which the Father was doing in Jesus do not stop short of that full realization. This is what Philip and the other disciples, and all would-be followers of Jesus in the future, ought to be believing.

The latter half of *v*. 10 ('the words that I say unto you I speak not from myself') invests the whole previous utterance with the authority of the Father. The thought that Jesus does not speak or act 'of Himself' is often noticeable in the Gospel (v. 19; vii. 17; viii. 28; xii. 49). From such passages as these we might get the impression that the words and works of Jesus are two different and independent aspects of His ministry, the one revealing to men the character and purposes of God, the other achieving those purposes, though both are alike in having behind them the authority of God. When Jesus speaks, God Himself is speaking through Him; When He acts, God Himself is acting in Him. The present passage carries us deeper into the thought of the Gospel. 'The Father abiding in me doeth his works.' The Father is performing His works at that very moment when Jesus is speaking, performing them in and through the words which Jesus speaks. Thus we ought not to draw a hard and fast distinction between words and works. The words of Jesus are not only informative but performative: they achieve results. By the same token the works of Jesus are not only effective but expressive: they convey a revelation of the will and purpose they are designed to implement. The works of God in St. John are His saving works, and the words of Jesus are a means by which the Father performs them. This is also the case with all the activity of Jesus. 'We must work the works of him that sent me, while it is day' (ix. 4). 'My meat is to do the will of him that sent me, and to accomplish his work (iv. 34). 'My Father worketh even until now, and I work' (v. 17). These works of God are saving works, which He performs in order that believers may have life; and they achieve that end, partly at least, because they reveal Him, enable Him to be 'seen'. Such works of God are the words which Jesus has just addressed to Philip. But the words are said to be works of God also because, besides their revelatory character, they belong together with the Passion, which they interpret, as effective means of bringing about the unity of believers with Jesus. Hitherto in the Gospel, it may be noted, the nature of the utterances of Jesus as being works of the Father has not been expressed in language of such intimacy as is employed now that Jesus is about to die: 'the Father abiding in me is performing his works.'

Once we have seen from the present passage how nearly interchangeable are the words and the works of Jesus, as means whereby

God both speaks and achieves His purposes, we can see that hints of this have been given earlier in the Gospel. In ix. 3, for example, we have been told that the affliction of the man born blind is to be seen as offering occasion to Jesus for making manifest the works of God. Here the emphasis is not so much on what the action of Jesus achieves as on what it reveals; the works of God are manifested when Jesus revealed Himself by utterance or by sign as the one sent by God to bring about the eschatological salvation. But we are reminded later in the same passage that the time for Him to do this is limited: 'the night cometh, when no man can work'. He must complete the work of God in the limited time available to Him, and this He does by His death. 'I glorified thee on the earth, having accomplished the work which thou hast given me to do' (xvii. 4; cf. xix. 30). The laying down of His life completes the works of God, because it is the act by which those who have accepted the revelation conveyed by His utterances and signs are drawn into unity with Him and so given eternal life.

'Believe me that I am in the Father, and the Father in me: or else believe me for the very works' sake' (v. 11). The disciples ought by now to have enough confidence in Jesus to recognise that He never speaks or acts without the backing of divine authority. But if this is too much to expect from them, the claims of Jesus can be supported in another way. The presence of God, the word of God, the activity of God, are self-authenticating, and can never be attested by any external guarantees. It should therefore be self-evident to the disciples that, whenever Jesus is either speaking or acting, God is at work in him; and it should be particularly evident that His approaching death is the crowning act of God. If this could be said only of isolated episodes in the life of Jesus, it might imply a union with God which was occasional or sporadic; but since it is true of all His words and works, they ought to deduce from this that the Father 'abides' in Him in a total and permanent union.

Everything that Jesus has said so far has been drawn from Him by the tentative questioning of Peter, Thomas and Philip, and He has spoken in mild rebuke. But now come assurances of an even more exalted kind. 'Verily, verily, I say unto you, He that believeth on me, the works that I do shall he do also; and greater works than these shall he do; because I go unto the Father' (v. 12). The basis of the assurance is that Jesus is now going to the Father, the very thing which made the disciples so dispirited. But what they regard as so grievous a loss is in fact to achieve for them the wonderful gain of doing the works of Jesus, and still greater works than His. We have just seen that the works of Jesus include both His words and His signs, the two together being regarded as necessary means whereby the Father performs His own work of revelation and redemption; both are needed to disclose the purpose of God and both are needed to accomplish it. To do the works of Jesus will, then, be to share His function as agent of the divine activity. Two conditions are stated for the fulfilment of this promise: a man must be a believer, and Jesus Himself must go to the Father. A believer is one who has accepted the joint revelation made by Father and Son of the reciprocal immanence which exists between them. The departure of Jesus to the Father is the act by which He prepares a place for such believers, to enable them to participate in the same union. It will then be true of them, as it has hitherto been true of Jesus, that the Father will have His permanent abode in them and in them continue to perform His own works. But the promise is that they will perform not only the works of Jesus, but even greater works! Here are arresting words indeed.

In an interpretation of this promise there are certain passages in the Gospel which may not be left out of account. 'And other sheep I have, which are not of this fold: them also I must bring, and they shall hear my voice; and they shall become one flock, one shepherd. Therefore doth the Father love me, because I lay down my life, that I may take it again' (x. 16-17). Further, the Evangelist tells us, in his own interpretation of the unconscious prophecy of Caiaphas, that Jesus would die 'not for the [Jewish] nation only, but that he might also gather together into one the children of God that are scattered abroad' (xi. 52). This is closely followed by the incident of the Greeks who want to see Jesus (xii. 21), which becomes the occasion for a new utterance of Jesus: 'And I, if I be lifted up from the earth, will draw all men unto myself' (xii. 32), with the explanatory comment of the Evangelist, 'This he said, signifying by what manner of death he should die'. According to these passages, then, the death of Jesus would lead to the widening of His saving activity in the world; and what we are now told in xiv. 12 is that this was to take place through the works of the disciples. Is it then really Jesus Himself who would perform the

works here spoken of, His disciples being regarded as organs of
His action? There would be truth in that, no doubt; for it was
Jesus who through His death was to bring the other sheep, to
gather the scattered children of God, to draw all men to Himself.
Yet so to put it would not have satisfied the Evangelist. In His
prayer Jesus speaks of '*their* word': 'Neither for these only do I
pray, but for them also that believe on me through their word'
(xvii. 20). Why *their* word? They are more than organs of the
word of Jesus; it is also their own, and so also are the works which
they are to do. They are to be works of Jesus in the sense that they
are to be like those which He has done, and again in the sense that
He will be doing them; and yet they are to be His disciples' own
works also. And they would be their works not merely in the
plain, matter-of-fact sense that the disciples would actually be
doing them, but theirs because, being themselves within the union
of Jesus and the Father, in doing the works they would be conveying to others the revelation of what they saw there, but also of
the fact that they had been there to see it. In dying Jesus would
cause His disciples to 'have part with' Him (xiii. 8), to be taken up
into His community of being and action with the Father. The
works they would do would be testimony borne to the 'seeing' or
'knowing' which they would enjoy from within their union with
Jesus and the Father. They were, then, to extend the revelation
of Jesus in the world after His departure; and they were to do it as
men participating in His own union with the Father and so in
His own knowledge of Him.

The saying at *v.* 12 is, however, only partly explicable in terms
of a revealing activity to be extended beyond the Jewish world by
the disciples of Jesus. Hoskyns indeed, with others before him,
was content with this explanation. 'The contrast is . . . between
the few disciples of Jesus and the vast number of those converted
by the preaching of His apostles; between the mission of Jesus to
the Jews and the mission of His disciples to the world' (*The
Fourth Gospel*, p. 538). But this does not appear to exhaust the
meaning. Not only was the original scope of the action of Jesus
in revelation to be widened, but the revealing works themselves
were to be in some other sense greater than those which Jesus had
accomplished during His ministry on earth. His going to the
Father would make their works greater than His own had been.
The Incarnation of the Logos in Himself, or, in the language of

M

the discourses rather than of the Prologue, the relationship of mutual indwelling between Himself and the Father, and what that relationship meant for mankind, had constituted His revelation. Were then His disciples by their greater works to accomplish a greater revelation than this? Were they to add to, were they to complete, an imperfect revelation? No, certainly not that. A revelation of which the Incarnation, Passion, and Resurrection made up the content could not be more complete than it was. He who believes in Jesus, Logos incarnate, crucified, and risen comes into possession of eternal life, and He who rejects Him is excluded from it (xii. 48). In what sense then, besides that of wider extension, would their revealing activity be greater than His had been? The revelation would be the same; the difference is that the disciples would be conveying it after His passion had taken place, and that His passion was to have as its fruit the incorporation of believers into His own union with the Father. Only the Passion does that for them. Before Jesus died the union with the Father was His alone; in dying He made all who believed in Him sharers in it. The real contrast, then, would appear to be between those works which Jesus was able to do on earth while the Passion was still in prospect and those which are possible once His union with believers has become an accomplished fact.

To prevent any possible misunderstanding of these greater works which the disciples are to do, Jesus at once adds that they are to be achieved only through prayer on their part and continued activity on His part. 'And whatsoever ye shall ask in my name, that will I do, that the Father may be glorified in the Son. If ye shall ask me anything in my name, that I will I do' (*vv.* 13–14). What then does it mean to pray in the name of Jesus? The phrase 'in my Father's name' had already been used in the Gospel in connexion with the mission of Jesus. 'I am come in my Father's name' (v. 43). 'The works that I do in my Father's name, these bear witness of me' (x. 25). In these passages Jesus is claiming to act with the full authority of the Father, whom He represents and reveals. They provide, therefore, no close parallel to those passages which speak of the disciples praying in the name of Jesus (xiv. 13, 14; xv. 16; xvi. 24, 26), since in prayer they are not acting with His authority, nor are they representing or revealing Him; and this is particularly so in the present passage, where the prayer is to be addressed to Jesus and answered by Him. We must fall back on the context for an explanation. The setting of the utterance indicates that prayers in the name of Jesus are prayers of men who believe in Him and have accepted His revelation of His own union with the Father and His offer of a share in that union. They are also prayers concerning the greater works which the disciples are to do, prayers for the continuance and success of the mission which is both His and theirs. Throughout His ministry Jesus has acted in total dependence on the Father. 'The Father abiding in me doeth his works' (xiv. 10). 'The Son can do nothing of himself, but what he seeth the Father doing. . . . The Father loveth the Son, and sheweth him all things that he himself doeth: and greater works than these will he shew him, that ye may marvel' (v. 19–20). When Jesus has prayed to the Father, it has been to put Himself wholly at the disposal of the divine will (xii. 27–28; cf. xvii. 1). In the same way, the disciples' prayers in the name of Jesus will put them at His disposal, in order that He may through them perform His greater works. They will be the prayers of those who have been drawn into unity with Him and so share His love for the world.

Jesus will answer such prayers, 'that the Father may be glorified in the Son'. When Jesus made the prayer to which we have just alluded ('Father, glorify thy name'), the answer came: 'I have both glorified it, and will glorify it again' (xii. 28). God had already glorified His name in the ministry of Jesus, because, through the giving of the glory of the Logos to Him and through the manifestation of it in His life and above all in His signs (i. 14; ii. 11), men had been able to see the glory of God (xi. 40). The giving of glory to the Son had thus been the winning of glory for the Father. St. John could quite consistently have said, therefore, that already the Father had been glorified in the Son. But the voice from heaven goes on to declare that God will glorify His name again in the death of Jesus, since that is the point at which the glory already imparted to Jesus is to be extended to believers (xvii. 22). The second prayer of Jesus begins: 'Father, the hour is come; glorify thy Son, that the Son may glorify thee' (xvii. 1). As we have seen in the discussion on xiii. 31–32, the glorification of the Son is His reception of believers into union with Himself through the Passion. But because the Son is in the Father and the Father in Him, once believers are in union with the Son, they are therefore in union with the Father also; and this is the Father's glorification. Thus it is true at the Passion that the Father is glorified in the Son. The present passage, however, carries us a stage further even than this. When the disciples begin to perform their greater works, we might have expected it to be said that God would be glorified in them; but instead it is said that the Father will be glorified in the Son. For the disciples themselves will then be 'in the Son', and their works will be the continuation and extension of the glorification begun in the Incarnation and Passion. This third and final glorification of the Father may be understood in two ways. On the one hand the greater works will be the product of the prayers of the disciples and the answer of Jesus, and these two together will bring glory to the Father by demonstrating to the world the truth of the claim that the disciples have been brought into union with Jesus. On the other hand the works will be an extension of Jesus' mission to the world, and will redound to God's glory by bringing a host of new believers into the same union.

Together with prayers offered in the name of Jesus, there is one further condition essential to the fulfilment of the promise of doing greater works. 'If ye love me, ye will keep my commandments' (v. 15). The bond by which the disciples are to be united with Jesus is a bond of love, on His part love to the uttermost displayed in His death for His friends (xiii. 1; xv. 13), on their part of love freely offered in return. Whether by loving Jesus, or by loving one another, they would be proving to the world the reality of their discipleship (xiii. 35). But what were the commandments? The only commandment which Jesus is said to have given His disciples already is the commandment that they love one another (xiii. 34; cf. xv. 12, 17). But this new commandment sheds singularly little light on the present passage. It is true that, in the thought of the Evangelist, love for Jesus and love for one's brother are at all times inseparable. But this is hardly the point under discussion here. It must be kept in mind that the future mission of the disciples is being contemplated, so that the likely meaning of the passage is: 'if you love me, you will keep the commandments which I shall give you in answer to your prayer in my name'. Largely, then, it would appear, the commandments in question are commandments which Jesus had not yet given; when He did give them, in response to prayer in His name, they would have to do with the necessities of the mission He has been entrusting to His disciples.

If this conclusion is well founded, it has one interesting corollary. Throughout the Gospel Jesus regularly speaks of His own obedience to the commandments of the Father, in such a way that it is clearly analogous to the obedience He here requires from His disciples (xv. 10). Everything He says (xii. 49), everything He does (xiv. 31), and above all His determination to go to the Cross (x. 18), are the outcome of this obedience. But to what commandments does He refer, and when were they given? Were they commandments given by God to the precosmic Logos? Were they commandments given once for all to the man Jesus at the outset of His public ministry? Or were they rather, as we may confidently suppose, commandments constantly given and as constantly obeyed throughout a life lived in unbroken communion with the Father? The parallel between the obedience of Jesus to the Father and the obedience of the disciples to Jesus is strongly in favour of this third interpretation. 'If ye keep my commandments, ye shall abide in my love; even as I have kept my Father's commandments, and abide in his love' (xv. 10). It would also be in full accord with the main thesis of this book, that the revelation imparted by Jesus consisted of truths learned by Him in the course of His human experience of union with the Father.

We come now to the first of the five utterances about the Paraclete. To assist them to pray in His name and to love Him, and so both to receive and to keep His commandments, when the old form of their companionship with Him is over, Jesus gives them a promise. 'And I will ask the Father, and He shall give you another Paraclete, that he may be with you for ever, even the Spirit of truth: whom the world cannot receive; for it beholdeth him not, neither knoweth him: ye know him; for he abideth with you, and shall be in you' (vv. 16–17). It will be best to make only a few provisional remarks about the term 'Paraclete' itself, until what is said in the other four explicit utterances about Him has been considered. The word is derived from the verb παρακαλέω, and originally it was used of 'one called in' to give support, and so of a pleader or advocate, 'a friend of the accused person, called to speak to his character, or otherwise to enlist the sympathy of the judges'.[6] It was used in this way, though apparently very seldom, in Greek courts of law; and so there was a tendency for the word to take on the active sense of one who intercedes for him whom

[6] Field, *Notes on the Translation of the New Testament*, p. 102.

he is called in to assist. The term is not used in the LXX, and in
the New Testament it is found only in the Fourth Gospel and
in 1 John ii. 1. It occurs as a Greek loan-word, transliterated into
Hebrew, in the rabbinic writings, with the sense of 'intercessor',
'pleader', and is used with reference to angels, to men, to sacrifice,
to repentance and good works, and in other connexions. A point of
special importance is that, although according to Strack-Billerbeck
(II 562) the Spirit is not expressly called 'Paraclete' in these
writings, the conception of the Spirit as 'intercessor' was not
unknown in later Judaism.

In the first of the Paraclete sayings Jesus promises the sending
of 'another Paraclete', the implication being that the relationship
of Jesus to His disciples hitherto and up to His departure from
them has been that of a Paraclete. It is obvious, however, that He
has not been a Paraclete in the sense of one called in by the
disciples to help them. 'Ye did not choose me, but I chose you'
(xv. 16). Nor has His relationship to them been that of a Paraclete
in the sense that of His own choice He has interceded or pleaded
for them before God. Moreover, the function of the Paraclete as
described here and in the subsequent Paraclete sayings is not
that of an intercessor or pleader for the disciples before God.
Hitherto Jesus had been their Paraclete in a sense to be inferred
from His words and acts of self-revelation in the Gospel: He had
been their helper towards their discernment of the self-revelation
of the Father in His own human-divine person. This helping
service in its old familiar form was now to come to an end; henceforth it was to be rendered by the Spirit whom the Father would
give to the disciples at the request of Jesus. The designation of the
Paraclete as 'the Spirit of truth' (cf. xv. 26; xvi. 13) points to a
function of the Spirit not as intercessor before God on account
of the sins of moral weakness of the disciples, but as mentor to
supply the deficiencies of their knowledge. Jesus has said of
Himself, 'I am the truth'. He embodied in Himself the divine
reality, the heavenly order of life or love. The Spirit of truth
belongs to this same heavenly order, and therefore is also able to
lead men to it by communicating to them the knowledge of it. But
Jesus *is* the truth. The Spirit therefore would lead men to the
truth through the deepened knowledge of Jesus which it would be
His function to impart. He would not convey a new revelation (cf.
xvi. 13). Whereas Jesus had not been with His disciples so very

long before He was to depart from them, they and all other believers would never be without the Paraclete; He would be with them, in them, always enlarging their knowledge of Jesus, always making more perfect their apprehension of the revelation of the Father given in the Incarnation and the Passion, and always intensifying their awareness of the union with Jesus and the Father into which these saving acts had drawn them. The world, as 'world', would neither see nor know the Paraclete, since it had neither seen or known Jesus, and therefore it is said that the world cannot receive Him. Yet in giving to His disciples His promise, Jesus is at the same time sending them into the world as the bearers of His revelation, in order that, through the double witness of their preaching and the Paraclete's illumination, the world may believe (cf. xvii. 21).

Jesus continues His work of solacing His disciples. 'I will not leave you desolate: I come unto you. Yet a little while, and the world beholdeth me no more; but ye behold me: because I live, ye shall live also. In that day ye shall know that I am in my Father, and ye in me, and I in you. He that hath my commandments, and keepeth them, he it is that loveth me: and he that loveth me shall be loved by my Father, and I will love him, and will manifest myself to him' (*vv.* 18–21). A moment before Jesus had put in prospect for His disciples the gift of 'another Paraclete' besides Himself. Now, however, He speaks of a coming of Himself to them of which they would be aware in a little while. How then are the coming of the Spirit and the coming of Jesus to be related? They cannot be simply identified, since the Spirit is called 'another Paraclete'. Is there then a suggestion in the order of the promises that the coming of Jesus depended upon the gift of the Paraclete? If this is so, the words 'I come to you' are not explicable simply from the resurrection appearances of Jesus, for His coming to the disciples then did not depend upon their possession of the other Paraclete. The same verb is indeed used in connexion with the appearances (xx. 19, 26). But the cessation of the appearances would then have left His disciples 'orphaned', bereft of His presence, desolate, contrary to His promise. There are some students of the Gospel who have tried to establish the view that the promise of Jesus to come again, here as at xiv. 3, refers to His coming in the definitive sense, His coming at the last day. They point out, as we have done, that the coming cannot be the resur-

rection appearances, since they were transitory, nor the coming of
the Spirit, since He is called 'another Paraclete'. But they add
that it cannot be a coming to the disciples in the period between
the resurrection and the last day, since there would then have been
no need for the sending of another Paraclete to take the place of
Jesus and represent Him. Only one possibility then remains, that
the disciples would continue to be bereft of the presence of Jesus
until the last day, notwithstanding the fact that the Paraclete
would be dwelling in them. But are the sayings in xiv. 18–21
agreeable to this reference of them to the coming on the last day?
Surely it is not so. 'In that day ye shall know that I am in my
Father, and ye in me, and I in you' (v. 20). Was this not to be
until the last day? If so, what becomes of the work of the indwelling Paraclete as described for instance in the second of the sayings
about His coming and function: 'But the Paraclete, the holy
Spirit, whom the Father will send in my name, he shall teach you
all things, and bring to your remembrance all that I said unto
you' (v. 26). No, the day of Jesus' coming to them was to be the
the day when they received the Spirit (xx. 19–23). Easter and
Whitsun coalesce in St. John, a fact which, together with the
function of the Spirit as expounder of the sayings of Jesus,
furnishes the standpoint from which the promise of Jesus' coming
is to be understood.

Since the Spirit was never to be withdrawn from the disciples,
the coming of Jesus likewise would never be broken off. How
may this invisible and continuous coming be conceived? It was
not to be just the same thing as the coming of the Spirit. The
Spirit was to bear witness to Jesus (xv. 26) and to glorify Jesus
(xvi. 14). What is meant by the coming of Jesus, in distinction
from the resurrection appearances, is the Spirit-aided realisation
on the part of the disciples that, in the language of v. 20, Jesus
was in His Father, and that they were in Jesus, and that Jesus was
in them. As we have now so often remarked, the relationship of
reciprocal indwelling between Jesus and the disciples was to be
brought to pass by His dying. It would be established because He
died and when He died, but the awareness of what He had done
for them would be a work of the Spirit within them, teaching
them all things and bringing to their remembrance everything
that Jesus had said to them (v. 26). Thus, as we concluded when
we had the story under discussion, the action of Jesus in washing

His disciples' feet was a revelation that His imminent Passion would make them fit to have part with Him; but they did not and could not grasp the revelation at the time. 'What I do thou knowest not now; but thou shalt understand hereafter' (xiii. 7), i.e. after the bestowal of the enabling Spirit.

We have concluded that the promise of Jesus' coming in v. 18 is to be explained in the light of the subsequent promise in v. 20: 'In that day ye shall know that I am in the Father, and ye in me, and I in you.' Their realisation of what the dying of Jesus had brought to pass between Him and themselves would be ensured by the revealing Spirit dwelling in them; and in that realisation they would experience the coming of Jesus. But v. 20 is also an explanatory comment on the immediately preceding verse. There is a deliberate substitution of one form of phrasing for another, by which the reader is given another instance of clarification of the Johannine conception of what it means to 'live' or to have 'life'. 'I live' is another way of saying 'I am in my Father; and 'you shall live' is another way of saying 'ye in me, and I in you'. A similar use of explanatory substitution is found in vi. 54, 56: 'He who eats my flesh and drinks my blood has eternal life. . . . He who eats my flesh and drinks my blood remains in me and I in him.' In one sense, of course, Jesus could have said, 'I live' at any time during His ministry, since from the start in discourse and sign He has been revealing that He is in the Father. But now it is with His dying at hand that He declares 'I live'. His union with the Father is indestructible by death. Not only so, but His dying would not separate Him from His disciples; on the contrary, they would be 'living' on account of it, and living because of a new and closer union with Him, as they would know by the aid of the Spirit.

There is a question whether v. 19 should be so punctuated as to make the second part of the verse a reason for the assurance given in the first part that the disciples would see Jesus, or whether they form an independent statement.

(a) 'Ye behold me, because I live and because ye also shall live.'

(b) 'Ye behold me: because I live, ye shall live also.'

In the former case, they were to see Him on the double ground that He would be living, i.e. would be in His Father, and they would be living, i.e. would be in Jesus and have Him in them. That is to say, because Jesus was in a union with the Father which His approaching death could not dissolve, and because His death, far from separating Him and them, would bring them into union with Him,—on these grounds they would assuredly see Him. Aided by the Spirit, they would see Him as He really was, united not merely with the Father but also, through the Passion, with themselves; and this would be His coming to them. It may to be sure look as if Jesus had only spoken of their seeing Him in the sense of their discerning His own union with the Father. But the words are uttered with the Passion regarded as an already accomplished fact; and so the knowledge of what it had achieved for them would also belong to the content of their seeing of Him. It is just because the Passion is being contemplated in retrospect that to 'I am in my Father' can be added 'and ye in me, and I in you'. Earlier in the Gospel similar language had twice been used of the relationship between Jesus and the Father (x. 38; xiv. 10). In neither instance was there the continuation 'and ye in me, and I in you'; for Jesus had still to die.

It is possible, however, that we should adopt the other punctuation of *v.* 19. In that case the sense will be: because Jesus is in imperishable union with the Father, His death will not dissolve the disciples' union with Him. Because His own union with the Father was indestructible, so would theirs be with Jesus from the moment of His dying, as they would know 'on that day', the day of His resurrection and of the communication of the Spirit. It is doubtful, but perhaps the other translation is rather more likely to be the right one.

Jesus now proceeds to a further and most illuminating variation on the same theme, which goes far towards clinching the case for the interpretation we have given to His coming. 'He that hath my commandments, and keepeth them, he it is that loveth me: and he that loveth me shall be loved of my Father, and I will love him, and will manifest myself unto him. . . . If a man love me, he will keep my word: and my Father will love him, and we will come unto him, and make our abode with him' (*vv.* 21, 23). The expression 'my commandments' in *v.* 15 and *v.* 21 is replaced in *v.* 23 by 'my word'. The commandments of Jesus are, as we have seen, those which He will give to His disciples during the unbroken communion with Him which they are to enjoy through His Passion and the gift of the Spirit. But His word, here and throughout the Gospel, covers His whole revelation of the Father through His revealing of Himself in utterance, sign and Passion. His commandments, then, are to be as comprehensive as His word. Just as the commandments which Jesus Himself obeyed (x. 18; xii. 49; xiv. 31; xv. 10) included everything He had to say or do in a life lived in harmony with the saving purpose of God, so His commandments will comprehend all that it means to be a recipient and a propagator of His word. By such conduct the disciples would be proving that they loved Jesus, and, more than that, that they had been taken up into the mutual love of the Father and the Son; and their obedience would be the occasion for the self-manifestation of Jesus.

It should be noticed how by comparison with *vv.* 18–20 the horizon widens in *vv.* 21 and 23. Jesus gives the assurance that He will love and manifest Himself not only to those whose feet He had washed, but to all other lovers of Himself who should become so by their response to the preaching of the Johannine 'word' (cf. xvii. 20 ff). Those who loved Him—the little group around Him and the many more to come—would be loved both by Jesus and by His Father. The sequel shows what this love involves. Jesus will love the one who loves Him by manifesting Himself to him. The love of Jesus and the Father will find expression in their coming to Him and taking up abode with Him. These variations of phrasing are so many attempts to show what it means to be loved by Jesus, to be loved by His Father; and only when the words 'we will make our abode with him' have been uttered has enough been said. Or conversely we may say that the experience of a love which is the inner being of the Godhead (xvii. 24–26) is the true content of the promise of Jesus to come again. The promise is given for the future; very soon indeed it would be in continuous fulfilment. Yet the fulfilment would not and could not set in until the Passion of Jesus had become an accomplished fact. The promise rests on the Johannine teaching that the death of Jesus glorifies Him, that is to say, that it unites believers with Himself, and further that it enables Him to impart to them the gift of the Spirit (vii. 39; xvi. 7). Only when the Spirit comes to aid their understanding will achievement of the Passion become real in their own experience.

Meanwhile there has been an interruption. 'Judas (not Iscariot) saith unto him, Lord, what is come to pass that thou wilt manifest thyself unto us, and not unto the world?' (*v.* 22). The question could not have been asked if the discourse of Jesus as a

whole had been understood, yet it shows a certain limited understanding which contributes to the argument. Judas is not rebuked
for supposing that the promised coming of Jesus would be a
private one and not a public manifestation. In this he has correctly
grasped the tenor of Jesus' words. The coming at the last day
would be a manifestation to the whole world, believing and
unbelieving alike (cf. v. 28–29). This coming is such that only
those will be aware of it whose powers of apprehension have been
informed by the gift of the Spirit. The world cannot receive the
Spirit (v. 17), and therefore cannot receive the coming manifestation of Jesus. In the answer given to Judas we are told the reason
why. 'He that loveth me not keepeth not my words: and the word
which ye hear is not mine, but the Father's who sent me' (v. 24).
The Spirit is given only to those who love Jesus, who are prepared
to be as obedient to and dependent on Him as He has been
obedient to and dependent on the Father.

A more definite indication of the function of the Paraclete in
providing the conditions for the coming of Jesus is given in the
second of the Paraclete sayings. 'These things have I spoken unto
you, while abiding with you (i.e. in the familiar manner of association). But the Paraclete, the Holy Spirit whom the Father will
send in my name, he shall teach you all things, and bring to your
remembrance all that I have said' (vv. 25–26). In the previous
passage the Paraclete was characterized as 'the Spirit of truth', the
Spirit coming from, and leading recipients into, the divine reality,
the reality of which Jesus on earth was Himself the embodiment
and revealer. How would the Paraclete lead men into this truth
which Jesus Himself is? He would not initiate the union of the
lovers of Jesus with Jesus and the Father; the dying of Jesus does
that. The Paraclete would bring them to the knowledge of the
union, and we are now told that He would do it by teaching them
'all things', and by recalling in their minds the teaching of Jesus.
Bernard (in loc.) wrote: 'This is the second side of the work of the
Spirit, who not only was to reveal what was new, but was to
recall to the memory of the apostles the old truths that Jesus had
taught.' This distinction between new and old is surely a false
one. 'All things' cannot mean a new revelation over and above
those things which the Spirit would bring to the disciples' remembrance; rather, the second clause is to be regarded as an expansion
and explanation of the first. For the revelation which Jesus accom-

plished on earth was not incomplete. 'He that hath seen me hath seen the Father' (*v.* 9). 'Not that any man hath seen the Father, save he which is from God, he hath seen the Father' (vi. 46). 'I speak the things which I have seen with my Father' (viii. 38). 'He that rejecteth me, and receiveth not my sayings, hath one that judgeth him: the word that I spake, the same shall judge him in the last day' (xii. 48). By being what He was, by His dying, by His self-revealing utterances and acts, Jesus fully revealed the Father. In the face of the passages just quoted we cannot take the words 'he shall teach you all things' to imply that the Holy Spirit would make complete a revelation left incomplete by Jesus Himself. On the other hand, the really appropriating response to it from His disciples, upon which depended their realisation of being in union with Him and the Father, had still to come. It was the Spirit who was to ensure the preservation and the understanding of all that Jesus had taught and done.

The Hebrew *shalom* (peace) was the common formula of courteous address at parting as well as at meeting (1 Sam. i. 17). With this familiar term Jesus now takes formal leave of His friends. 'Peace I leave with you; my peace I give unto you: not as the world giveth, give I unto you. Let not your heart be troubled, neither let it be fearful' (*v.* 27). But on His lips it becomes more than a common salutation. For the word *shalom* is also used in the Old Testament in the sense of salvation. 'The chastisement that brought us peace was upon him' (Isa. liii. 5). 'I will hear what God the Lord will speak: for he will speak peace unto his people, and to his saints; but let them not turn again to folly. Surely his salvation is nigh them that fear him' (Ps. lxxxv. 8 f.). The peace which Jesus leaves to His disciples is the peace of being in union with Himself, which is the true eschatological salvation according to St. John. But it is also His own peace that He gives, a share in His own union with the Father. He does not give His peace as the world gives its peace. He gives at the uttermost cost, gives by dying; so that only He can give the peace which is His peace. The world's peace is but a spoken word, an expression of good will at parting; the peace which Jesus gives is eternal life through union with Himself and the Father. The disciples need not be troubled or disturbed at His departure, for instead of separating them from Him it will bind them to Him in the bonds of His peace.

In bequeathing to the disciples His own peace Jesus has been setting before them in yet one more guise the promise of His coming again, and to that promise He now explicitly reverts. 'Ye heard how I said to you, I go away, and I come unto you. If ye loved me, ye would have rejoiced, because I go unto the Father: for the Father is greater than I' (v. 28). On whose account would they have rejoiced, on His, or on their own? Many commentators have assumed that it is on Jesus' account that they should have been rejoicing. 'It would be selfish as well as cowardly, after His explanations, to continue to lament His departure, since they knew from His own lips whither He was going. His destination, He had told them, was His Father's house: the inconceivable joy and glory of the Divine presence. It must be a most imperfect, a most blind and erring love, that grudged Him this, and would detain Him here, when the greatness of the Father's Right Hand lay before Him there'.[7] 'Jesus has told them that they must not be cowards; now He tells them that they must not be selfish. His departure means for Him the resumption of the Divine glory.'[8] 'He is released from further humiliation and re-established in His original glory.'[9] We may seem to be dwelling unduly on a small point. But the remarks just quoted show that upon the way the question is answered may depend our understanding of the very heart of St. John's message. For they imply that the Incarnation of the Logos involved the relinquishment of the glory which He enjoyed in the presence of the Father before the world was made, and this is not the inference to be drawn from xvii. 5. The Logos became flesh retaining His original glory and able to manifest it in His incarnate life (i. 14; ii. 11). He continued throughout His earthly life to be 'in the bosom of the Father' (i. 18; cf. iii. 13). Jesus does indeed receive glory when He dies, the glory which is the union of Himself and His disciples. His going to the Father, from whom death cannot separate Him, is also their going to the Father through their union with Him. It would seem, therefore, to be no less on their own account than on His that they ought now to be joyful over His departure, as they would be if they loved Him enough to understand His promises.

[7] Swete, op. cit., p. 61 f.
[8] Bernard, in loc.
[9] Hoskyns, in loc.

A further reason is now added why the disciples should have rejoiced: 'the Father is greater than I'. It is difficult to see what the connexion of thought could be if we assumed that the disciples were expected to rejoice unselfishly over Jesus. But if the interpretation we have been giving to the previous saying is not at fault, the connexion is clear enough. The disciples ought not to be dismayed at the prospect of losing Jesus; no, they should be rejoicing over the fact that in dying He would not only be uniting them with Himself, but taking them with Him to One greater than Himself, to One to whom He, from the point of view of His manhood, owes His own possession of the life, the love, the peace, which He is now able to communicate to them. The union with the Father which, through the initiative of the Father, Jesus enjoys on earth, and which, as He dies, He knows that He will always enjoy, is everything to Him; it is also the end to which He brings His disciples, and all believers who come after them, through their union with Himself.

In spite of all that Jesus has said, His death will still be to all outward appearance a loss which will leave the disciples bereft. 'And now I have told you before it is come to pass, that, when it is come to pass, ye may believe' (*v.* 29). Only to faith will His coming again have the all-sufficient reality He has been describing. At the outset the disciples have been assured that they believe both in God and in Jesus; but it is plain that their faith has a long way to go before it becomes the full and mature understanding and acceptance of His promises. Only through the possession of the Spirit would they attain to that mature, discerning faith; and then only because the Spirit would be able to remind them that Jesus had known and foretold in advance the whole course of the saving activity of the Father.

For further enlightenment the disciples will now have to await the coming of the Spirit, for the time at the disposal of Jesus is being cut short. 'I will no more speak much with you, for the prince of this world cometh: and he hath nothing in me; but that the world may know that I love the Father, and as the Father gave me commandment, even so I do' (*vv.* 30–31). It looks as if we are meant to understand that the men who serve as the instruments of Satan for his assault upon Jesus are preparing to seize Him (cf. vi. 70; viii. 44; xiii. 2, 27). The disciples, we may suppose, would have been more fearful than ever at the knowledge that behind the impending departure of Jesus stood Satan. Would he have his way with Jesus? They hear the words of reassurance: 'He has no claim on me.' There was no sin of Jesus for Satan to light upon, nothing akin to himself to enable him to bring Jesus within his power. His death might look like a triumph for the prince of this world, but the appearance was the reverse of the truth. Satan's greatest assault upon Him was also His own greatest opportunity to obey the Father's will. 'Now is the judgement of this world; now shall the prince of this world be cast out' (xii. 31). The Passion of Jesus would decide the issue between Himself and Satan, between Himself and the world. 'In the world ye have tribulation: but be of good cheer; I have overcome the world' (xvi. 33). In the judgement of the Cross the world and the world's prince were to lose their case. The coming of Satan, just because it would give Jesus the opportunity to show the perfection of His love and obedience to the Father's will, would spread throughout Satan's domain, the world, the knowledge that his conqueror had come. Henceforth all who believed in Him would be in union with the Victor in the decisive conflict; and to that union Satan's fatal power could not extend. It remained true indeed that 'the whole world lieth in the evil one' (1 John v. 19), but no longer need it be so; and it is so, we should understand, only to the extent that the Son of God is rejected or unknown.

15

THE TRUE VINE

The vine had long served as an emblem of the chosen people, the people of God. 'Israel is a luxuriant vine, which putteth forth his fruit' (Hos. x. 1). 'I planted thee a noble vine, wholly a right seed: how then art thou turned into the degenerate plant of a strange vine unto me?' (Jer. ii. 21; cf. Isa. v. 1–7; Ezek. xv. 1–8). 'Thou broughtest a vine out of Egypt: thou didst drive out the nations and plantedst it. Thou preparedst *room* before it, and it took deep root, and filled the land. . . . Turn again, we beseech thee, O God of hosts: Look down from heaven, and behold, and visit this vine, and the stock which thy right hand hath planted, and the branch that thou madest strong for thyself' (Ps. lxxx. 8–15). In the Targum to this psalm *vv.* 14–15 become a petition for 'the vine shoot which thy right hand hath planted and the King Messiah whom thou hast established for thyself', the Branch being taken to be a technical term for the Messiah, with the result that a parallelism between vine and Messiah is set up. The Apocalypse of Baruch (xxxix. 7) uses 'vine' (along with 'fountain') as a simile for 'Messiae mei principatus'. The Christian church is described as 'the holy vine of David' in *Didache* ix. 2 (cf. Justin, *Dial.* 110; *Acts of Thomas* 146).

In claiming to be 'the true vine' Jesus is disclosing His unity with the whole body of believers present and to come. We are expected to have in mind the moment at which the saying is uttered, when the Passion is being treated as though it were an already accomplished fact, and to interpret it in the light of the Johannine teaching that the dying of Jesus makes Him one with all believers. By this act of love to the uttermost (xiii. 1) He becomes to the whole body of believers the source and giver of life, and therefore declares Himself to be 'the true vine'. In the sixth chapter of the Gospel Jesus appears as 'the true bread', which is then defined as the bread which 'gives life to the world'; and He is so on the double ground that, first, He is the Son, and therefore in the Father, having life in Himself by the Father's gift (vi. 40; x. 38; v. 26), and then, later in the discourse, because by His

N

Passion He unites believers with Himself. For the same two reasons Jesus is here said to be the true, the life-giving vine. There is also a contrast intended here parallel to that between the manna which Moses gave and the true bread. To belong to the vine of Israel was no guarantee of the gift of life. Israel was no more the true vine than the Torah was the true manna (cf. i. 17 –18; v. 39–47).

It is important to recognise that the figure of the vine depicts the objective reality of the new union established by the Passion, if we are to appreciate the purport of the qualifications which follow. 'I am the true vine, and my Father is the husbandman. Every branch in me that beareth not fruit, he taketh it away: and every *branch* that beareth fruit, he cleanseth it, that it may bear more fruit' (*vv.* 1–2). The branch is part of the vine, whether or not it shows signs of life and fruitfulness; but the vine-dresser removes the unfruitful branches and prunes the others to improve their yield of fruit. The death of Jesus has established a union between Him and His disciples, irrespective of any response they may be required to make. But the Father will not allow this union to continue, unless they show by their 'fruit-bearing' that they have appropriated the life that Jesus has to give, and have allowed it to come to effective expression. The absence of 'fruit' would show that their relationship with Jesus was only empty appearance, and the Father, whose care it was to watch over the relationship, would abolish it.

What then does it mean to 'bear fruit', and what is symbolized by the barren branch? In part a barren branch is a disciple to whom the Holy Spirit has come for His work of actualizing the hidden union created by the Passion, but has come ineffectually. To be a barren branch will mean to be a follower of Jesus without being awakened to the fact of union with Him, to be on the vine without receiving as a conscious possession the life that flows from it. Such a disciple has not entered receptively into the promises made by Jesus in the last chapter; he does not love Jesus, the word of Jesus has not come home to him, the Spirit has sought unavailingly to be his teacher. But there is still more meaning in the figure. Of Himself Jesus had said: 'Except a grain of wheat fall into the earth and die, it abideth by itself alone; but if it die, it beareth much fruit. . . . And I, if I be lifted up from the earth, will draw all men unto myself' (xii. 24, 32). In His case fruit-bearing is clearly the opposite of remaining alone, and is therefore synonymous with drawing all men into union with Himself. Equally clearly the fruit-bearing of the branches must be homogeneous with and consequent upon the fruit-bearing of the vine. For the disciples it will mean in part, as we have seen, their allowing Him to draw them into unity with Himself. But it will also involve their acting as His agents in the continuing mission by which He is to draw to Himself the rest of humanity. The barren branch is a disciple who, lacking any effective share in the life which Jesus alone is able to communicate, is also necessarily unfitted for the mission to the world; he cannot do the 'greater works' than those of Jesus (xiv. 12), by bringing others into the union with Jesus to which the Passion has opened the way. That this is the intended meaning of 'fruit-bearing' becomes apparent later in the chapter: 'Ye did not choose me, but I chose you, and appointed you, that ye should go and bear fruit' (v. 16). The going here spoken of is to be understood in the light of xvii. 18: 'As thou didst send me into the world, even so sent I them into the world'. Through their missionary preaching and through the influence of lives such as even the world can see to be in union with Jesus (xiii. 34–35) they will incorporate others into the vine. A disciple who is a barren branch can bear no fruit in this sense, for he bears no fruit in the other sense of being through the helping Spirit in living union with Jesus. Upon him the judgment of God would fall; he would be excised from the vine. For the fruit-bearing branches too there is the pruning knife: by painful discipline the great Vine-dresser ensures that the true disciple is rid of whatever in him prevents a more abundant fruit-bearing in each of the senses we have been describing.

A fortifying encouragement follows the solemn warning. 'Already ye are clean, because of the word which I have spoken unto you' (v. 3). Naturally it is not the intention to declare the disciples 'clean' simply because 'the word' has been spoken to them; it depended upon the response to it whether or not the hearers became 'clean', be it in the sense of freedom from defilement (cf. xiii. 10), or also, as the context here suggests and usage allows, in that of fitness for bearing fruit.[1] Moreover, 'the word' is no mere verbal utterance, spoken by the lips and heard by the

---

[1] Cf. Xenophon, *Oeconomicus* xx. 20, where vines are said to be καθαραί when the soil they grow in has been cleared of weeds.

ear; it is the whole content of the revelation given by Jesus, the disclosure that in His person the eschatological and saving action of God is taking place, which enables Him to make the disciples 'clean' by His dying. The Word which Jesus is He speaks not only with His lips but with His life, and above all with His death. Because they have accepted that word, the Father has already made the disciples clean; but He will go on cleaning them, as by the help of the Spirit they more and more firmly appropriate the benefits of the Passion.

Of this increased fruit-bearing the necessary condition on their side is that they hold fast to their union with Jesus. 'Abide in me, and I in you. As the branch cannot bear fruit of itself, except it abide in the vine; so neither can ye, except ye abide in me. I am the vine, ye are the branches: he that abideth in me, and I in him, the same beareth much fruit: for apart from me ye can do nothing' (vv. 4–5). Just as the sap rising from the root of a vine flows to the branches, thus supplying them with the power to bear fruit, so it is with the disciples of Jesus: it is the life that flows to them from their union with Him that enables them to carry out their mission. They are not being asked to achieve anything by virtue of their own vitality or effort, but to allow themselves to become channels for the activity of Jesus. There is no dichotomy, nor even tension, between the inward turning of their relationship to Jesus and the outward turning of their mission to the world. The mission can have no success unless it is a mission in which Jesus, and therefore the Father, is active; and to be united with Jesus is to be united with Him and with the Father in their saving love for the world.

There has been an allusion already to the fate of the barren branch; now comes a figurative description of it in some detail, to quicken in a disciple the sense of his peril in being on the vine and yet not bearing fruit. 'If a man abide not in me, he is cast forth as a branch, and is withered; and they gather them, and cast them into the fire, and they are burned' (v. 6). In Greek the verbs 'cast forth' and 'withered' are in the aorist, apparently to indicate how certainly a disciple will fall under the divine judgment, when once it is evident that he is not bearing fruit. On the other hand, disciples who have remained in Jesus may have confidence that all their prayers will be granted. 'If ye abide in me, and my words abide in you, ask whatsoever ye will, and it shall be done unto you' (*v.* 7). Having regard to the context, we may judge that the prayers will be prayers which arise out of the disciples' union with Jesus and have to do with their fruit-bearing (cf. xiv. 13–14). It will be noticed that, whereas hitherto Jesus has spoken of His disciples' remaining in Him and His remaining in them, now there is a change: they must allow His words to remain in them, the utterances which make up His whole revelation. The variation in the phrasing is not without significance. Jesus (it is being suggested) remains in disciples who possess His revelation, with Spirit-illumined apprehension of it (cf. xiv. 26). The union of the disciples with Jesus, the branches with the vine, is not to be experienced apart from their adherence to and understanding of His teaching.

The mention of the disciples' prayers recalls one of the themes of the previous chapter, that through the answers given to their prayers the Father would be glorified in the Son (xiv. 13). We saw there that the Father may be said to glorify His name, or to win glory for Himself, when His glory, the glory of the eternal Logos, is revealed to the world by being imparted to Jesus, through Him to the disciples, and through them (particularly through their prayers) to the rest of mankind. What was there said in compressed and enigmatic form is now expressed more directly. 'Herein is my Father glorified, that ye bear much fruit; and *so* shall ye be my disciples' (*v.* 8). The Father is to win glory for Himself by means of the fruit-bearing of the disciples, and that for two reasons. The fruit-bearing of the branches is at the same time the fruit-bearing of the vine, the process by which Jesus ceases to be alone in His union with the Father and draws men into His own corporate manhood; and to this mission the disciples are to contribute, both by their preaching and their prayers. But it is also the process by which they will demonstrate the genuineness of their discipleship, will prove that their union with Jesus is being allowed to unfold towards its perfection through the work of the Paraclete.

To speak, as we have constantly done, of the union of Jesus with His disciples could give the impression that St. John had in mind some impersonal, quasi-physical fusion of being. The next saying guards against any such misapprehension. 'Even as the Father hath loved me, I also have loved you: abide ye in my love' (*v.* 9). The union into which Jesus has brought the disciples by His Passion is a union of love; more than that, it is an extension of that which the Father had brought to pass between Jesus (as the incarnate Logos) and Himself. The Father had loved Jesus: what are we expected to understand from such a sparing use of language? Several times in the Gospel the Father's love of Jesus has been spoken of, and it will be well to bring the instances together and consider them. 'The Father loveth the Son, and hath given all things into his hand' (iii. 35). 'The Son can do nothing of himself, but what he seeth the Father doing: for what things soever he doeth, these the Son also doeth in like manner. For the Father loveth the Son, and sheweth him all things that he himself doeth' (v. 19–20). 'Therefore doth the Father love me, because I lay down my life, that I may take it again' (x. 17). These three passages make it clear that the love of the Father for the Son involves not merely a personal intimacy, but also a sharing of a common activity and purpose. To the Son the Father commits His whole plan of salvation for the world, and the Son responds by totally identifying Himself with the Father's love for the world. Because the Son lays down His life in obedience to the Father's commandments, and so finishes the work which the Father gave Him to do, he remains in the Father's love (x. 17–18; xiv. 31; xv. 10; xvii. 4). Similarly, the love of Jesus for His disciples will involve not only a relationship of mutual indwelling, but also His sharing with them all that He Himself is doing; and it is in this sense that they are asked to remain in His love. To complete the picture we must refer to one further passage. 'The glory which thou hast given me I have given unto them . . . that the world may know that thou . . . lovedst them, even as thou lovedst me' (xvii. 22–26). Here the glory of the eternal Logos, which has been bestowed on Jesus in the Incarnation and on the disciples through the Passion, is being reinterpreted in terms of love. In the same way in xv. 9 St. John has dropped the imagery of the vine and the branches in favour of the language of personal relationship. A Jew might claim to belong to the vine of Israel by physical descent. But a man could be a branch on the true vine only by the personal act of self-sacrificing love by which Jesus had drawn him into unity with Himself, and by his own personal act in choosing to remain there.

How could they remain in the love of Jesus? Upon what on their side did their remaining in His love depend? 'If ye keep my commandments, ye shall abide in my love; even as I have kept my

Father's commandments, and abide in his love' (xv. 10). In the
last chapter we have already had occasion to discuss what is meant
by keeping the commandments of Jesus, but it will be well to see
whether an independent study of the present passage confirms our
conclusions there. From v. 12, where the singular is used, we
might get the impression that the only commandment under
consideration was that of mutual love among disciples. But vv.
14–15 suggest that something more is intended. There we are told
that the disciples are friends of Jesus because He has made known
to them everything that He has heard from His Father, and that
they are His friends if they do what He commands them. There is
surely an indication here that what He commands them to do is
what He has made known to them, namely, the whole relevation
He has accomplished, His word comprehensively understood. By
His obedient response to all that He has heard from the Father,
that is, to the Father's purpose of salvation, Jesus has remained
in the Father's love; and He is now calling for a similar response
from the disciples, once the Spirit has enabled them to make it
(cf. xiv. 26).

A share in the love and purpose of Jesus carries with it also a
share in His joy. 'These things have I spoken unto you, that my
joy may be in you, and that your joy may be fulfilled' (v. 11).
Jesus has already spoken of the joy which the disciples ought to
have experienced at His departure (xiv. 28), but now it appears
that what they were then being offered was a participation in His
own joy—the joy of His own union with the Father, but also the
joy of accomplishment, since He had kept the Father's commandments and had completed the work which the Father had given
Him to do (xvii. 4). His own perfection of joy was communicable;
it was for them as well as for Himself, for all who remained in His
love, as fruit-bearing branches in the vine, since they would be
taking part in His own completed work.

In expounding His allegory Jesus has so far been speaking of
the union between Himself and the disciples, and of what was
needful on their part, if it was to endure and unfold towards its
perfection; now His concern is with the relationship between the
disciples themselves which follows from their union with Him.
'This is my commandment, that ye love one another, even as I
have loved you' (v. 12). It is not enough that they be affectionately
disposed towards one another, or that they treat one another with

self-sacrificing goodwill, or even that they be ready, if need be, to give their lives for one another. Though all that is demanded of them, they must also cherish the union with one another into which He has brought them. The love they were to render to one another was to be a self-communication, as had been His own love of them. In Him they were one already; they must let the fact become a conscious and manifest actuality. So they would be loving one another as He had loved them.

In words which have a double reference, Jesus goes on to speak of the completeness of the self-sacrifice which His love of them, His communication of Himself to them, requires of Him, and which His commandment will require of them. 'Greater love hath no man than this, that a man lay down his life for his friends' (v. 13). Jesus dies for His 'friends'. Are earlier sayings in the Gospel being traversed? It has been represented that His mission is to give life to the world (iii. 16; vi. 33); and that He lays down His life not only for the sheep who are already in the fold, but for other sheep also (x. 14–16). There is no contradiction; for the friends of Jesus, as we are about to be told in v. 15, are those who respond with obedience, not only to the commandment of love, but to His whole revelation. Anyone who receives the word of Jesus, anyone who believes in Him, Jew or Gentile, of any time, is a friend of Jesus; for him Jesus dies, thereby loving him in the sense of communicating Himself to him, of establishing union with him. Is it, then, the very perfection of love that Jesus should die for His friends? Is it not greater love to die for enemies? The question is an irrelevant one. By an enemy of Jesus the Evangelist would have understood one who, on being confronted with the revelation of Jesus, whether by Jesus Himself or in the apostolic preaching, rejected it. How could Jesus so love as to unite with Himself one in whom His word, His revelation found no lodgment? In dying He could be loving only His friends, for to love as He now loved was to impart Himself, or to establish the union figured in this allegory of the vine and the branches. The common criticism that love for friends is a narrower thing than love for enemies only points to a faulty understanding of Johannine thought. It is indeed the perfection of love that Jesus should die for His friends, and this not only because it is love at such a cost, but because it is love which brings its objects into the union with Himself which is eternal life.

The friends of Jesus are those who do what He commands
them to do, not slavishly with blind obedience, but with an understanding of the purpose that lies behind them. 'Ye are my friends,
if ye do the things which I command you. No longer do I call you
servants; for the servant knoweth not what his lord doeth: but I
have called you friends, for all things that I heard from my Father
I have made known to you' (*vv.* 14–15). A man may demand
obedience from a slave simply on the grounds of his authority; but
he may ask obedience from a friend only if he is prepared to take
him fully into his confidence, to open his heart to him, to disclose
all his intentions and aspirations. It is this mature and informed
obedience that Jesus claims from his disciples. In an earlier
discourse (viii. 31–36) He has contrasted the slave who has no
security of tenure in the household with the Son who has the
freedom of the house, and has promised His hearers that the truth
will make them free. It is this same truth that here constitutes the
difference between a slave and a friend, the truth which is nothing
less than the whole counsel of God divulged once for all in the
person and mission of Jesus.

The disciples must not however suppose that they owe it to
themselves that they have ceased to be slaves and have become
friends of Jesus, or that they are so for their own sakes alone. 'Ye
did not choose me, but I chose you, and appointed you, that ye
should go and bear fruit, and that your fruit should abide: that
whatsoever ye shall ask of the Father in my name, he may give
it you' (*v.* 16). There is a return here to the two main themes in
the imagery of the vine: the total dependence of the branches on
the vine, and their function as the bearers of fruit. Whatever
response may be required of the disciples, it is from start to finish
the work of Jesus that has made them what they now are, and they
must therefore allow their lives to be conformed to the pattern and
purpose of His. He had made known to them everything He had
learned from the Father, and He was to die for them, to make
them His friends, to obtain for them their freedom in His Father's
house, to impart life to them; and all these benefits they must
extend to others in their apostolic mission. Hoskyns rightly
observed that 'the appointment of the chosen disciples to lead the
mission to the world is the direct outcome of the death of Jesus'
(pp. 103–107; and cf. xvii. 18–19). He also points out (*in loc.*) that
the Evangelist has used the same Greek word for the 'appointing'

of the disciples as for the 'laying down' of the life of Jesus; and, in a book which makes such frequent use of double meanings, it may well have been with deliberation that he did so. Their appointment to the mission was at the same time appointment to the life of prayer; they were to pray to the Father for their success in fruit-bearing, for the growth of the church; and further, as it would seem, their fruit-bearing would itself constitute a ground of certainty that the Father would grant all such petitions. But the success of the mission will also depend on the quality of their common life, and it is no doubt for this reason that the commandment to love one another is repeated so soon (v. 17; cf. xiii. 35).

The reality of the disciples' union with Jesus would thus be attested by the success of their mission; but, in quite a different way, it would also be attested by its failure. 'If the world hateth you, ye know that it hath hated me before *it hated* you' (v. 18; cf. vii. 7; xvi. 33). In a world which has crucified Jesus they must expect hostility. The world of men, far from God, opposed to Him, ignorant of Him, remains the object of His love, exerted to the full in the mission of His Son (iii. 16–17; iv. 42; xii. 47); and in the mission of the disciples divine love for the world would continue to be put forth. But they are warned beforehand that they will draw the world's hatred upon themselves, and this not only on account of their association with Jesus, but because of what they have become in themselves. 'If ye were of the world, the world would love its own: but because ye are not of the world, but I chose you out of the world, therefore the world hateth you (v. 19). Not to be of the world means not to derive one's life and nature from the world, not to be what the world is. But it is to be noted that, though the disciples are not now of the world, they have not always been so; they have been chosen out of the world. The distinction, therefore, between those who are of the world and those who are not of the world, however absolute it may appear, is not necessarily a permanent one. The disciples are living proof that those who once were of the world may come to be not of the world. How then had their new origin and so their new being come about? By Jesus' choice of them more is meant than the calling of disciples at the beginning of the ministry, for in this sense Judas too had been chosen (cf. vi. 70). He could not so choose them that He could say of them, 'Ye are not of the world,' unless His choice was to take effect through His revelation of what He had heard from the Father and through His drawing of them into union with Himself by the Passion. His own origin—His only origin, which was not so in the case of the disciples—was heavenly; and only when He had brought them into union with Himself, who was not, and never had been, of the world, could it be said that they too were not of the world. We are expected then to understand that the choosing here in question had required—in order to be effectual, to take them out of the world—that He should convey to them His revelation (*v.* 15) and that He should die for them (*v.* 13).

Jesus has just said, 'I no longer call you slaves' (*v.* 15); and He is not going back on this declaration when He now calls to mind an earlier saying that 'a servant is not greater than his lord' (*v.* 20; cf. xiii. 16). A simple point is being made, without the kind of reflexion which the proximity of *vv.* 15 and 20 starts in the mind; they must not expect the world to treat them any better than it treated Jesus. Just as surely as Jesus had been persecuted, so would they be; and just as little, or as much, as His word was heeded, so would theirs be too. We are to understand that the hatred the disciples were to experience would come to them above all from the Jews. 'They shall put you out of the synagogues: yea, the hour cometh that whosoever killeth you shall think that he offereth service unto God. And these things will they do, because they have not known the Father, nor me' (xvi. 2–3). In St. John the Jews represent that which is meant by the world, for they do not know God and they therefore act in opposition to Him, even when they claim to be serving Him. The warning which Jesus is giving is intended to encourage the disciples. They are to recognise that whatever in the way of suffering might come to them on their mission would be on account of their confession of Jesus; and that the reason for their persecutor's action would be ignorance of God. 'But all these things will they do unto you for my name's sake, because they know not him that sent me' (*v.* 21).

This theme of the world's ignorance of God is pursued in the noteworthy verses which follow. 'If I had not come and spoken unto them, they had not had sin: but now they have no excuse for their sin. He that hateth me hateth my Father also. If I had not done among them the works which none other did, they had not had sin: but now have they both seen and hated both me and my Father. But this cometh to pass, that the word may be fulfilled that is written in their law, They hated me without a cause' (*vv.* 22–25). It is expected of the reader that he will let the record of the works and words of Jesus given in the Gospel supply 'if I had not come and spoken' with content. If the Incarnation of the Logos had not taken place, and if the incarnate Logos had not revealed to men that His humanity had been taken into unity with the Father, and what it meant for them that it should be so, then they would not 'have had sin.' Here is something to give the reader pause. Was it then the coming of Jesus which alone created the possibility of 'having sin'? What of the time before the Incarnation? Could there have been no 'having sin' in the pre-Christian world? How very un-Pauline it sounds! Could St. Paul ever have written what we here find in St. John (cf. Rom. i. 18–iii 20)? It is a question however how the phrase 'have sin' should be understood (cf. ix. 41; xix. 11). Of course it is not to be taken to imply that men before the Incarnation were without sin, in the sense of being alienated from God, far away from Him, in ignorance of Him, living in defiance of His will for them. As the world's light Jesus was the antithesis of what the world was in itself before He came, and of what it still was apart from Him now that He had come. Light was an accepted symbol of salvation; and the figure of darkness was applicable to the world, because it lacked the life which Jesus alone could give. Men before the coming of Jesus were indeed in a lost condition, but whether finally so or not only their acceptance or rejection of Jesus would determine, be it there and then when He spoke and by signs revealed His glory, or at the last day when all who were in the tombs would 'hear his voice' (v. 28–29). The situation of the world in relation to God before the Incarnation—its ignorance of Him, its being without life, its self-sufficiency, its going its own way and not His—called forth the compassion rather than the anger of God. This was the world which God loved enough to send His only Son. There is indeed, according to St. John, only one sin which is finally mortal in its consequences, and this is the sin of rejecting the offer of life by rejecting the One whom God has sent to accomplish for the world the purpose of its creation.

The sin for which there is now no excuse is the sin of remaining in ignorance of God once Jesus has made Him known. The implication is that before the Incarnation the sin in question was not inexcusable. Now they have no excuse, but formerly they had one. They have none now because God as He is has made Himself knowable in Jesus; formerly they had an excuse, because God as He is had not been knowable. Not only was it the case that no man had ever seen God (i. 18; vi. 46); no one could have seen Him until He was revealed in Jesus. Before the Incarnation there was an excuse for sin; but sin there was, notwithstanding the statement that, apart from the coming of Jesus, men would not have had sin. The difficulty is relieved by the consideration that the sin for which there was the excuse that God was not yet knowable might or might not become the sin of refusing the knowledge of Him which Jesus made available; only the opportunity to receive or to reject it would decide that. But the former sin of not knowing God, and so of behaviour which was not in accordance with His will for men, was not mortal in the sense that it deprived men of the ability to know God as He is when once He had willed in Jesus so to be known. Apart from the coming of Jesus men would not have had the mortal sin of rejecting the knowledge of God which He brought, the sin which disables men from ever having life. They would not to be sure have found a way to life, if Jesus had not come; but before the Incarnation they were not, and could not be, in a finally lost condition; their fate was still to be decided. The coming of Jesus does decide it, turning into mortal sin the former, excusable sin of those who reject Him.

Jesus is loved in the reception of His word and hated in the rejection of it (cf. xiv. 21–23). But His word is the word of the Father who sent Him xiv. 24). To hate Jesus is to hate the Father whose revealer He is; and to hate the Father is to reject the saving love which has prompted the sending of Jesus. This is the one mortal sin, the sin for which there is no excuse. It is the repudiation not only of the word of Jesus, but also of those unprecedented works, which, no less than His words have been a revelation of the Father.

The chapter comes to a close with the third saying about the Paraclete. 'But when the Paraclete is come, whom I will send unto you from the Father, even the Spirit of truth, which proceedeth from the Father, he shall bear witness of me: and ye also bear witness, because ye have been with me from the beginning' (vv. 26–27).

The connexion of thought with what has gone before will be that for its hostile attitude towards the disciples on their mission the world would have no excuse. Jesus had made ignorance of God inexcusable, mortal sin. The disciples on their mission would be confronting the world with the same revelation, and the consequences of rejecting it would be the same. But why should the preaching of the disciples be so fateful for those who refused it? What would make the situation of the hearers of it just as critical as if Jesus had gone to them Himself? It was that the Paraclete would be bearing witness to Him. The witnessing of the Paraclete to Jesus would give to the disciples' word the same decisive character as had belonged to the word of Jesus. We are not to infer that the Paraclete would perform His role of witnessing independently of that of the disciples. Jesus was to send the Paraclete to them. The Paraclete would only be given to those who believed in Jesus, which means those who, on account of the Passion, were in union with Him. He would have no other organs of activity in the world except believers. He would bear witness to Jesus before the world, but it would be through the disciples' preaching of the word and the appeal of their unity in love (cf. xiii. 7). The Paraclete, as has been said in the second of the promises of Jesus about Him, would teach the disciples everything (xiv. 26); He would bring them to the understanding of the words which Jesus had uttered and of the works He had performed; He would disclose to them the full meaning of the self-testimony of Jesus. It would be in this sense that He would bear witness to Jesus: anyone who accepted the preaching of the apostles would do so because he was convinced by the double witness of the human speaker and the interpreting Spirit.

16

VICTORY OVER THE WORLD

Jesus has been warning the disciples about a conflict with the hostile world which lies in store for them. Now he begins to show them in greater detail what form the conflict will take. 'These things have I spoken unto you, that ye should not be made to stumble. They shall put you out of the synagogues: yea, the hour cometh, that whosoever killeth you shall think that he offereth service unto God. And these things will they do, because they have not known the Father, nor me' (xvi. 1–3). The hostility will come not from men who are openly and obviously evil, but from those who hold positions of responsibility and authority, who are accustomed to command respect and obedience, and who, in excommunicating or securing a death sentence on the disciples, will be acting in good conscience and, as they suppose, in the best interests of the people of God and of true religion. Unless they were forearmed by the warnings of Jesus, the disciples might, in the face of such impressive opposition, be tempted to 'stumble', to waver in their confidence that Jesus was right and the world wrong. But those who stumble only betray the fact that they are walking in darkness, devoid of the light of life, ignorant of their destination (xi. 10; xii. 35). The disciples will be safe against the world's seductions and intimidations only if they hold fast to the settled conviction that they are walking in the light and know where they are going, while the world's enmity arises out of its ignorance of God.

Of the sufferings which the future would bring to them Jesus had not spoken from the beginning; there had been the less need to do so because He had been together with them, so that He could have been their solace if such sufferings had befallen them. But now that He is about to leave them, He must and does speak of these things, so that when persecution comes to them they may remember His prophecy and draw strength from His words.

'But now I go unto him that sent me; and none of you asketh me, Whither goest thou? But because I have spoken these things unto you, sorrow hath filled your heart' (vv. 5–6). But had not

Peter just asked this question (xiii. 36; cf. xiv. 5)? He had certainly used the selfsame words, but it does not follow that in using them he was asking the question that Jesus now wanted him to ask. His question had been dictated by the sorrow of prospective parting, by the bitter regret of imminent loss. We are to observe that in the present verse Jesus tells His disciples where He is going and then, with that said, wishes that they would ask Him about it. A responding 'Where goest thou?', in the sense He desired, would have meant: 'Tell us, Lord, about your going to Him who sent you, and what it will mean for us. We want to understand you.' Peter's earlier question had not been an asking for enlightenment on that subject. The disciples ought to be rejoicing over the departure of Jesus to the Father (cf. xiv. 28); but as it is they are full of concern about the impending loss of Him and the dark future they suppose to be in prospect for them.

What the disciples are thinking to be sheer loss will in fact be gain. 'It is expedient for you that I go away: for if I go not away, the Paraclete will not come unto you; but if I go, I will send him unto you' (v. 7). They have enjoyed the presence of Jesus among them and are desolated at the thought of His departure. What they do not realise is that His going away is His Passion, in which He goes to the Father, at the same time drawing believers into union with Himself; and that only when He has won for Himself this glory (cf. vii. 39) can He send the Paraclete and so guarantee to them His own coming again, of which He has been speaking, in a lasting and effective union, far more intimate than the friendship they have so far experienced.

The Paraclete will not only be the defender of the disciples against the hostile attacks of the world; He will carry the battle into the enemy's camp. 'And he, when he is come, will convict the world in respect of sin, and of righteousness, and of judgement: of sin, because they believe not on me; of righteousness, because I go to the Father, and ye behold me no more; of judgement, because the prince of this world hath been judged' (vv. 8–11). In the intention of the Evangelist the immediate reference of the term 'world' is to the Jews, as may be seen from the matters of Jewish concern to be settled by the Paraclete: for the Jews believed that sin was disobedience to the Law, that righteousness was obedience to it, and that divine judgement would be determined by its standards; and accordingly, they saw Jesus as a sinner unworthy of their faith, His going to the Father as a well-deserved criminal execution, His exaltation on the Cross as a victory for the ruler of this world. But what would the activity of the Paraclete do for this unbelieving world? Was He to convict the world, in the sense of bringing about its final condemnation (so RV, quoted above)? Or was He to convince the world of its errors, and so to secure its conversion?

The possible meanings of the verb ἐλέγχειν are: to bring to light, prove, demonstrate; or to point out a person's bad conduct to him, to censure him for it, to call him to account. The context alone determines whether the person concerned allows himself to be convinced and turns over a new leaf, or disregards the reproof and perhaps lays himself open to a conviction by a judge. Usage alone, then, does not enable us to decide which of these two possibilities was intended by St. John; that depends not simply on the immediate context, but on our understanding of his theology as a whole. Until we have examined the passage in greater detail, we must be content with a neutral rendering: it will be the function of the Paraclete to prove the world wrong in respect of sin, of righteousness, and of judgement.

The Paraclete will prove the world wrong about sin. But does the clause 'because they believe not on me' indicate the content of the sin of which the world is proved guilty, or does it indicate the reason why the world has in fact been in error on this subject. Some students of St. John have taken the first view, that the sin in question is the sin of not believing in Jesus, the sin with which nothing could be done, the sin of which Jesus says 'your sin remains' (ix. 41; cf. xv. 22–24). This understanding of the sin intended would imply that the mission of the Paraclete was only for the confirmation of the world in its darkness. But the other alternative has more to be said for it. The world had a false conception of sin long before the coming of Jesus. The darkness was there before the coming of the light. Only the coming of the light could show the darkness up for what it was. Only through belief in Jesus could the world discover its own ignorance of God, and therefore the true nature of sin, which is opposition to God. The sin, then, which the Paraclete was to expose was the sin of not knowing God, which characterized the world before Jesus came, and which continued to characterize it now that He had come, in so far as it had still to have presented to it His revelation of God in the revelation of Himself.

O

The Paraclete will prove the world wrong about righteousness, and this because Jesus is going to the Father and His disciples are to see Him no more. Here too the subordinate clause gives, not a definition of the righteousness of Jesus, but a reason why the world will prove to have been wrong. Jesus was now on the point of dying. Had His grave been the grave of a criminal, as many had supposed? No, in dying He had been going to the Father; His standing with Him had been the reverse of what His enemies thought. The Cross had been proof of His righteousness, proof, that is, that He had been in the right with the Father, for it was there that He had performed His supreme act of obedience to Him (cf. x. 17-18; xiv. 30-31). The true righteousness was not to be found in obedience to the Law which Jesus had been accused of breaking, but in His constant obedience to the Father's saving purpose, even when it led Him to the Cross. On that understanding of the verse, the Paraclete would bring about an overthrow of existing ideas about what constituted acceptability to God, in order that those who allowed themselves to be convinced might come to share the righteousness of Jesus Himself. For it was to the Father that Jesus was going, and this, as we have seen, was to be the point at which He would draw all men to Himself.

The Paraclete will prove the world wrong about judgement, because 'the prince of this world hath been judged'. At his final assault upon Jesus the prince of this world encountered One he could not conquer. Into the world, the domain of Satan, the disciples would bring by their preaching the knowledge of Satan's defeat. 'Now is the judgement of this world; now shall the prince of this world be cast out. And I, if I be lifted up from the earth, will draw all men unto myself' (xii. 31-32). This Spirit-led preaching would secure in the world a reversal of the verdict which God might have seemed to have passed on Jesus, and which His enemies believed had been passed on Him, at the Crucifixion.

We are to keep in mind that it is a question of the Spirit's bearing witness to Jesus in the world through the disciples' proclamation of His word after His death, and perhaps also through their love of one another (cf. xiii. 35). Would then the Spirit, with the disciples as His organs, convict the world of sin, in the sense of bringing the sin to light, exposing it? This to be sure would be the case. What more should be said? The sin of the world would in any event be left without excuse (xv. 22), made mortal, if persisted in. As we noticed in considering the sayings in xv. 22–24, the existing sin—the ignorance of God and the wrong behaviour corresponding to it—of the hearers of the words of Jesus and the beholders of His works is turned into mortal sin by their rejection of Him. So would it be again, just as surely, in the case of the witnessing of the Spirit to Jesus, if it should not be heeded. But are we to understand that the putting of the world in the wrong by the Spirit, besides convicting it, might also convince it? Are we to say that the world was not only to have its ignorance of God and the wickedness flowing from it exposed, but was to be brought to the acknowledgement that it did not know Him and was not doing His will? This would be as much as to say that the Spirit was to bring about His proof that there might be acceptance of Jesus in the world, and it will be right. The Spirit was not to bear witness to Jesus through the disciples in order that the world might have its sin made mortal by the refusal of the witness, and there an end. Fateful in the result though rejection of it would be, the purpose of the witnessing was to be the liberation of the world from its sin, the removal of its ignorance of God, the gaining of believers (cf. i. 29; iv. 42; xii. 47; xv. 8, 16; xvii. 20–23).

Since the world will not be convinced by the Paraclete of its triple error independently of the preaching of the disciples, His whole work in the end issues from His illumination of them. 'I have yet many things to say unto you, but ye cannot bear them now. Howbeit when he, the Spirit of truth, is come, he shall guide you into all the truth: for he shall not speak from himself; but what things soever he shall hear, these shall he speak: and he shall declare unto you the things that are to come. He shall glorify me: for he shall take of mine, and shall declare it unto you. All things whatsoever the Father hath are mine: therefore said I, that he taketh of mine, and shall declare it unto you' (*vv.* 12–15). In this fifth utterance about the Paraclete, the last of the series, the disciples receive an assurance that they will be brought by the Paraclete to the understanding of the word they are to take to the world. The opening words may seem to imply that a revelation given in the events of the Incarnation, the Passion, and the Resurrection, and in the words and acts by which Jesus disclosed their meaning, is not regarded in St. John as a complete revelation, but one still in need of an enlargement, which it would be a work of the Spirit to supply. In the sense intended, however, the utterance has to do with the disciples' need of a deepened understanding of a revelation which Jesus left complete (cf. xv. 15; xvii. 6-8, 14) and would expound to them through the Spirit. In consideration of this teaching function, the Paraclete is once more called the Spirit of Truth. We are not to suppose that it would be in the power of the Spirit to do more for the disciples in this respect than Jesus, the Truth incarnate, had been able to do for them. The point is that, until they were in Jesus and He in them, there was much in His revelation which they could not grasp. Once the union was established by His dying, the work of the Paraclete in the enlightenment of the disciples could begin. He would lead them 'into all the truth', which is a repetition of the promise of xiv. 26 that He would 'teach them everything'—everything concerning the meaning of the self-revealing words and works of Jesus, of His person, and of His Passion. (There is also a variant reading 'in all the truth', which has a good claim to acceptance: the Spirit would be their guide in the whole field of reality. Whichever reading we adopt, we are to observe the reference of the term 'truth' to Jesus. By recourse to Him the content of 'truth' is to be filled in. The Spirit would be the guide of the disciples in or into the whole range of reality embodied and revealed in His person and works.)

If then the Spirit is not to be regarded as an independent source of revelation, what are we to make of the statement that He will 'declare unto you the things that are to come'? Our difficulty here is one frequently met in biblical references to the future: is the time spoken of future to the writer and his readers, or future only to the speaker (cf. Heb. x. 1). If the task of the Paraclete was to reveal things which were still future at the time of His coming, He could hardly be said to speak only what He had heard in the revelation of Jesus. It is interesting, however, and hardly without significance for the interpretation of v. 13, that the same phrase (things to come) occurs again at xviii. 4, the reference there being to the things which were about to happen to Jesus and are told of Him in chapters 18 and 19. If, as may well be, the allusion of the phrasing is the same each time, we must understand that the Spirit would interpret to the disciples the betrayal, arrest, trial, scourging, mockery, and Crucifixion of Jesus, reversing for them a shattering surface-meaning of these events, and teaching them that the seeming defeat of love in this supreme instance of it was in reality the occasion of its greatest victory. He would guide them to publish the sufferings and death of Jesus as good news for the world, the best news that the world could possibly hear.

This interpretation receives strong support from the succeeding two verses. By receiving and interpreting the tradition derived from Jesus the Spirit would lead the disciples into a knowledge of the Father's true purpose, and so into the whole field of reality. In so doing He would glorify Jesus; that is to say, He would make a manifest actuality to them of the fact that Jesus by His dying had incorporated them into His own union with the Father.

How necessary the interpretative work of the Paraclete would be is now demonstrated by the incomprehension of the disciples. 'A little while, and ye behold me no more; and again a little while, and ye shall see me. Some of his disciples therefore said one to another, What is this that he saith unto us, A little while, and ye behold me not; and again a little while, and ye shall see me: and, Because I go to the Father? They said therefore, What is this that he saith, A little while? We know not what he saith' (vv. 16–18). Only when the promise becomes an actual experience, when through the operation of the Paraclete they become aware of the presence of the risen Jesus with them and in them, will their perplexity be resolved. Until then they cannot understand that Jesus is speaking of two different modes of 'seeing': in a little while they would see Him no more, in the material sense of 'seeing'; a little while longer and they would 'see' Him again, not just in the temporary seeing of His risen body, but with the eye of understanding enlightened by the Spirit.

The lamentation of the disciples over the dead Jesus (cf. Jer. xxii. 10) will be turned to joy as swiftly as the labour-pains are forgotten by a woman at the birth of her child. 'Jesus perceived that they were desirous to ask him, and he said unto them, Do ye inquire yourselves concerning this, that I said, A little while, and ye behold me not, and again a little while, and ye shall see me? Verily, verily, I say unto you, that ye shall weep and lament, but the world shall rejoice: ye shall be sorrowful, but your sorrow shall be turned into joy. A woman when she is in travail hath sorrow, because her hour is come: but when she is delivered of the child, she remembereth no more the anguish, for the joy that a man is born into the world. And ye therefore now have sorrow: but I will see you again, and your heart shall rejoice, and your joy no one taketh away from you. And in that day ye shall ask me nothing. Verily, verily, I say unto you, If ye shall ask anything of the Father, he will give it you in my name. Hitherto have ye asked nothing in my name: ask, and ye shall receive, that your joy may be fulfilled' (*vv.* 19–24). In a Johannine adaptation of late Jewish thought about the 'travail pains of the Messiah' (for a Pauline one see Gal. iv. 19), the grief of the disciples over the sufferings and death of Jesus is figured as birth-pangs of their new relation to Him.

In the RV translation *vv.* 23 and 24 appear to involve a self-contradiction, but the Greek in fact uses two different verbs for 'ask'. 'And on that day you will ask me no questions' (*v.* 23). The day being spoken of is the day of the appearance of the risen Jesus to the disciples and of their reception of the Spirit from Him (xx. 19–23), the day of the events which would establish them in knowledge that He was in the Father, one with Him, and that by His dying He had made them participants in that union. Once they were in this relation to Him, and in possession of the Spirit, Jesus would no longer be incomprehensible to them. Then the disciples will stop having to ask questions and begin instead to ask for an answer to their prayers. The prayers, like those mentioned in xv. 16, are to be prayers concerning the 'greater works' (xiv. 12), prayers with a missionary range of reference, prayers which, once granted, as such prayers offered in the name of Jesus would be, were to bring to the disciples the joy of union with their converts in the faith; and this added joy would make complete the joy of their union with Jesus Himself. Hitherto the disciples have made no petitions in the name of Jesus. They could not have done so, for prayer in the name of Jesus is prayer offered within the union with Him and by the enlightenment of the Spirit, which are the product of His death and resurrection.

The inability of the disciples to understand what Jesus has been saying in the Last Discourse is thus fully explained (xiii. 36–38; xiv. 5–9, 22; xvi. 17–20). 'These things have I spoken unto you in proverbs: the hour cometh, when I shall no more speak unto you in proverbs, but shall tell you plainly of the Father. In that day ye shall ask in my name: and I say not unto you, that I will pray the Father for you; for the Father himself loveth you, because ye have loved me, and have believed that I came forth from the Father. I came out from the Father, and am come into the world: again, I leave the world, and go unto the Father. His disciples say, Lo, now speakest thou plainly, and speakest no proverb. Now know we that thou knowest all things, and needest not that any man should ask thee: by this we believe that thou camest forth from God' (vv. 25–30). The word παροιμίαι (proverbs, parables) is here being used in the sense of dark sayings, utterances which have had in them meanings hidden so far from the disciples (cf. Sir. xxxix. 3). What Jesus has told them about their new relationship to Him will remain a dark riddle until, after His death and resurrection, they come through the gift of the Spirit to experience the reality of union with Him and the Father. We have seen that the gift of the Spirit would be the prerequisite for a 'coming' of Jesus to them (xiv. 16–18). Similarly, in the instruction of the Spirit, Jesus would be telling them about Himself (cf. vv. 12–16), and therefore about the Father.

When the time comes for Jesus to tell the disciples plainly of the Father, and for them to make requests in His name, He will not pray to the Father for them, and this because His death, resurrection, and imparting of the Spirit will have brought them into the relation of love as it exists between the Father and Himself. At xvii. 9 Jesus does pray for them, because these events have not yet taken place.

When Jesus speaks of His public ministry and of its ending at His death within the setting of an announcement concerning His heavenly origin and destination (v. 28), His disciples are not perplexed by Him, and they infer from the utterance that He knows everything; i.e., so we are expected to understand, they are professing themselves sure at last that all the 'I am' sayings of Jesus were true and that His whole ministry of utterance, sign, and accepted Passion was a ministry of One whose knowledge in the region of truth was perfect—knowledge which, on being disclosed and received, was for man saving knowledge. But their confidence is scarcely justified, as the sequel shows. They believe that Jesus is already speaking plainly, but their belief is at once called in question. 'Do ye now believe? Behold, the hour cometh, yea, is come, that ye shall be scattered, every man to his own, and shall leave me alone: and yet I am not alone, because the Father is with me' (vv. 31–32). Their faith is not yet firmly enough based

to bring them into union with Him and so into full comprehension˙
They will leave Him alone, deprived of human company, since
none of them could yet go where He was going (xiii. 36; xiv. 6).
In this sense only by His death could He cease to be alone, through
the drawing of all men into union with Himself (xii. 24, 32). In
another sense, to be sure, He is never alone, not even on the Cross.
The Father would be with Jesus in His Passion, accomplishing
His will that Jesus should become to the disciples the source of
peace—peace in the full biblical sense of salvation. Jesus calls the
present faith of the disciples in question only to give them the
assurance that it would not die out under the test now coming to
it nor lose its reward. For Johannine faith in its fulness was only
possible from within the union with Jesus which His dying would
bring to pass, and by the work of the Spirit still to be given.

NOTE. Jesus' Knowledge of His Origin and Destiny.

At xvi. 28 Jesus uses a formula which has a 'gnostic' ring about
it: 'I came out from the Father, . . . and go unto the Father.' A
similar formula has already been used more than once in the
Gospel. The claim of Jesus to be the bread of life was made
within a framework of announcement about His heavenly origin
and destination (vi. 33, 62). He has defended the truth of His
claim to be the light of the world on the grounds that 'I know
whence I came and whither I go' (viii. 14). It was in the perfection
of knowledge that He had come from God and was going to God
that He washed the disciples' feet (xiii. 3). All this suggests that
St. John may have been turning to account a 'gnostic' belief,
attested by Christian and pagan sources, that a man who came
to know the origin and destination of his soul thereby gained the
knowledge that saved him and could save others.

We consider first the occurrence of the formula in the *Evangelium Veritatis*. In this work the destination of man is the place of
his origin, which is the unknown inner being of God, 'the Father
of Truth'; he gets there through the reception of the true 'gnosis'.
This saving gnosis was contained in what the writing calls the
'Book of the Living', by which is meant the hidden thoughts and
purposes of the Father of Truth concerning man (xix. 35 ff.).
The gnosis was for those who had had their names inscribed by
Him in the Book (xxi. 23 ff.). The contents of the Book—that is,
what the true gnosis was and who they were who would receive it

when it was disclosed—the Father of Truth had reserved to Himself till He committed the revelation of the gnosis to Jesus (xx. 1 ff.; xl. 23 ff.), the Son, the Logos, on earth (xvi. 34 f.; xxxvii. 8 ff.). No other could receive the Book. What qualified Jesus to do that and to communicate it ? His precosmic relation to the Father of Truth (xvi. 33 ff.), who brought Him forth from within the depths of His being,[1] in order to make Himself known by Him in a universe[2] produced from within Himself (xvii. 5), which remains within Him (xix. 34), but which exists in ignorance[3] of its origin in Him, as also of its destination in Him (xvii. 10 *et passim*). But Jesus had a further qualification for revealing the Father of Truth: His patient acceptance of suffering and death. This, He knew (xx. 14), would mean life for many. He died, it is said (xx. 10 ff.), so as to obtain the Book, that is, so as to be able to impart the true gnosis. How much more did His voluntary dying do according to the *Evangelium Veritatis*? In what way did it help recipients of His gnosis to make their return to the Father of Truth? It is clear that without the dying of Jesus the return could not be made. If He had not accepted His death, no true gnosis could have been found anywhere. But did His dying belong to the content of the gnosis itself? In a sense it did; for His willingness to die that many might live (xx. 14) was a revelation of the nature of the being of that Father from whom man had come and to whom he would return, if he received the gnosis of Jesus. In this sense the dying of Jesus belonged to the gnosis. But it remains that in the *Evangelium Veritatis* salvation is by gnosis, by revelation in a teaching, by disclosure in this way of the nature of God and of the essentially divine nature of man. In this connexion the material in xx. 15–30 is of interest. As it would seem, though the matter is not altogether clear, the universe did not know its own worth so long as the Father was hidden from it. But it was His decree that He should no longer be incomprehensible, and this decree Jesus fastened to the Cross. (Any reminiscence of Col. ii. 14 is purely superficial.)

[1] The name of the Father of Truth, it is said, is the Son (xxxviii. 6 ff.), i.e. the willed Self-manifestation of Him. Cf. Philo's identification of the Logos with the name of God (*De confus. ling.* 28).

[2] That is, the heavenly world, the Pleroma. Matter is a work of 'Error' (xvii. 15 ff.), not of the Father of Truth; it is called a 'defect', a 'fault' (xxxv. 6). See Sagnard, *La Gnose Valentinienne*, 1947, pp. 649–651).

[3] Ignorance of the Father of Truth was of His own ordaining. In creating the 'universe' He withheld from it perfection, i.e. the knowledge of Him, to foster in it the need of Him and longing search for Him (xviii. 35; xix. 1, 5).

What more particularly is the saving gnosis in the *Evangelium Veritatis*? Bearing in mind that the Book of the Living contains both it and the names of such as are divinely appointed to receive it, we may find an answer in the following passage. 'He who in this manner (i.e. from Jesus) knows (i.e. has received gnosis), recognises whence he came and whither he goes. He recognises it as one who has been drunk and has come back out of his drunkenness' (xxii. 14 ff.). This return to sobriety is called 'a return to himself', by which is meant that he had had his origin in the being of the Father of Truth. Elsewhere (xxi. 5 ff.) it is said that those whose names are inscribed in the Book of the Living receive from Jesus instruction about themselves, and this in a context which makes the resulting self-knowledge at the same time an ascent to the Father of Truth. Or again, we find this from another summary of the gnosis of Jesus: the Son will speak about the place from which each man has come forth, and he, if his name is in the Book, will be in haste to return to the place of his origin (xli. 5 ff.). There he will receive 'what is his own' (xxi. 12; xxii. 18). This is to be near to the Father of Truth (xli. 31); no longer to be in troubled search of Him (xlii. 25); to have the Father in him and to be in Him inseparably (xlii. 27 f.); to be 'with the true brothers upon whom the love of the Father flows forth' (xliii. 5 f.); to be 'in the true and eternal life' (xliii. 10).

This idea that one who knows his (heavenly) origin and (heavenly) destination is in possession of knowledge which gives salvation appears to have been a commonplace in Christian and pagan 'gnostic' circles. Thus, in the account Irenaeus (I 25, 5) gives of the Marcosian Gnostics we read: 'I go again to my own whence I have come . . . I know myself and I know the origin of my being.' Ignatius, writing to the Philadelphians about the Spirit (7, 1), shows himself familiar with the same idea in the form that knowledge of one's origin and destination is a guarantee that one has the perfection of knowledge about any sacred matter in hand: 'The Spirit is not deceived, being from God; for he knows whence he came and whither he goes.' This is confirmed by the 'gnostic' sources themselves. 'But it is not only the washing— i.e. baptism—that is liberating, but the knowledge of who we were, and what we have become, where we were and where we were placed, whither we hasten, for what we were redeemed, what birth is and what rebirth' (*Excerpta ex Theodoto*, 78). '[Thou,

O Lord] hast shown me how to seek myself and know what I was, and who and in what manner I now am, that I may again become that which I was' (*Acts of Thomas*, 15). And the proof that this is not an idea peculiar to Christian 'gnosticism' is found in the *Corpus Hermeticum*: 'But if you . . . say . . . "I know nothing . . . I cannot mount to heaven; I know not what I was, nor what I shall be"; then, what have you to do with God?' (XI, 21). 'If then, being made of Life and Light, you learn to know that you are made of them, you will go back into Life and Light' (I, 21).

Not all occurrences of this formula, to be sure, are to be regarded as 'gnostic'. In the *De Somniis* of Philo (I, 53 ff.; cf. 211–212) knowledge of the self is held to be necessary for knowledge of God, but here there is no thought that the knowledge in question is knowledge of our oneness with Him. Philo says of Abraham that 'when most he knew himself, then most did he despair of himself, in order that he might attain to an exact knowledge of Him who really is'. This clearly is not 'gnostic'. Similarly in *De Migratione Abrahami* (184–195) Philo commends the worth of exploration of the self in the quest for knowledge of God, but again, as the context shows, he is not being 'gnostic'.

In *Pirke Aboth* (iii. 1) we read: 'Mark well three things and thou wilt not fall into the clutches of sin: know whence thou art come, whither thou art going, and before whom thou are destined to give an account and reckoning. "Whence art thou come?" "From a putrid drop." "Whither art thou going?" "To a place of dust, worm, and maggot." "And before whom art thou destined to give an account and reckoning?" "Before the King of kings, the Holy One, blessed be He." ' Is this deliberately anti-gnostic? At any rate, a 'gnostic' type of answer to these questions would have been utterly alien in a treatise founded on the idea of Torah as the perfect divine revelation.

In certain Stoic writings (e.g. Seneca, *Epistles* lxxxii. 6; Persius, *Satires* III 66–72; Marcus Ant. VIII 52; Epictetus I vi. 25; II x; II xxiv. 19–23) are passages concerning man which might appear to belong together with the 'gnostic' material we have had before us, but it turns out, at a reading of them, that the strictly 'gnostic' significance attaching to the knowledge of man's origin and destination is absent.

The question before us then is to what extent a knowledge of the strictly 'gnostic' belief has left its mark on the form of the

presentation of the Christian faith in St. John. The passage at
viii. 12 ff. forms a good test case. Jesus, knowing where He had
come from and where He was going, had the saving knowledge
to impart to man. And what was it? Not here, as in the *Evangelium
Veritatis*, man's forgotten origin in the being of God, to which a
properly qualified revealer of it could get him back by teaching
him about it, by bringing him in that way out of his 'drunkenness'
to 'sobriety'. No, that was not the saving knowledge that Jesus
had to communicate. He had the knowledge that He was the light
of the world, the supreme source of felicity for men. The content
of the saving gnosis is Jesus, and this not because He is the
disclosure of man's true identity, but because He is the embodiment of God's purpose (now for the first time) to impart His own
life to men and to take men into unity with Himself.

It is tempting to think that St. John was aware of a pagan
gnosis to which he was deliberately opposing his own doctrine,
that amongst the hoped-for readers of the Gospel were some who
took their 'gnostic' formula seriously and would therefore see the
point and perhaps be persuaded to forsake their own gnosis for the
Johannine.

As we have noticed earlier, in the *Evangelium Veritatis*, the
dying of Jesus is very important in the sense that without it He
would never have had to offer to man what is there regarded as the
true gnosis; but in St. John His dying is the act by which He
releases and communicates the life which was in Him to those
who receive His gnosis (so to call it), that is, His word, His self-
disclosure. By His dying He draws believers into the union with
Himself and so with the Father which is the life offered to man in
the gospel. Thus the believer is saved, not by a knowledge of
eternal truths veiled by man's fall into sinfulness, but by a knowledge that God's purpose of love has become an earthly reality in
the life, death, and resurrection of Jesus.

17

THE PRAYER OF JESUS

The great prayer of Jesus is both the climax and the summary of St. John's theology. In the foregoing chapters we have regularly had occasion to turn to it for a key to unlock the intricacies of the evangelist's thought, and it now remains to be seen whether the prayer as a whole justifies the use we have made of its parts. Two principles of interpretation may be laid down in advance, one concerning the structure of the prayer, the other concerning its temporal standpoint. Structurally the prayer appears to fall into three sections: in *vv.* 1–5 Jesus prays for Himself, in *vv.* 6–19 for those disciples who have been the companions of His earthly ministry, and in *vv.* 20–26 for the larger body of believers who are to be brought into union with Jesus through the preaching of the church. These divisions are not, however, to be pressed. Already in the opening section Jesus prays not as an individual, but as the inclusive representative of all who through His Passion are to be drawn into that love relationship with Himself and the Father which is eternal life; so that the second and third sections should be regarded as the unfolding of ideas already implicit in the first five verses.

It has often been held, largely because of the complexity of St. John's use of tenses, that the temporal standpoint, not only of this prayer but of the Gospel as a whole, is that of the evangelist's own day, that he puts into the mouth of Jesus sayings which reflect the conditions of the time of writing, not of the time when they purport to have been spoken. In dealing with earlier passages in the Gospel, and particularly iii. 13, we have argued that this view is mistaken, and that the sayings of Jesus in the Fourth Gospel are always to be interpreted to fit the situation at the time when they are spoken. The prayer of Jesus can be so interpreted, provided that we keep in mind two Johannine uses of the aorist and perfect tenses. These tenses can be used for one of two reasons to describe events which from the point of view of the speaker are still future: either because the event is considered to be determined by the predestining will of God, or because the human agents have so fully committed themselves to a course of action that the result can be treated as already accomplished (cf. especially xiii. 31).

The opening paragraph of the prayer contains examples of both these usages. 'Father, the hour is come; glorify thy Son, that the Son may glorify thee: even as thou gavest him authority over all flesh, that whatsoever thou hast given him, to them he should give eternal life. And this is life eternal, that they should know thee the only true God, and him whom thou didst send, *even* Jesus Christ' (xvii. 1-3). The hour is the hour of the Passion, for which the reader has been prepared since its first mention at the wedding in Cana. It follows that the glory which the Father is to bestow on the Son and the Son on the Father is a glory brought to pass by the dying of Jesus. Since the glory which Jesus has possessed and manifested in His ministry can be shown to be His filial love-union with the Father, we have argued (pp. 36-40) that the glory for which He now appeals is His analogous union with believers, which brings them also to share His own union with the Father. We can now see how fully the context bears out this interpretation. For the appeal is made on the grounds that[1] the Father has already granted to the Son sovereignty over all mankind and has given to Him all those[2] who now or in the future are to be recipients of the gift of eternal life. The glory which Jesus asks for Himself must therefore be the implementation of the divine purpose to impart to men that life which has already been imparted to Jesus (v. 26), and the proper sequel to the giving of these men into the charge of Jesus. In the second section of the prayer (v. 6) it will be made clear that those who are said to be given to Jesus are believers in whom the Father had previously wrought a work of preparation which had made them His own (cf. pp. 93-95); and the giving of them to Jesus may be assumed to have occurred at the point when He accepted the commission to be the bringer of life to the world. But the ability of Jesus to receive a new access of glory, and so to impart life to the world, depends also on His possessing sovereignty over mankind. It is conceivable that this sovereignty too came to Him with His initial commission (cf. v. 27). But when we remember that until

---

[1] For this meaning of καθώς see Blass-Debrunner, 453, 2.

[2] For the neuter used of persons here and in *v.* 24 see Blass-Debrunner, 138, 1.

the death of Jesus sovereignty over the world is exercised by Satan, 'the ruler of this world', it seems more likely that the grant of sovereignty to Jesus is to be made at the Cross, and that the overthrow of Satan by Jesus at and because of His dying is being presupposed as already accomplished, since both Jesus and Satan, in the person of his minion Judas, have committed themselves to their course of action. The Father had already accepted the self-consecration of Jesus as His conquest over the ruler of this world and granted Him world sovereignty as its consequence.

This interpretation is borne out by the words of Jesus two verses later: 'I glorified thee on the earth, having accomplished the work which thou hast given me to do' (v. 4). Here again the aorist is used to depict as already complete an event which has still to take place. To be sure Jesus had throughout His life manifested the glory that befitted an only Son, and so had made it possible for the world to see the glory of God (i. 14; ii. 11; xi. 40), and in all His words and deeds He had been doing the work of God (v. 17). But here He speaks of a glory given to the Father by His finished work, and this can only be a reference to the Cross. Insofar as the glorification of the Father rests on the obedient self-surrender of Jesus, it can be spoken of as already achieved. Yet at the same time Jesus can confidently pray the Father to endorse His action, because it has been undertaken in accordance with the Father's own commission.

The winning of a new glory for the Father and the Son through the Cross is, then, one side of the process whereby men are brought to share the Son's relationship with the Father, and therefore to share also His eternal life. The other side of the process is described in terms of their knowledge. 'This is life eternal, that they should know thee the only true God, and him whom thou didst send, *even* Jesus Christ' (v. 3). Taken by itself this verse might be interpreted in a somewhat Gnostic fashion, as though eternal life consisted in the contemplation of God's changeless perfections. But this is not what St. John has in mind. God is to be known as the One who has sent Jesus and has thereby accomplished the salvation of the world, as the One who in the Incarnation has taken the manhood of Jesus into union with the Logos, and who in the Cross will make that manhood inclusive of all believers. Such knowledge is necessarily an experimental knowledge, available only to those who by the death of Jesus have been united with Him and by the aid of the enlightening Paraclete know themselves to be so united. They can know the common purpose, the mutual love, and the reciprocal glories of the Father and the Son only from within their relation of oneness with the Father and Jesus which the dying of Jesus has gained for them.

All this does not, however, exhaust the significance of the prayer of Jesus for His own glorification. 'And now, O Father, glorify thou me with thine own self with the glory which I had with thee before the world was' (v. 5). This petition is liable to two forms of misinterpretation. The glorification of Jesus in His death is also the point at which He leaves the world to go to the Father (vi. 62; vii. 33; xiii. 1, 33, 36; xiv. 2, 12; xvi. 17, 28). But it would be wrong to think that Jesus is therefore praying simply for the restoration of the *status quo* described in the first two verses of the Prologue. The speaker is not the Logos but the Logos incarnate, the man Jesus, who can claim to have had glory before the world was because he has accepted what God has willed—His total identification with the Logos. It would be equally mistaken, however, to think that Jesus is praying to be Himself endowed with the eternal glory of the Logos. This He has already possessed in virtue of the Incarnation: throughout His earthly life He has been in the bosom of the Father (i. 18), in heaven (iii. 13), in the Father (x. 38; xiv. 10). His prayer is based on the fact that, committed as He is to the Cross, He has completed the work of drawing men into union with Himself (xii. 32). It is a prayer to be received into the presence of God not merely as man, but as the inclusive representative of humanity.

Jesus now turns His attention to the intimate circle of disciples, who are to be the first recipients of His gift of life and glory. 'I manifested thy name unto the men whom thou gavest me out of the world: thine they were, and thou gavest them to me; and they have kept thy word' (v. 6). The utterance offers a supporting ground for the petition in v. 1 as well as for that in v. 5. It enumerates four reasons why the disciples are qualified to be included in the new glory of the Son: the divine preparation which has marked them out as belonging to God, the commission of Jesus to make them His own, His revelation of the Father, and their own response of faith. By the 'name' of the Father which Jesus had made known is meant the Father Himself as revealed to Jesus in the relation of oneness which He had caused to exist between Himself and Him.

Accordingly, it is said that the Father had shared His name with Jesus (*vv.* 11-12), and that the words of Jesus had been words which the Father had given to Him (*v.* 8). The self-revelation of the Father to the world took place in the self-revelation of the Son. The disciples can be said to have kept the Father's word because they have come to recognise and to accept the unity of purpose and action which exists between Son and Father. 'Now they know that all things whatsoever thou hast given me are from thee: for the words which thou gavest me I have given unto them: and they received them, and knew of a truth that I came forth from thee, and they believed that thou didst send me' (*vv.* 7-8). The disciples have not only received the words of the Son, but have received them as words of the Father. At the end of the farewell discourse the faith of the disciples and their knowledge of God have been called in question (xvi. 27-32); there could not be a fully saving faith or knowledge without the death of Jesus and the sending of the Paraclete. But here they can be regarded as adequate grounds for the inclusion of the disciples in Jesus' own prayer for glory, because the Cross and its consequences are assumed to be accomplished.

Now for the first time it is explicitly said that the prayer of Jesus is not for Himself alone, but for believers. 'I pray for them: I pray not for the world, but for those whom thou hast given me; for they are thine: and all things that are mine are thine, and thine are mine: and I am glorified in them' (*vv.* 9-10). In *v.* 6 the disciples '*were* thine' because of the divine preparation which preceded and made possible their call by Jesus. Now it is said that 'they *are* thine', because Jesus has made them His own, and because everything that belongs to Jesus belongs also to God. The Father and the Son have their possessions in common (cf. xvi. 15). Accordingly, the glory for which Jesus has been praying is a glory He has won for Himself in the persons of His followers, the glory of having brought them into union with Himself (cf. xiv. 13). For the time being the world is expressly excluded from the prayer because, being ignorant of the God self-revealed in the self-revelation of Jesus, and hating both Jesus and the Father (xv. 24), it is disqualified from such a union. But the disqualification is not to remain permanent, for the world is still the object of God's redemptive love (iii. 16), and it is to be given a further opportunity of coming to faith through those who are the direct concern of

P

Jesus' prayer (xvii. 21, 23). Only through them can His work in and for the world be completed. 'And I am no more in the world, and these are in the world, and I come to thee. Holy Father, keep them in thy name which thou hast given me, that they may be one, even as we are' (v. 11). As long as Jesus was in the world, He was maintained in unity with the Father through sharing His name—His whole revealed character and purpose; and the disciples are to be maintained in the same unity by the same means. The mission of the disciples as servants of the word of the Father given them by Jesus begins to come under allusion at this point. On account of the hostility of the world it is a mission involving danger and difficulty, and so the Father is addressed as 'Holy Father' in acknowledgment that He is at once other than the world and all that in Jesus He has revealed Himself to be. The title carries its own guarantee of protection from the assaults of the world (cf. v. 15), to take the place of the protection afforded by the earthly presence of Jesus. 'While I was with them, I kept them in thy name which thou hast given me: and I guarded them, and not one of them perished, but the son of perdition; that the scripture might be fulfilled' (v. 12). Only in the case of Judas Iscariot had the protecting ministry of Jesus been unavailing, as was inevitable, since the Father, by a decree recorded in Scripture, had not 'given' him to Jesus (cf. vi. 39, 44, 64 f.; xiii. 18).

In xv. 1–10 Jesus had spoken of the responses required from His disciples if His purpose of making them sharers in His own joy was to be achieved. To these conditions He now adds the efficacy of His own prayer. 'But now I come to thee; and these things I speak in the world, that they may have my joy fulfilled in themselves' (v. 13). Like all the other fruits of His union with the Father, His joy is communicable to them. It is also a joy independent of outward circumstance. 'I have given them thy word; and the world hated them, because they are not of the world, even as I am not of the world. I pray not that thou shouldest take them from the world, but that thou shouldest keep them from the evil *one*. They are not of the world, even as I am not of the world' (vv. 14–16). The hatred of the disciples by the world and by its ruler, the Evil One, will make itself felt as soon as they begin their apostolic mission, but, like all other consequences of the passion, it is here spoken of in the past tense. Jesus will offer no Petition to the Father for their removal from the world. The world's hatred of them will merely be the proof that they are 'not of the world', that by the choice of Jesus and by the efficacy of His death they have been made sharers of His life, and therefore of His victory over the world and its ruler (xvi. 33). The statement that 'they are not of the world, even as I am not of the world' is made twice with different emphases. At *v.* 14 the words serve to explain the hatred of the disciples by the world, which loves only its own (vii. 7; xv. 19). At *v.* 16 they are the ground for the following petition that the Father should consecrate the disciples by accepting what Jesus has done for them.

The words that follow have already been singled out as the most striking evidence that the death of Jesus is regarded in the Fourth Gospel as representative and inclusive (cf. pp. 49–53), and it will suffice here to summarize our earlier argument. 'Sanctify them in the truth: thy word is truth. As thou didst send me into the world, even so sent I them into the world. And for their sakes I sanctify myself, that they themselves also may be sanctified in truth' (*vv.* 17–19). The parallelism at *v.* 18 (cf. xx. 21) shows that, when St. John speaks of Jesus as sent into the world by the Father (which he does more than forty times), he is thinking not of His nativity but of His public mission. Already, before that mission began, He had been consecrated by His permanent union with the Logos (x. 36). Humanly speaking, that union has been manifested in a life of obedience to the redemptive purpose of God's love; and, when Jesus completes His obedience by the acceptance of death, He is completing also His consecration. But the consecration is said to be for the sake of the disciples, 'that they themselves also may be consecrated in truth'. Their consecration is included in His. His self-offering as their representatives is the ground for His petition to the Father to 'sanctify them in the truth'. For the truth in which they are to be consecrated is the word of God; and Jesus is both Word and Truth (i. 14; xiv. 6).

From the mission of the disciples, which will depend on their solidarity with Himself and the Father, Jesus turns to contemplate the host of believers whom the mission will win. 'Neither for these only do I pray, but for them also that believe on me through their word; that they may all be one; even as thou, Father, art in me, and I in thee, that they also may be in us: that the world may believe that thou didst send me' (*vv.* 20–21). Two points which have been implicit in the prayer from the beginning are now for the first time made explicit: that the range of reference of the prayer is intended to include converts made to the faith by the witness of the first disciples; and that the glorification or consecration of Jesus will involve the bringing of all disciples into unity with one another, because they will be given a share in the unity subsisting between Father and Son.[3] Indeed, it now appears that unity, glory, life and love, are interchangeable terms for the relationship between Father and Son into which believers are to be admitted by the death of Jesus, either directly in the case of the first disciples, or indirectly in the case of future converts. 'And the glory which thou hast given me I have given unto them; that they may be one, even as we are one; I in them, and thou in me, that they may be perfected into one; that the world may know that thou didst send me, and lovedst them, even as thou lovedst me' (*vv.* 22–23). It is perhaps worth while to reiterate here the warning already given about St. John's use of tenses. We are not to suppose from the use of the perfect tense that Jesus has already, in advance of His death, communicated to believers the glory of His own filial relation to the Father. He has said in so many words that the disciples cannot come to the Father until He has prepared the way for them by His death (xiii. 36–xiv. 6); and in any case the majority of those to whom He now refers were not even born at the moment when He was speaking. It is because He has committed Himself to the Cross, by which He will draw all believers, present and future, into union with Himself, that He can speak as though the gift of glory were already made, even in the course of the prayer which begins with a petition for that very glory to be given to Jesus on their behalf. The glorification of Jesus by the Father and His gift of glory to the disciples are but aspects of the same event, which includes also the glorification of the Father (cf. *v.* 1). For God's glory is but another name for His love, and is displayed precisely in the act of being imparted, first to Jesus, and through Him to others, so that they are enabled to share in the oneness and love which are constitutive in the Godhead. Such oneness among believers would be a cardinal influence in the world for the awakening of belief in Jesus as the agent of the divine purpose and the recipient and mediator of the divine love. For it would prove that the Father had drawn them into the same love relation with

---

[3] The reading in which ἕν is repeated before the second ὦσιν disturbs the simplicity of the thought.

Himself as that into which He had brought Jesus, sent by Him to this end.

Up to this point the prayer has been concerned with the union of life and love which, established by the Cross and illuminated by the Paraclete, the believer will be able to enjoy without being taken out of the world. Now for a moment it moves on to hint at a more ultimate bliss. 'Father, that which thou hast given me, I will that, where I am, they also may be with me; that they may behold my glory, which thou hast given me: for thou lovedst me before the foundation of the world' (v. 24). These words recall the promises of the last discourse that Jesus will come again, not only in the repeated experiences of earthly faith, but also at the last day when faith gives place to sight in the Presence Chamber of God (cf. xiv. 3). The eternal love of God and the Logos will reach its fulfilment only when mankind has been included eternally within its scope.

Even in the face of the world's enmity and His own ensuing death Jesus can cling to this vision of world salvation, because His confidence rests wholly in God. 'O righteous Father, the world knew thee not, but I knew thee; and these knew that thou didst send me; and I made known unto them thy name, and will make it known; that the love wherewith thou lovedst me may be in them, and I in them' (vv. 25–26). The world has demonstrated its ignorance of God by its refusal of the knowledge of God offered to it in the self-revelation of Jesus (cf. i. 10). but it will hardly be the case that the Father is addressed as 'righteous' in the expectation that He will condemn the world for its rejection of Him, especially in view of the concern just shown for the conversion of the world by the mission of the disciples. Rather Jesus utters His trust in the righteousness of the Father because He knows the will and the power of the Father to carry out His promise of granting to all believers present and to come the supreme good of being with Jesus where He is (for this sense of 'righteous' cf. Isa xlv. 21; Ps. cxv. 4–5). The world's ignorance of God is mentioned only to throw into relief the more important fact that Jesus knows Him and can share His knowledge with others. During His earthly life He has made the Father's name known to His disciples; and, when He is no longer in the world, but has gone to the Father, He will continue to make it known through their proclamation of the word, which the Father had given to Him and He to them (cf. vv. 6–8,

14). His purpose in so doing will be to make all recipients of the revelation sharers in the oneness of love that exists between Himself and the Father. But not even this declared purpose speaks more eloquently of the effects of His Passion than the claim that in the mission of the disciples He will be still at work in them as the one revealer of the Father.

INDEX LOCORUM

1. Biblical References

Old Testament

New Testament

2. NON-BIBLICAL REFERENCES